Ethics for Journalists

Ethics for Journalists critically explores many of the dilemmas that journalists face in their work and supports journalists in good ethical decision-making. From building trust, to combatting disinformation, to minimizing harm to vulnerable people through responsible suicide reporting, this book provides substantial analysis of key contemporary ethical debates and offers guidance on how to address them.

Revised and updated throughout, this third edition covers:

- the influence of press freedom and misinformation on trust;
- the novel ethical challenges presented by social media;
- the need for diversity of sources and in the newsroom, specifically relating to gender, ethnicity, sexual orientation and disability;
- issues around vulnerable people—reporting traumatic events, bereaved people, suicide and privacy;
- health journalism and reporting a pandemic; and
- the impact of regulation on professional standards.

Taking an accessible and engaging approach, including expert reflections on personal and professional experience, *Ethics for Journalists* provides a wealth of insight for those in journalism, from students and trainees to specialist correspondents and experienced editors.

Sallyanne Duncan was a senior lecturer in journalism/journalism ethics at the University of Strathclyde, and also worked as a regional newspaper journalist.

Media Skills

Edited by Richard Keeble, Lincoln University

The *Media Skills* series provides a concise and thorough introduction to a rapidly changing media landscape. Each book is written by media and journalism lecturers or experienced professionals and is a key resource for a particular industry. Offering helpful advice and information and using practical examples from print, broadcast and digital media, as well as discussing ethical and regulatory issues, *Media Skills* books are essential guides for students and media professionals.

English for Journalists
Twentieth Anniversary Edition
Wynford Hicks

Researching for the Media
Television, Radio and Journalism, second edition
Adele Emm

Subediting and Production for Journalists
Print, Digital and Social, second edition
Tim Holmes

Magazine Production
Second edition
Jason Whittaker

Interviewing for Journalists
Third edition
Sally Adams and Emma Lee-Potter

Designing for Newspapers and Magazines
Second edition
Chris Frost

Sports Journalism
The State of Play
Tom Bradshaw and Daragh Minogue

Freelancing for Journalists
Lily Canter and Emma Wilkinson

Writing for Journalists
Fourth edition
Matt Swaine with Harriett Gilbert and Gavin Allen

Ethics for Journalists
Third edition
Sallyanne Duncan

For more information about this series, please visit: www.routledge.com/Media-Skills/book-series/SE0372

Ethics for Journalists

THIRD EDITION

Sallyanne Duncan

Routledge
Taylor & Francis Group
LONDON AND NEW YORK

Designed cover image: XtockImages, Getty Images

Third edition published 2023
by Routledge
4 Park Square, Milton Park, Abingdon, Oxon, OX14 4RN

and by Routledge
605 Third Avenue, New York, NY 10158

Routledge is an imprint of the Taylor & Francis Group, an informa business

© 2023 Sallyanne Duncan

The right of Sallyanne Duncan to be identified as author of the editorial material, and of the authors for their individual chapters has been asserted in accordance with sections 77 and 78 of the Copyright, Designs and Patents Act 1988.

All rights reserved. No part of this book may be reprinted or reproduced or utilised in any form or by any electronic, mechanical, or other means, now known or hereafter invented, including photocopying and recording, or in any information storage or retrieval system, without permission in writing from the publishers.

Trademark notice: Product or corporate names may be trademarks or registered trademarks, and are used only for identification and explanation without intent to infringe.

First edition published by Routledge 2001

British Library Cataloguing-in-Publication Data
A catalogue record for this book is available from the British Library

Library of Congress Cataloging-in-Publication Data
Names: Duncan, Sallyanne, author.
Title: Ethics for journalists / Sallyanne Duncan.
Description: Third edition. | Abingdon, Oxon ; New York, NY : Routledge, Taylor & Francis Group, 2022. | Series: Media skills | Includes bibliographical references and index. |
Identifiers: LCCN 2022027669 (print) | LCCN 2022027670 (ebook) |
Classification: LCC PN4756 .K37 2022 (print) | LCC PN4756 (ebook) |
DDC 174.90704–dc23
LC record available at https://lccn.loc.gov/2022027669
LC ebook record available at https://lccn.loc.gov/2022027670

ISBN: 978-1-138-58354-2 (hbk)
ISBN: 978-1-138-58526-3 (pbk)
ISBN: 978-0-429-50538-6 (ebk)

DOI: 10.4324/9780429505386

Typeset in Goudy
by Newgen Publishing UK

For Al and Portia
and
Peter and Doreen

Contents

	List of contributors	ix
	Acknowledgements	xi
	Introduction: Core principles of ethical journalism SALLYANNE DUNCAN	1
1	Trust, information disorder and freedom of expression: Influences on ethical journalism SALLYANNE DUNCAN	12
2	Regulating the mainstream media: Who guards the guardians? SALLYANNE DUNCAN	30
	Ethics in action: Aidan White, founder of the Ethical Journalism Network	45
3	Journalists and social media: Entering an 'ethical vacuum'? FRANCES YEOMAN	58
	Ethics in action: Jim Waterson, media editor of The Guardian	74
4	Sources: The lifeblood of journalism JACKIE NEWTON	83
	Ethics in action: Gerard Ryle, director of the International Consortium of Investigative Journalists	94
5	Privacy and intrusion: Navigating the muddy waters of conflicting rights SALLYANNE DUNCAN, WITH ADDITIONAL RESEARCH BY ANNA BRYAN	101
	Ethics in action: Joshua King, head of digital engagement and development at the Scotsman	118

6	Covering death and trauma: Focus on compassion and respect SALLYANNE DUNCAN	128
	Ethics in action: Jo Healey, journalist, author and founder of Trauma Reporting training	*142*
7	Reporting suicide responsibly: A force for good SALLYANNE DUNCAN	151
	Ethics in action: Gordon Allan, who was bereaved by suicide	*164*
8	Diversity in the news: Seeking fair representation and inclusivity SALLYANNE DUNCAN	174
	Ethics in action: Barnie Choudhury, editor-at-large of Eastern Eye	*187*
9	The ethics of health journalism: Reporting a pandemic PETYA ECKLER AND OZAN B. MANTAR	199
	Ethics in action: Helen McArdle, health correspondent at The Herald	*210*
10	Battling for news: Reporting war and conflict RICHARD LANCE KEEBLE	222
	Ethics in action: Lara Pawson, former BBC World Service correspondent	*234*
	Index	244

Contributors

Sallyanne Duncan was a senior lecturer in journalism/journalism ethics at the University of Strathclyde, and also worked as a regional newspaper journalist.

Petya Eckler is a senior lecturer in journalism, media and communication at the University of Strathclyde. She researches health communication and social media and is a fellow of the university's Centre for Health Policy. She is the founder of the Working Group on Body Image and Eating Disorders, which includes academics, clinicians, health charity professionals, bloggers and people with lived experiences. She has contributed to the Scottish Government's Healthy Body Image for Children and Young People Advisory Group, which produced a detailed report with recommendations in March 2020.

Richard Lance Keeble is a professor of journalism at Lincoln University and visiting professor at Liverpool Hope University. He is the author of the first two editions of *Ethics for Journalists* and has written or edited 38 books on journalism and other topics including peace journalism, newspaper skills, literary journalism, profiles, and the secret state and the media and George Orwell. He is joint editor of *Ethical Space: The International Journal of Communication Ethics* and *George Orwell Studies*. In 2013, the Association for Journalism Education gave him a Lifetime Achievement Award.

Ozan B. Mantar is PhD student, researching "The role of online discussion forums in decision-making and attitude formation about childhood vaccination".

Jackie Newton is a senior lecturer in journalism at Liverpool John Moores University. She previously worked as a feature writer and features editor, senior subeditor and a designer at the *Liverpool Daily Post and Echo*. She has also freelanced for national newspapers and lifestyle magazines. Jackie researches comparative ethics in reporting tragedy and media relations with the bereaved. She has co-authored the book, *Reporting Bad News*, with Dr Sallyanne Duncan.

Frances Yeoman is a senior lecturer and head of journalism at Liverpool John Moores University. Her research focuses on news literacy, working with Ofcom, DCMS and the News Literacy Network. Previously, Fran worked for more than a decade in national newspapers. She was an assistant editor of *i*, worked for the *Independent* and *The Times* as a news editor and reporter, and spent a year as a Westminster political reporter.

Acknowledgements

Although this is the third edition of *Ethics for Journalists*, it is my first. It's been quite a journey. It has given me the chance to dive deeply into my favourite subject: journalism ethics. Therefore, I begin by thanking Richard Lance Keeble, the author of the first two editions, for trusting me with his book. Richard suggested to Routledge that I take on the third edition, and in doing so paid me an enormous compliment.

In the beginning, there were two of us. My friend and research colleague, Jackie Newton, was my co-creator in the early stages of this project. I am deeply indebted to her for her insights and ideas in the planning of this book. Thanks also to Jackie for writing the chapter on Sources, one of the essential sections, and the book would have been the poorer without it.

Special thanks go to my good friend Jo Healey who has been an enthusiastic supporter and motivator over the gestation of this edition. I am hugely thankful to Jo for sharing her expertise with me regarding the Covering Death and Trauma chapter, both as a contributor and a critic, although she was never critical.

I am immensely grateful to Gordon Allan, who generously agreed to read the chapter on Reporting Suicide Responsibly. Gordon made excellent suggestions that added dimensions to the chapter that had not occurred to me, and in doing so has set me on a path for future research. I was also incredibly touched when he gave me permission to include his own personal love story, which for me is one of the highlights of this book.

Numerous hands have toiled in the making of this edition. All of them have given unsparingly of their time, and for that I thank them profusely. Five specialist authors wrote chapters that were beyond my scope, and I really appreciate their contributions. Thanks to Frances Yeoman, Petya Eckler and Ozan B. Mantar, and of course Jackie and Richard for their chapters. I also express my gratitude to all the ethical experts who agreed to contribute an interview or story to show ethics in action. Thanks go to Aidan White, Jim Waterson, Gerard Ryle, Joshua King, Barnie Choudhury, Helen McArdle, Lara Pawson, and of course Jo and Gordon.

My thanks also to Anna Bryan, who was my research assistant for the Privacy and Intrusion chapter. Anna's hard work and solid research skills provided a robust foundation for this important part of the book.

I am grateful to Priscille Biehlmann, Elizabeth Cox and, previously, Margaret Farrelly, at Routledge for their guidance and patience in getting the manuscript into print.

Immense thanks to Al and Portia for their unyielding support, which made it so much easier to get this book done.

Sallyanne Duncan

Introduction
Core principles of ethical journalism

Sallyanne Duncan

A long time ago, when I was a journalist, an editor told me that I didn't need to know about ethics: that was his responsibility. His view was that he made all the hard decisions and my job was to carry them out, unquestioningly.

Oh, how things have changed. Ethics are everyone's responsibility in journalism—from the trainee or work experience intern to the managing editor or proprietor—no one should shirk that obligation. After all, journalism is a collaborative process and with that comes collective responsibility for the actions taken in the name of the news outlet. Nowadays, with fewer staff in the newsroom, increasing numbers of freelance media workers and greater autonomy being placed on younger staff at earlier stages in their careers, ethics are everyone's concern. Of course, editors still play a vital role in ethical decision-making and in setting the moral compass of their news organisation, but this now filters down—and up—to others too.

I also believe he was wrong. Every decent human being has their own personal code of ethics, and sometimes, more often than not, that coincides with their professional norms and practice. They bring their value systems to the job, and they use those to interpret the standards of behaviour expected of their calling. So conceivably, ethical imperatives are inherent in every decision a journalist makes about their work. Academic and former journalist, Tony Harcup, elaborates with this insight:

> Whether we recognise it or not, ethics are involved in every story we follow up or ignore; every interview we request; every conversation with a confidential source; every quote we use, leave out or tidy up; every bit of context we squeeze in, simplify or exclude; every decision to create (sorry, report) a "row"; every photograph we select or "improve"; every soundbite we choose to use; every approach from an advertiser trying to influence editorial copy; every headline we write; every question we ask or don't ask. For the ethical

journalist, it is not enough to have a bulging contacts book or a good nose for news; being an ethical journalist also means asking questions about our own practice.

2007, p. 6

To his list we could add, every clickbait story we write; every tweet we send; every post we take from social media; every piece of user-generated content we upload to our news sites; every time we use drone footage; and many more "everys" that you can come up with yourselves.

So ethics are at the heart of everything that journalists do. They are about trying to take the right action in often difficult circumstances, but it is not always clear what the right action is, or how we arrive at that. So invariably, it depends on the particular circumstances. My fellow academic and author of the first two editions of this book, Richard Lance Keeble, wrote:

Ethical inquiry is crucial for all media workers—and managers. It encourages journalists to examine their basic moral and political principles; their responsibilities and rights; their relationship to their employer and audience; their ultimate goals. Self-criticism and the reflective, questioning approach are always required. And journalists need to be eloquent about ethics and politics, confident in articulating and handling the issues—and imaginative in their promotion of standards, both individually and collectively.

2009, p. 1

And that's what I hope this book will enable you to do. Of course, no book on journalism ethics can cover every possible dilemma or debate, and so this one is selective in its topics. The content also differs from previous editions—although I hope it is true to the spirit of the others—and that is partly because some issues have faded from the ethical journalism landscape whilst others have come into sharp focus. Central to them all, however, are fundamental ethical principles that form the basis of professional standards and ethical codes of conduct or practice.

The core principles of ethical journalism

Five core principles help inform journalists' ethical decision-making. These have been cogently classified by the founder of the Ethical Journalism Network (EJN), Aidan White. They are: truth and accuracy; independence; fairness and impartiality; humanity; and accountability (Ethical Journalism Network, 2022; White, 2015). These are generally accepted worldwide as the essential values that journalists should adhere to if they are to report responsibly.

Truth and accuracy

The EJN's first core principle states:

> Journalists cannot always guarantee "truth" but getting the facts right is the cardinal principle of journalism. We should always strive for accuracy, give all the relevant facts we have, and ensure that they have been checked. When we cannot corroborate information, we should say so.
>
> *Ethical Journalism Network, 2022*

Truth is a very long word that gets us into abstract discussions about what it is and is not, says Aidan White (2015, 00:25), and instead, he advises we focus on accuracy as an ethical concept. This is echoed by the Society of Professional Journalists (SPJ), who stress the importance of accuracy in their code of ethics, but also headline their first principle as "seek truth and report it" (SPJ, 2014). White stresses that there should be "no deceptive handling of the facts" as journalists work in fact-based information (2015, 00:34). The importance of fact-based journalism was heightened during the early stages of the COVID-19 pandemic when the media embraced its public service role to provide anxious audiences with credible information. Consequently, it has been perceived as a sustainable opportunity for news organisations to build trust with their audiences (see Chapter 1 on Trust). In doing so, they fulfil the first article of the International Federation of Journalists (IFJ) Global Charter of Ethics for Journalist. It states: "Respect for the facts and for the right of the public to truth is the first duty of the journalist" (IFJ, 2019). The IFJ also emphasise honesty in news processes and publication, as well as clearly distinguishing factual information from fair commentary and criticism, although those lines are blurring in some online content. Whilst checking information for accuracy has always been a journalism fundamental, verification has increasingly become more necessary with the rise of false information through misinformation, disinformation and malinformation, and in response to this, we have seen a growth in fact-checking services like Full Fact (https://fullfact.org/) and The Ferret Fact Service (https://theferret.scot/ferret-fact-service/). But accuracy also applies to what reporters leave out of their stories. Are they suppressing essential information by excluding specific details? And when they include certain material or viewpoints, are they reliably reporting them including people's posts on social media? Therefore, their selection and rejection of information should be fair, logical and balanced.

Independence

Regarding independence, the EJN advises:

> Journalists must be independent voices; we should not act, formally or informally, on behalf of special interests whether political, corporate or

> cultural. We should declare to our editors–or the audience–any of our political affiliations, financial arrangements or other personal information that might constitute a conflict of interest.
>
> *2022*

Independence means that journalists can undertake their work as watchdogs without fear or favour, without appearing surreptitiously partisan or without seeming to be part of a propaganda machine for governments, business or other special interest groups, nor acting as an instrument of the police or security services, particularly in relation to revealing the identity of sources or handing over information from them. In other words, avoid real or perceived conflicts of interest, refuse gifts, inducements or special treatment and resist internal or external pressure to influence coverage (SPJ, 2014). Independence supports the notion of a free press in that it endorses transparency in newsgathering, production and publication for the benefit of the public (see Chapter 1 on Freedom of Expression/Free Press). This need for transparency extends to being honest and clear about respecting the use of off-the-record or anonymity agreements with sources and the terms of embargoed information. The IFJ's Global Charter comments: "Journalism is a profession, which requires time, resources and the means to practise–all of which are essential to its independence" (2019, preamble).

Fairness and impartiality

The core principle on fairness and impartiality says:

> Most stories have at least two sides. While there is no obligation to present every side in every piece, stories should be balanced and add context. Objectivity is not always possible and may not always be desirable (in the face for example of brutality or inhumanity), but impartial reporting builds trust and confidence.
>
> *Ethical Journalism Network, 2022*

From this principle, it is clear that journalists are responsible for thinking about balance, which does not only mean getting one perspective and then the opposite view as there can be many different standpoints that need to be included in a story for it to be fair and impartial. Aidan White comments: "What are the other sides of this story? Here is one story that's being told but what are the other opinions that I need to bring in to make the story whole?" (2015, 01:18). Fairness extends to the methods that journalists use too. They should always declare who they are and who they work for, avoiding misrepresenting themselves as someone other than a journalist. This includes omitting to or avoiding to tell those they encounter in their newsgathering. It is not for potential sources to ask if the person contacting them is a journalist. This must be a proactive action by the journalist. Of course, there are circumstances when such a declaration is ill-advised, such as undercover investigations or hidden recordings, but the ethical approach for these exceptions should be discussed in detail by the reporters and editors involved. Additionally, such approaches need to be justified in the public interest, a theme that occurs throughout this book (for example, see Chapter 2, *What is the public interest and what does it have to do with codes?*). Regarding impartiality, journalists are expected to abstain from benefitting from any unfair advantage or personal gain as a result of what they do or do not publish. By doing so, they do not have any obligations to anyone regarding their reporting (as noted in the section on *Independence* above). Avoiding such conflicts of interest assists journalists to be impartial, thus reinforcing their credibility and integrity.

Humanity

The principle on humanity states:

> Journalists should do no harm. What we publish or broadcast may be hurtful, but we should be aware of the impact of our words and images on the lives of others.
> *Ethical Journalism Network, 2022*

This principle is about minimizing harm to those affected by news outlets' content, whether that is text, pictures, video including drone footage or material produced using virtual reality, augmented reality or artificial intelligence. It is one that is of great concern to news subjects, audiences and the general public, especially when the media are perceived as overstepping the boundaries. Minimizing harm applies to many of the ethical concerns discussed in this book and so is a recurring theme, such as misuse of social media, privacy, treatment of and by sources, covering death and trauma, responsibly reporting suicide, discrimination, accuracy in health and science journalism and reporting war and conflict. Aidan White says that journalists are expected to show humanity in their work. They should be aware of the consequences of what they publish or broadcast and the potential harm that their words or pictures can cause (2015, 01:28). However, it is important to recognise that journalists and their news organisations cannot anticipate all the consequences of their coverage but they can and should consider the obvious ones. White observes:

> It's not the job of a journalist to do undue harm. It's our job to protect people. And it's very important that when we are reporting we don't indulge in a hate speech, we don't show obscene images, we don't show unnecessarily

explicit images of violence and so on, because we are part of a humanitarian process and that's what journalism should be.

2015, 01:49

The SPJ code echoes this core principle in their article on minimizing harm. They also emphasise compassion and not "pandering to lurid curiosity, even if others do". Additionally, they warn about the long-term implications of "the extended reach and permanence of publication", plus the need to update with accurate information, offering the example of public shaming where journalists' comments on social media can result in a viral storm that can be extremely harmful to public figures and private citizens alike (SPJ, 2014). The IFJ also pick up on this point, advising that journalists take care that their coverage does not contribute to hatred, prejudice or discrimination (IFJ, article 9). Privacy is a major concern in terms of minimizing harm, possibly because of intrusion into individuals' personal lives. Sometimes, this is in the public interest and other times it is not, so that justification needs to be used as a test for intrusion. But it is also about ensuring that potential sources realise that the conversation that they are having with a journalist is intended for publication. This is particularly important with vulnerable interviewees or people who are not used to dealing with the media (IFJ, article 8). Additionally, the SPJ advises that journalists need to balance the public's need to be informed against potential harm caused by the reporting. They say: "Pursuit of the news is not a licence for arrogance or undue intrusiveness" (SPJ, 2014).

Accountability

The last EJN core principle states:

> A sure sign of professionalism and responsible journalism is the ability to hold ourselves accountable. When we commit errors, we must correct them, and our expressions of regret must be sincere not cynical. We listen to the concerns of our audience. We may not change what readers write or say but we will always provide remedies when we are unfair.
>
> *Ethical Journalism Network, 2022*

Aidan White believes this is probably the most difficult principle for journalists to implement. He says:

> We're not a humble group. We find it difficult to say sorry and to admit our mistakes even though we can be lacerating in our criticism of others. But we have to do that. We have to engage with the audience and we have to correct our mistakes. We have to be prepared to provide remedies when we get it wrong and do damage.
>
> *2015, 2:16*

As far as the IFJ are concerned, mistakes can result in serious professional misconduct, especially when it involves plagiarism, distortion of the facts, unfounded accusations and defamation (IFJ, 2019). It's about journalists and their news organisations taking responsibility for their work and clearly explaining their decisions to the public, according to the SPJ. However, the media have a poor track record in shining a light on their decision-making or indeed how news is made. Some advocates of news literacy consider explaining the processes and production of news as part of the journalist's accountability role. Maksl, Ashley and Craft argue that the promotion of a news literate population is for journalists both a pragmatic and an ethical duty. It is, they say, "partly a matter of economic survival, a way of sustaining demand for the type of content professional journalists provide, but also of fulfilling its role to help citizens be adequately informed to participate in democratic life" (SPJ, 2014; Maksl, Ashley and Craft, 2015, p. 29; personal research note from Frances Yeoman, 2020).

(For more from Aidan White, see the *Ethics in Action* section in Chapter 2.)

The structure of this book

This book contains 10 chapters and this introduction. Chapters 2–10 explore specific ethical issues that media workers encounter on a regular basis. The format for these is:

- A general discussion of the topic
- An Ethics in Action section, where an ethical "expert" gives their take on the topic, drawing on their professional or personal experience of the media
- An Ethical Workout, which provides a series of questions that journalism educators can explore with their students, or that readers can investigate for themselves
- Five takeaways from the chapter, which summarises its key points
- An Ethics Toolbox, a list of resources for readers to research and extend their understanding of the chapter's topic.

Firstly, a broader approach is taken in Chapter 1, which considers three dominant influences on journalists' ethical choices. These are trust, information disorder and freedom of expression. Journalists build trust with their audiences and wider communities through ethical reporting but that can be undermined by information disorder. An antidote to this burgeoning problem is freedom of expression and with it press freedom that enables responsible news organisations to seek truth and report it accurately.

In Chapter 2, UK codes of conduct and their associated regulatory bodies are critiqued as fundamental tools for maintaining professional standards, alongside other means of promoting responsible reporting including readers' editors, professional networks, monitoring groups and public pressure via social media. It also discusses the importance of the public interest. In the *Ethics in Action* section, Aidan White of the EJN, explores the effectiveness of current regulatory systems and codes, the role of the EJN in maintaining standards and the challenges for journalists after the COVID-19 pandemic.

Frances Yeoman, in Chapter 3, investigates how social media has not only revolutionised newsgathering and news publishing but also created novel ethical challenges. Also, in this chapter, in the *Ethics in Action* section, Jim Waterson, media editor at *The Guardian*, reflects on the profound effect that social media has had on journalism, and how ethical journalists navigate their way through it. Frances is a senior lecturer and head of journalism at Liverpool John Moores University. Her research focuses on news literacy, working on projects with Ofcom, DCMS and the News Literacy Network. Previously, she was assistant editor of *i*, worked for the *Independent* and *The Times* as a news editor and reporter and was also a Westminster political reporter.

In Chapter 4, Jackie Newton, also of Liverpool John Moores University, explores the relationship between journalists and their sources. She examines how the choice of sources can shape news and influence the news agenda, sometimes to the detriment of wider society. In the *Ethics in Action* section, Gerard Ryle, who led the worldwide teams of journalists working on the Panama Papers, Paradise Papers and Pandora Papers investigations, discusses using anonymous sources, protection of sources and the ethics of handling large data sets involving news outlets and journalists from all over the world. Jackie is a senior lecturer in journalism who previously worked as a feature writer and features editor, senior sub-editor and a designer at the *Liverpool Daily Post and Echo*. She has also freelanced for national newspapers and lifestyle magazines. Jackie researches comparative ethics in reporting tragedy and media relations with the bereaved. She has co-authored the book *Reporting Bad News* with Dr Sallyanne Duncan.

Privacy is one of the most controversial issues in media reporting, and one that splits public opinion. Chapter 5 starts by discussing rights and regulation, then explores intrusion into celebrities' private lives, particularly the Duchess of Sussex' call for a basic right to privacy, as well as the influential Sir Cliff Richard case. Intrusion into ordinary people's privacy is also explored before concluding the chapter with a discussion of taking care over children's privacy. In the *Ethics in Action* section, head of digital engagement and development at the *Scotsman*, Joshua King, outlines some key considerations for journalists weighing up privacy and intrusion.

The theme of intrusion is further explored in Chapter 6, but this time in relation to coverage of death and trauma. Deaths that happen in public places and some that occur in private, such as celebrity deaths, are newsworthy, so journalists have a duty to report them but equally those who experience death and trauma have a right to privacy. This chapter looks at approaching traumatised people, using social media and covering funerals. It examines specific types of trauma including responsibly reporting road crashes and violent crimes, like murder, coercive control, murder-suicide and mass shootings. In the *Ethics in Action* section, journalist, author and trauma training specialist Jo Healey gives her insights into ethically reporting people's personal tragedies.

Minimizing harm to vulnerable people is a dominant theme within Chapter 7 on media reporting of suicide. A lot of suicide coverage globally contains shocking, graphic depictions, but media reporting of suicide can be a force for good, if it is reported responsibly. This chapter examines the ethical concerns raised by media coverage of suicide and explains the Responsible Suicide Reporting model, a tool for hard-pressed journalists to report ethically whilst under pressure of deadline. Using this model as a foundation, the chapter explores balancing accurate, truthful reporting with minimizing harm to vulnerable people; concerns about descriptions of method and location; copycat suicides and contagion; avoiding stigma; speculation, blame and simplistic reasons for suicide; and the necessity of using helplines. The *Ethics in Action* section has a poignant, personal story from Gordon Allan, who was suddenly thrust into the media spotlight when his wife Sally went missing and later died by suicide.

Diversity, a significant ethical issue for news outlets, is discussed in Chapter 8. Numerous minorities are under-represented in UK news and worldwide, and indeed in newsrooms. This chapter explores the effects of this lack of diversity, some of the attitudes that prevail and some ways that news organisations can overcome a diversity deficit. It examines the current position regarding discrimination and perspectives on unconscious bias. Specifically, it also looks at media treatment of women, people with disabilities, LGBTQ+ communities and ethnic minorities. In the *Ethics in Action* section, Barnie Choudhury, editor-at-large of *Eastern Eye*, discusses the media's relationship with diversity. He offers insight into the mainstream media's reporting of race and on the approach of publications that have diversity at their heart, like *Eastern Eye*.

The COVID-19 pandemic has had a profound effect on our world and indeed the world of journalism. In Chapter 9, Dr Petya Eckler and Ozan Mantar of the University of Strathclyde discuss health journalism as a unique specialism and the frequent ethical decisions health journalists grapple with, particularly resulting from the pandemic. In the *Ethics in Action* section, health correspondent at *The*

Herald (Glasgow), Helen McArdle, explains her approach to covering major health stories, including the need to rigorously check data to present accurate information to the public. Petya is a senior lecturer in journalism, media and communication, researches health communication and social media. She is the founder of the Working Group on Body Image and Eating Disorders and has contributed to the Scottish Government's Healthy Body Image for Children and Young People Advisory Group. Ozan Mantar is a PhD student, researching "The role of online discussion forums in decision-making and attitude formation about childhood vaccination".

In the final chapter, Prof Richard Keeble explores some ethical issues involved in reporting conflict. He focuses on the corporate media and the emergence of the professional war correspondent. Along with a critique of professionalism, Chapter 10 takes in the alternative media and considers the opportunities for progressive journalism within the mainstream. The crucial ethical responsibilities of journalists in both the corporate and alternative sectors in bringing to light the warfare activities of the secret state are also highlighted. In the *Ethics in Action* section, former BBC World Service correspondent, Lara Pawson, reflects on the ethical choices she made while reporting from Africa. Richard is a professor of journalism at Lincoln University and visiting professor at Liverpool Hope University. He is the author of the first two editions of *Ethics for Journalists* and has written or edited 38 books on journalism and other topics including peace journalism, newspaper skills, literary journalism, profiles, and the secret state and the media and George Orwell. He is joint editor of *Ethical Space: The International Journal of Communication Ethics* and *George Orwell Studies*.

And so you have it. The contributors and I hope that by reading this edition of *Ethics for Journalists* you will discover and agree with us that ethics in journalism is everyone's responsibility. How journalists report stories, how they treat their sources and vulnerable people or people from diverse backgrounds, how they give voice to those who we normally don't hear from, how they hold those in power to account and how they tell people's precious stories all matter. Being an ethical journalist matters, now more than ever when audiences are hungry for responsible, fact-based journalism. We hope that this book will help you to be ethical, or at least to think about it.

References

Ethical Journalism Network. (2022) 'Our five core principles of ethical journalism'. Available at: https://ethicaljournalismnetwork.org/who-we-are (Accessed: 13 January 2022).

Harcup, T. (2007) *The ethical journalist*. London: Sage.

International Federation of Journalists (IFJ). (2019) 'Global charter of ethics for journalists'. Available at: www.ifj.org/who/rules-and-policy/global-charter-of-ethics-for-journalists.html (Accessed: 13 January 2022).

Keeble, R.L. (2009) *Ethics for journalists*. 2nd ed. Abingdon: Routledge.

Maksl, A., Ashley, S. and Craft, S. (2015). 'Measuring news media literacy'. *Journal of Media Literacy Education*, 6(3), pp. 29–45. Available at: https://digitalcommons.uri.edu/jmle/vol6/iss3/3 (Accessed: 14 January 2022).

Society of Professional Journalists (SPJ). (2014) 'SPJ code of ethics'. Available at: www.spj.org/ethicscode.asp (Accessed: 13 January 2022).

White, A. (2015) *The 5 core values of journalism*. 19 February. Available at: www.youtube.com/watch?v=uNidQHk5SZs (Accessed: 13 January 2022.

Yeoman, F. (2020) Email to Sallyanne Duncan, 24 August.

1
Trust, information disorder and freedom of expression
Influences on ethical journalism

Sallyanne Duncan

There are several influences on the ethical choices made by news organisations and journalists, but three in particular have dominated in recent years. They are trust, information disorder and freedom of expression. Journalists build trust with their audiences and wider communities through ethical reporting but that can be undermined by information disorder—misinformation, disinformation and malinformation—from untrustworthy sources. An antidote to information disorder is freedom of expression and with it press freedom that enables responsible news organisations to seek the truth and report it. This chapter examines these influences and the debates around them.

Why is trust important?

Trust is fundamental to journalism. It is associated with all five core principles of ethical journalism: truth and accuracy; independence; fairness and impartiality; humanity; and accountability (Ethical Journalism Network, 2022; White, 2015). Seeking the truth and reporting it accurately are the tools that build trust in journalism. Fact-based journalism grounded on honest reporting where journalists admit openly when they are unable to corroborate information is key to developing trust with audiences. Acting independently to hold those in power to account, avoiding biases and actively listening to those who are under-represented in the media engenders trust amongst audiences and wider communities. Striving for fairness by providing a range of voices and opinions in stories as well as necessary context aids impartial reporting that builds trust and confidence. Equally, journalists who seek to minimize harm to those who appear in or are affected by their stories—and therefore consider humanity and dignity in their reporting—will be trusted over those who are ethically casual regarding the consequences of their coverage. Lastly, journalists and

DOI: 10.4324/9780429505386-2

news outlets that are transparent about their sourcing or admit their mistakes and correct them swiftly and sincerely are acting responsibly. By holding themselves to account, they encourage trust in their product.

But this ethical optimism is marred by two factors: not all news outlets are trustworthy, and there is a lack of trust, or low level of trust, in the media among the population globally. News outlets can damage trust when they adopt fervent agenda-setting to influence the public agenda on certain controversial topics, such as migrants' attempts to reach the UK, and report them inaccurately or in a biased way. Individual journalists can also be deemed untrustworthy if their reporting is consistently inaccurate, discriminatory, gratuitous or sensational. Both news outlets and journalists will lose the public's trust if they regularly employ poor journalistic practices that breach professional standards and industry codes of conduct or even break the law. This happened after the phone-hacking scandal involving News Corp tabloids in the UK in 2011. A YouGov survey for US public service broadcaster, PBS, shortly afterwards, found that 58% of UK respondents said they had lost trust in the British press as a result of the scandal, while 51% said they were less likely to trust any UK news organisations (Robinson, 2011).

Creating distrust and false realities

However, distrust in the news is not only a British phenomenon. Nor is it confined to the media alone. It is part of a general, global decline in institutional trust relationships across social and political establishments that people believe have failed them (Robinson, 2019; Lewis, 2020). Scholars have identified low and declining rates of trust in news in various countries worldwide, falling on average by five percentage points across 18 countries since 2015, although it is not universal and is dependent on age (Hanitzsch, Van Dalen and Steindl, 2018; Jones, 2018; Fletcher, no date, para 2). The effect of this decline on trust and by turn credibility is a major problem for the journalism profession. Reed et al (2020, p. 41) observe that "without credibility, facts lack impact. And without trust, there is little chance of credibility." It is also seen to be a symptom of a bigger problem: the "worshipping of the individual at the expense of community"—a potential erosion of social cohesion—where public conversations take place on social media in "niche-oriented groups" susceptible to commercial and political manipulation that encourages people to "assume binary interests and pick sides to protect discursive territory" (Usher, 2018; Robinson, 2019, p. 56).

Distrust in the media has been an ongoing problem for decades, although the reasons for this are numerous and diverse. Erosion of trust is partially due to changing structures, technological and economic challenges, the obscuring of journalism's professional boundaries and increasing production pressures on staff working in a 24/7 news cycle that are reshaping the roles, routines and financial models of news organisations (Usher, 2014, 2018; Lewis, 2020). A lack of trust can affect the media's ability to function as watchdogs or curators of shared experiences (Carey, 1992; Schudson, 2000) so there is a mismatch between public expectations and journalism's ability to deliver (Karlsson and Clerwall, 2019). But as Fletcher notes, trust in the media is not solely the responsibility of news organisations and journalists. Some people are indifferent to journalism and others see trust in the media as linked to trust in politics where even quality news coverage can be construed as biased when politics is polarised. Public understanding of journalism, therefore, can be swayed by their perception of other institutions and by signals from politicians and other leaders, "who in some countries increasingly aggressively and explicitly attack independent news media and question journalists' integrity and motives" (Fletcher, no date, para 4). To counter this, Robinson suggests that journalists could distance themselves from "their synergetic relationships with institutionalized power elites and turn towards communities" (2019, p. 56).

One of the most corrosive challenges to trust is the pervasive use of the term fake news by particular individuals or groups to condemn legitimate news coverage that they disagree with, and "to construct the idea of a parallel, false reality built by a liberal elite with socialist aims" (Reed et al., 2020, p. 41). Responsibility for the widespread use of fake news and its associated term, alternative facts, lies with former US President, Donald Trump, who in the first 100 days of his presidency made 492 false or misleading statements, according to *The Washington Post* (n.d.). Trump also used the term, fake news, to undermine the professional work of journalists who held him to account. In doing so, he created "a sense of uncertainty about whether any facts are knowable at all" (Lewandowsky, Ecker and Cook, 2017, p. 361). The issue of fake news, or false news, and information disorder will be discussed later in the chapter.

Trust in journalism begins to recover

Public trust in journalism has seen a slight recovery in 2021 as populations affected by the coronavirus disease 2019 (COVID-19) pandemic sought out reliable—and trusted—information to deal with the crisis. There was a hunger for fact-based reporting that eschewed political spin and partisan agenda setting. The Reuters Institute Digital News Report for 2021 found that although the crisis led to the closure of numerous newspaper print editions, it did highlight the importance of accurate, reliable information at a time of national and international catastrophe. People turned to trusted brands (Newman et al.,

2021) that prioritised truth-seeking and accuracy alongside holding those in power to account. During 2020–2021, journalism's public service function was foregrounded, underpinned by the UK government's designation of journalists as key workers whose work was "critical to the Covid-19 response" (Tobitt, 2020) and who provided trusted, independent news that in some cases enabled people, organisations and governments to make momentous, life-changing decisions. However, the Reuters Institute researchers emphasised that this loyalty to trusted brands varied throughout the world and it also revealed "worrying inequalities in both consumption and trust with the young, women, people from ethnic minorities, and political partisans often feeling less fairly represented by the media" (Newman et al., 2021, p. 9). They did note that trust in the news had increased on average by six percentage points during the pandemic. A total of 44% of their global respondents reported that they trusted most news most of the time, which after years of decline returned public trust to 2018 levels. In terms of individual countries, Finland ranked the highest at 65%, whilst the USA was the lowest at 29%. Regarding the UK media, trust increased by eight percentage points to 36% but remains low, being 14 percentage points lower than in 2016, prior to the Brexit referendum. The report also found that audiences in countries where there is a strong, independent public service media placed greater importance on accurate, reliable news sources from recognised, dependable news products during the pandemic than on social media and aggregated news sites. However, they added the caveat that: "The pattern is less clear outside Western Europe, in countries where the Coronavirus crisis has dominated the media agenda less, or where other political and social issues have played a bigger role" (Newman et al., 2021, p. 9).

News outlets, at least in the UK, appear to be embracing this challenge to continue to provide fact-based reporting as the pandemic moves into further stages. While the spread of information disorder—misinformation, disinformation and malinformation—and the use of untrustworthy sources continues to dominate news during the pandemic, some media leaders are optimistic about the situation. Reuters editor-in-chief, Alessandra Galloni, sees a commercial opportunity in offering rigorously fact-checked, fact-based, impartial journalism, particularly as politics and society become more polarised. She said:

> The news business is being tested by the impact of platforms, the proliferation of misinformation and the continuing challenges to press freedom around the world. However, journalists are resilient and, as an industry, we have demonstrated our ability to learn, adapt and improve. I am confident that the world is starting to recognise the real value of news—and trusted, independent journalism—as both a product and a public service.
>
> *Tobitt and Turvill, 2021*

What is information disorder? Why is it a threat to trust?

Firstly, what it is not: it is not fake news. It is much more than this misleading term, and despite the sanguinity of some trusted news brands, it remains a major threat to trust. By 2021, 41% of people continued to struggle in determining whether information about coronavirus was true or false, according to an Ofcom survey (Tobitt, 2021).

Information disorder is a collective term that embraces misinformation, disinformation and malinformation, all of which can undermine trust in varying degrees. Misinformation involves an element of unintended consequences. Disinformation and malinformation appear to be more sinister in that their use involves a deliberate act to harm.

Misinformation is often shared by people on social media who do not realise that the content is false or misleading. Their intention may be to help people in their networks or communities by sharing information, but in doing so they are giving this false information greater circulation. And since journalists use social media to source stories they may come across it then publish it more widely, especially if it is humorous or contains pictures or videos. Of course, reporters should do due diligence and verify the content using rigorous fact-checking techniques, but under the pressure of deadlines or the need to find quick content, they may well take the risk and use the content without verifying its authenticity in order to complete the task.

Disinformation, as noted above, aims to do harm. It is content that is deliberately false and damaging when it is taken at face value as being authentic. Those who create disinformation are motivated by three factors, according to First Draft, an organisation that aims to combat the circulation of harmful, false and misleading information by providing people, including journalists, with the knowledge and tools to debunk it. The factors are: to make money; to obtain domestic or foreign political influence; or to maliciously make trouble (Wardle, 2019, p. 8). Sometimes, disinformation is shared innocently and consequently takes on the form of misinformation. However, other times it is deliberately and malevolently circulated to cause harm.

Malinformation is equally devious in that it is genuine information that is used to harm a person's reputation, possibly by making private information public. Because it contains some truth, people are more likely to believe it. Most false information falls into this category, Wardle says. "We are increasingly seeing the weaponization of context, the use of genuine content, but content that is warped and reframed" (2019, p. 8).

Information disorder in the time of COVID-19

The rise of widespread information disorder has gained significant prominence during the COVID-19 pandemic, a worrying trend that can undermine public health messages and impact on saving lives. The denigration of experts and scientific facts as a result of sharing false information impinges on the confidence that news consumers have in the information provided by news outlets through a general erosion of trust. Professor Devi Sridhar, chair of global public health at the University of Edinburgh, who has first-hand experience of information disorder, believes that the line between facts and lies has disintegrated.

> Years of experience in infectious disease control and a doctorate or medical degree quickly become equivalent to the influencer on YouTube or Facebook who has garnered hundreds of thousands of followers by promoting exciting-but-untrue "facts".
>
> *Sridhar, 2022*

She has been subjected to lies where her expertise has been attacked, with false claims that she has no published scientific papers or that she is a philosopher rather than a scientist because she has a DPhil from the University of Oxford. She adds: "It's easy to laugh at such obvious untruths, until it sinks in that this clickbait gets shared thousands of times. People believe it, and then they too share it" (Sridhar, 2022).

But the media also have to take some responsibility for the circulation of false information about COVID-19. Research from Princeton University's Empirical Studies of Conflict Project (ESOC) found that one in eight news outlets helped disseminate misinformation on COVID-19. They examined a database of 5,613 false news narratives from news organisations, social media and fact-checking initiatives and identified 737 that were distributed by news outlets; some of these were the source of the false information, notably in countries where the media are strictly controlled. Although only 16 bogus storylines emerged from the UK, they included narratives that coronavirus originated from people eating bats in China (*Daily Mail*, 31 January 2020) and people who were over six feet tall were twice as likely to get the virus (*Telegraph*, *Daily Mirror* and *Mail Online*, 10 August 2020; the *Daily Mirror* article was amended later to clarify the facts; Majid, 2021b). Another study by Cornell University's Alliance for Science examined 1.1 million English language stories in the mainstream media between January and May 2020 and found that only 16% were "fact-checking" in nature, leading the researchers to conclude "that the majority of Covid-19 misinformation is conveyed by the media without question or correction" (Evanega et al. 2021, quoted in Majid, 2021b). Also, research by fact-checking organisation, Full Fact, for *Press Gazette*, found that most false information in mainstream media was a result of journalists' misreporting or misunderstanding scientific research and academic findings. They found that around 25 out of the 102 media errors they examined were due to miscommunicating science (Majid, 2021a; see Chapter 9 for further discussion of health reporting).

Different types of false information

First Draft breaks down the three categories of information disorder further to assist people in identifying variations in false information. These range in severity from low harm to high harm and are, starting with low harm, satire or parody; false connection; misleading content; false content; imposter content; manipulated content; and fabricated content, which has the highest harm level (Wardle, 2017). With satire/parody, there is no intention to cause harm but it has the potential to trick people. Magazines like *Private Eye* and *The Onion* are well-known for their satirical content and parodies of public figures, so in this context it is a recognised form of journalism that audiences understand. But when satire is misused, potential harm can increase. Those with malevolent intentions can evade fact-checking systems, spread rumours and propagate conspiracy theories under the guise of satire, claiming that any misrepresentation was unintentional. Additionally, as satire is circulated on social media, it progressively loses its original context and source, especially if it is shared as a screenshot or meme, and so people fail to recognise it as satire. The visual or contextual cues that would be apparent in a printed edition are absent when it is reshared numerous times online (Wardle, 2017, 2019).

False connection also has a lower harm level and occurs when headlines, images or captions do not reflect the accompanying content, causing a mismatch. Thus, news outlets need to take some responsibility for the occurrence of this form of false information (Wardle, 2017). Using clickbait to drive traffic to online news sites is a particular concern. Wardle describes exploiting sensational language to tease audiences into clicking through to content that fails to fulfil their expectations as "a form of pollution" even though audiences may be familiar with the practice (2019, p. 19). In turn, this can undermine trust in the journalism profession and lead people to reject a news outlet.

Misleading content is the ambiguous or misrepresentative framing of an issue or an individual. It is difficult to pin down as it can include writing a headline that reframes a story, using partial quotes to support a wider point, including statistics to support a particular viewpoint rather than in an impartial manner and avoiding covering a perspective because it undermines an argument

(Wardle, 2017, 2019, p. 24). Several of these practices would result in biased reporting. Wardle explains:

> There is clearly a significant difference between sensational hyperpartisan content and slightly misleading captions that reframe an issue and impact the way someone might interpret an image. But trust in the media has plummeted. Misleading content that might previously have been viewed as harmless should be viewed differently.
>
> *2019, p. 24*

With false context, real content is interspersed with false contextual information in dangerous ways and shared (Wardle, 2017, 2019). It is most prevalent in photographs and video where a genuine image can be re-captioned with a fabricated description, or an authentic picture can be taken out of context and used in an unrelated story so that it is passed off as representing that story.

Real information is also utilised in imposter content where genuine sources or trusted news organisations are impersonated. News from reputable journalists or branding designs, for example, logos, of respected, established outlets are added to false and misleading statements or images to pass them off as genuine content from the outlet that is shared on social media (Wardle, 2017). Some contain hyperlinks that actually go to the impersonated news outlet's real site. Others involve photoshopping in additional, harmful information into a genuine story then sharing it on social media with the fabricated content in place. Journalists have also been targeted with their real Twitter handle, photograph and bio being put on to fake tweets so that it looked like they had made some shocking statement (Wardle, 2017). The result is that with information overload people may fail to spot that their trusted news outlets or journalists are being abused by imposters.

Again, authentic information or images are a factor in manipulated content, but these are specifically engineered to deceive people. Here, a component of authentic content is altered so that it tells a lie. Often, this occurs when two real images are edited together in a montage without acknowledging that the technique has been used. It can also be applied to audio to discredit someone's reputation. The audio of a speech given by the US House of Representatives Speaker, Nancy Pelosi, in 2019, was manipulated by slowing it down slightly so that it made her appear to slur her words as if she was drunk (Wardle, 2019).

Lastly, the most harmful category, fabricated content, is entirely false and is conceived to dupe people and cause harm (Wardle, 2017). One noteworthy example was the false claim by WTOE 5 News that Pope Francis had endorsed Donald Trump's candidacy for the US presidential election in 2016. However, the story was debunked by Snopes, a fact-checking site, who described WTOE

5 News as a "one of many fake news sites that masquerade as local television news outlets and do not publish factual stories" (Evon, 2016; Wardle, 2019). Artificial intelligence (AI) is now being used to create fabricated content of public figures saying or doing outrageous things. Known as deepfakes, they use deep learning, a form of AI, to create images of false events. One of the most well-known examples is a version of former US President Barack Obama that was created by Jordan Peele in 2018 where he appeared to disparage Donald Trump. Another was Meta Platforms co-founder and CEO, Mark Zuckerberg, seemingly admitting that Facebook's true aim was to manipulate and exploit its users. The problem is growing exponentially, and news organisations need to be increasingly vigilant in identifying this false content as it becomes increasingly more sophisticated. In 2019, there were 7,964 deepfake videos online, but that almost doubled in nine months to 14,678, according to AI company Deeptrace (Sample, 2020; Toews, 2020). A consequence is that their circulation could create a "zero-trust society, where people cannot, or no longer bother to, distinguish truth from falsehood" (Sample, 2020). This could lead to a culture of plausible deniability where doubt is cast on genuine video footage by claiming it was a deepfake, which may be difficult to prove otherwise.

Why is freedom of expression so vital to press freedom and a free press?

If information disorder erodes trust, then free expression has the ability to fortify it. Freedom of expression is a universal human right, protected by Article 19 of the Universal Declaration of Human Rights, which should be enjoyed by every citizen but sadly is not, whether this is for political or economic reasons, or due to state oppression.

There is a long tradition of freedom of expression in Western society, stretching from the ideas of philosopher John Locke and poet John Milton in the 1600s, who were at the forefront of early debates about freedom of expression, to its incorporation as a right in the Human Rights Act 1998 (HRA) in the UK. The HRA is an interpretation of the treaty that covers all European citizens, the European Convention on Human Rights, which is similar to the US Bill of Rights (Frost, 2016). It states:

> Everyone has the right to freedom of expression. This right shall include freedom to hold opinions and to receive and impart information and ideas without interference by public authority and regardless of frontiers. This Article shall not prevent States from requiring the licensing of broadcasting, television or cinema enterprises.
>
> *HRA, Article 10.1, 1998*

The Act acknowledges an individual's right to have their own views and to express them to others. One of the most noted defences of freedom of expression as a right came from John Stuart Mill's 1859 essay *On Liberty*. He argued that without freedom to express ideas, humanity could not progress science, politics or law. Truth, he stated, drives out falsity and discussing ideas freely, whether they are true or false, should not be feared as this prevents "the deep slumber of decided opinion" (2016, p. 34). He added:

> The peculiar evil of silencing an expression of opinion is that it is robbing the human race; posterity as well as the existing generation; those who dissent from the opinion, still more than those who hold it.
>
> 2016, p. 17

Therefore, freedom of expression is a necessary function of democracy. As part of that right, citizens are entitled to *receive* information in order to assist them in engaging in democratic, autonomous decision-making. Central to that is a free press that can seek truth and report it as well as share a variety of ideas, comment and analysis, and hold those in power to account. According to philosopher Professor Onora O'Neill, there are three classic arguments of why we need press freedom, although she sees flaws in all of them. These include the protection of individual's rights to self-expression, but the media is concerned with communication rather than self-expression; the needs for truth-seeking, which she says is too narrow because truth is not the issue in all media content, for example, horoscopes; and most notably, "that our social, cultural and political life needs media communication that is not only accessible and intelligible but can be assessed for its reliability and provenance". Nonetheless, she adds, some news organisations do not do enough to make their communication assessable (O'Neill, 2012).

Journalism's responsibilities

So, as Frost (2016) notes, press freedom acquires its authority from the individual right to freedom of expression and opinion (p. 39), but journalists have no special privileges in the UK, and in their work, they implement the same rights as they do as a citizen.

> Journalists have always resisted attempts to make them different, partly because if the media were to have special privileges it might also be expected to have special obligations. However, this is not the case throughout the world and in some European countries journalists have special rights and special rights of access to information unavailable to the general public.
>
> Frost, 2016, p. 52

That said, Frost posits that there may be a distinction between personal freedom of expression and press freedom of expression as Article 10 of the HRA does not refer specifically to freedom of the press. Additionally, personal freedom of expression can be seen as an individual claim whilst press freedom is a collective entitlement. But journalists do carry special responsibilities, however, to guard the public's right to "seek, receive and impart information and ideas through any media and regardless of frontiers", as enshrined in Article 19 of the Universal Declaration of Human Rights (United Nations, n.d.). Frost observes:

> It is the right to receive information that is the true driving force behind media freedom in the UK. If we are to receive information, we must receive it from the media and so to prevent the media telling the public things, unless it is to protect some other right (reputation, privacy, life or fair trial), would be to breach the rights of many citizens to freely receive information.
> 2016, p. 45

But given the commercial nature of most media, not all information that citizens receive is worthy or assists them in their democratic decision-making. The mainstream media operate in a profit-oriented economy where their primary purpose is to satisfy shareholders rather than citizens, and for some news outlets, that means their focus is celebrity-driven news. Within this context, the right to freedom of expression can be cited as justification for potentially ethically dubious acts, such as harm caused from intense media scrutiny of stars, personalities and public figures or devious reporting methods that harm ordinary people. Indeed, Lord Leveson warned the media not to take liberties with the free expression justification. He said that freedom for commercial news organisations was not the same as freedom of individual self-expression—one was corporate, the other was personal—and the need for free speech to be available to "powerless" individuals was not a claim for the need for free speech for powerful news corporations". He added: "The need for a free press is not to provide the media with a free voice, but to provide a means of communication that will give others the opportunity to have their free voice heard" (Leveson, 2012, p. 62, quoted in Frost, 2016, p. 47).

Limits to free expression

Evidently, a free press is not always a responsible press, and so limits to free expression need to be placed on the media. The first is that press freedom must operate within the law, whether that is in relation to defamation, data protection, trespass and harassment, anti-terrorism, confidence and privacy, copyright and court reporting, or other legislation. If news outlets fail to do this, then they risk losing their moral credibility—and trust—as an instrument of information amplification. Additionally, their reporting must be in the public interest, a concept that sits alongside a free press (Frost, 2016, p. 49). Freedom of expression does not give news outlets the right to publish anything they want; there needs to be a moral justification to inform citizens, and therefore, content should be in the public interest, albeit that it should be engaging, and not merely of interest to the public such that it satisfies their curiosity or entertains them. Therefore, for democracy to function effectively so that people receive the information they need to make decisions, journalists need to base their reporting choices on solid ethical evaluation. But freedom of the press means different things to different people. One person might see it as the freedom to publish the truth, another might view that pursuit of the truth as a gross invasion of their private life. Proprietors might perceive it as a way to increase profits, a journalist might consider it as a means to secure an exclusive or win an award, whilst another journalist might see it as a conduit to exposing corruption or other wrongs and to holding those in power to account. Frost warns journalists to take care when deciding to publish something in the public interest because of its potential to cause harm. He reminds them of their obligation to take responsibility for their actions where necessary and to defend their decisions to circulate information more widely (2016).

Freedom of expression in times of crisis

There are times, however, when the media and the public might accept limits to their freedom of expression. The COVID-19 pandemic was one such crisis. Reporters without Borders (RSF) found that press freedom was constrained in 75% of the world during the pandemic, leading to a dramatic deterioration in press freedom (Holt, 2021, p. 1695). Such limits need to be justified; otherwise, essentially temporary restrictions could result in a loss of freedom and an erosion of individual rights and press freedom. As noted in the section on trust, it is evident that journalists have performed a public service role as key workers in disseminating information from authorities, particularly during the early stages of the pandemic. Their crucial role on ensuring that the public received accurate information in a time of calamity has been recognised by health experts and clinicians. Rebecca Vincent, director of international campaigns at RSF Reporters without Borders told *The Lancet*:

> There is an interconnection between freedom of information and public health, and this pandemic has highlighted how important freedom of information is in a public health emergency. Journalists need to be allowed to give accurate information freely to the public so that people can inform themselves and take appropriate steps in an emergency.
>
> Holt, 2021, p. 1696

However, some governments have used the pandemic as an opportunity to implement emergency powers that stifle critics and abuse press freedom, including physically attacking and jailing journalists. The World Press Freedom

Index 2021 found that even in Norway, the country deemed to have the greatest amount of press freedom in the world, reporting restrictions had affected coverage and some journalists experienced a lack of access to vital information, undermining relationships between the media and authorities (RSF, 2022). News outlets in the UK also experienced difficulties with the authorities over-reporting the pandemic but other issues dominated. These include the UK government's use of an obscure unit called The Clearing House, which circulates freedom of information requests from journalists and others to government departments and advises on their response. Julian Richards, the editor-in-chief of openDemocracy, the global media platform that first raised concerns about the unit in 2018, described it as "a toxic culture of secrecy and evasion that has to stop" (Siddique, 2021). The continued detention of WikiLeaks publisher, Julian Assange, in a British high-security prison also undermined the UK's press freedom ranking. He is to be extradited to the USA after losing a legal battle in December 2021 to face charges of conspiracy to hack into American military databases in order to obtain top secret information on the wars in Afghanistan and Iraq, which he published on the WikiLeaks website. Amnesty International described the extradition ruling as a "travesty of justice" (Morton, 2021). Also, journalists in Northern Ireland who cover paramilitary activities and organised crime continued to be at risk two years after journalist Lyra McKee was killed when she was covering riots in Derry (RSF, 2022).

Is there a totally free media?

It appears that no country in the world has a totally free media, according to Frost. In Western democracies, restrictions are imposed by proprietors and advertisers, and even by journalists who decide which angle to take in a story, or by governments who try to manage the circulation of information about themselves (Frost, 2016). Oppressive regimes strictly control information flow by instructing news organisations on the content and approach to their reporting so that they only produce beneficial coverage. They clamp down on resistance by journalists who pursue press freedom, but some take action against this through their reporting like the journalist and media company CEO Maria Ressa from the Philippines and Russian editor Dmitry Muratov, who shared the Nobel Peace Prize in 2021. They received the award for "their courageous fight for freedom of expression in the Philippines and Russia". The Norwegian Nobel Committee said the two were representatives of all journalists who champion free expression where "democracy and freedom of the press face increasingly adverse conditions". Independent, fact-based journalism, like that undertaken by Ressa and Muratov, was a safeguard against abuse of power, lies and propaganda, Berit Reiss-Andersen, the chair of the Norwegian Nobel committee said (Ratcliffe, 2021; Nobel Peace Prize, 2021).

Maria Ressa is the co-founder and CEO of *Rappler*, an investigative journalism digital media company based in the Philippines. It was set up in 2012 with the desire to search out the truth and to embrace social media. *Rappler* is known for its uncompromising journalism and analysis "that inspires smart conversations and a thirst for change" (Rappler, 2011). More than 4.5 million people follow it on Facebook and around 3.5 million on Twitter. Despite their public profile, Ressa and the news site have been subject to numerous criminal investigations and subsequent charges after publishing stories that criticised the country's president, Rodrigo Duterte. Their reports have concentrated on his government's controversial anti-drug campaign that conducts extrajudicial killings against suspected drug dealers and users. They have also covered the regime's use of social media to spread fake news, to intimidate rivals and to manipulate public discourse. As a result, Ressa has been issued with many warrants for her arrest involving her in numerous legal battles with the Philippine government. In 2020, she was convicted, along with former *Rappler* writer, Reynaldo Santos Jr, of cyber libel for an article in *Rappler* in 2012 about the apparent involvement of rich Filipino businessman, Wilfredo Keng, in murder, drug dealing, human trafficking and smuggling. The pair, who are out on bail, face a six-year prison sentence (CBC Radio, 2021).

Dmitry Muratov founded the Russian independent newspaper, *Novaya Gazeta*, in 1993, with colleagues. He became editor-in-chief in 1995, a post he held for 24 years. Known for its criticism of those in power, it has reported on corruption, police violence, unlawful arrests, electoral fraud and "troll factories" and the deployment of the Russian military in and outside the country (Nobel Peace Prize, 2021). Six of its journalists have been killed since its inception, including Anna Politkovskaya who wrote exposés on the war in Chechnya. The committee said: "The newspaper's fact-based journalism and professional integrity have made it an important source of information on censurable aspects of Russian society rarely mentioned by other media" (Nobel Peace Prize, 2021). In his Nobel lecture, Muratov said that Russia was going through "a dark valley" regarding its treatment of journalists and news outlets. This extended to human rights supporters and NGOs, who have been branded as "foreign agents", which he commented meant "enemies of the people" (Nobel Prize, 2021).

After the announcement that Ressa and Muratov had won the peace prize, Agnès Callamard, Secretary General of Amnesty International, said:

> Maria Ressa and Dmitry Muratov's Nobel Peace Prize win is a victory not only for independent, critical journalism in The Philippines and Russia, but for the fight for justice, accountability and freedom of expression all over the world.
>
> *Amnesty International, 2021*

References

Amnesty International. (2021) 'Maria Ressa and Dmitry Muratov's Nobel Peace Prize win is a victory for press freedom globally'. Available at: www.amnesty.org/en/latest/news/2021/10/maria-ressa-and-dmitry-muratovs-nobel-peace-prize-win-is-a-victory-for-press-freedom-globally/ (Accessed: 14 January 2022).

Carey, J.W. (1992) *Communication as culture* (Revised Edition: Essays on Media and Society). London: Routledge.

CBC Radio. (2021) 'Facing possible jail time totalling 100 years, journalist Maria Ressa says she won't stop fighting for justice', 8 October. *The Current, CBC Radio*. Available at: www.cbc.ca/radio/thecurrent/the-current-for-june-18-2020-1.5616058/facing-possible-jail-time-totalling-100-years-journalist-maria-ressa-says-she-won-t-stop-fighting-for-justice-1.5617289#:~:text=Update%2C%20Oct.,sentence%20has%20been%20handed%20down (Accessed: 15 January 2022).

Ethical Journalism Network. (2022) 'Our five core principles of ethical journalism'. Available at: https://ethicaljournalismnetwork.org/who-we-are#Mission (Accessed: 6 January 2022).

Evanega, S., Lynas, M., Adams, J. and Smolenyak, K. (2021) 'Coronavirus misinformation: Quantifying sources and themes in the Covid-19 "infodemic"', quoted in 'Tall stories: News media's role in spreading misinformation during Covid-19 charted', *Press Gazette*, 9 September. Available at: https://pressgazette.co.uk/news-media-covid-misinformation/ (Accessed: 6 January 2022).

Evon, D. (2016) 'Pope Francis shocks world, endorses Donald Trump for president'. 10 July. Available at: www.snopes.com/fact-check/pope-francis-donald-trump-endorsement/ (Accessed: 6 January 2022).

Fletcher, R. (no date) 'Trust will get worse before it gets better'. Available at: www.digitalnewsreport.org/publications/2020/trust-will-get-worse-gets-better/ (Accessed: 4 January 2022).

Frost, C. (2016) *Journalism ethics and regulation*, 4th ed. Abingdon: Routledge.

Hanitzsch, T., Van Dalen, A. and Steindl, N. (2018) 'Caught in the nexus: A comparative and longitudinal analysis of public trust in the press', *The International Journal of Press/Politics*, 23(1), pp. 30–23. https://doi.org/10.1177/1940161217740695

Holt, E. (2021) 'Media restrictions have "cost lives"', *The Lancet*, 397(10286), pp. 1695–1696. https://doi.org/10.1016/S0140-6736(21)01053-9

Human Rights Act. (1998), a.10. Available at: www.legislation.gov.uk/ukpga/1998/42/schedule/1 (Accessed: 9 January 2022).

Jones, J.M. (2018). 'US media trust continues to recover from 2016 low', *Gallup*, 12 October. Available at: https://news.gallup.com/poll/243665/media-trust-continues-recover-2016-low.aspx (Accessed: 4 January 2022).

Karlsson, M. and Clerwall, C. (2019) 'Cornerstones in Journalism', *Journalism Studies*, 20(8), 1184–1199. https://doi.org/10.1080/1461670X.2018.1499436.

Leveson, L.J. (2012) 'An inquiry into the culture, practices and ethics of the press: Report'. London: The Stationary Office, quoted in: Frost, C. (2016) *Journalism ethics and regulation*, 4th ed. Abingdon: Routledge.

Lewandowsky, S., Ecker, U. K. H. and Cook, J. (2017). 'Beyond misinformation: Understanding and coping with the "post-truth" era', *Journal of Applied Research in Memory and Cognition*, 6(4), 353–369. https://doi.org/10.1016/j.jarmac.2017.07.008

Lewis, S. C. (2020) 'Lack of trust in the news media, institutional weakness, and relational journalism as a potential way forward', *Journalism*, 21(3), 345–348. doi: 10.1177/1464884918807597.

Majid, A. (2021a) 'Covid-19 and the rise of misinformation and misunderstanding', *Press Gazette*, 15 April. Available at: https://pressgazette.co.uk/covid-19-rise-in-news-misinformation-data/ (Accessed: 6 January 2022).

Majid, A. (2021b) 'Tall stories: News media's role in spreading misinformation during Covid-19 charted', *Press Gazette*, 9 September. Available at: https://pressgazette.co.uk/news-media-covid-misinformation/ (Accessed: 6 January 2022).

Mill, J.S. (2016) (first published in 1859) *On liberty*, Los Angeles, CA: Enhanced Media.

Morton, B. (2021) 'Julian Assange can be extradited to the US, court rules', *BBC News*, 10 December. Available at: www.bbc.co.uk/news/uk-59608641 (Accessed: 11 January 2022).

Newman, N., Fletcher, R., Schulz, A., Andi, S., Robertson, C. and Nielsen, R. K. (2021) *Reuters Institute Digital News Report 2021* (June 23, 2021). Available at: SSRN: https://ssrn.com/abstract=3873260 (Accessed: 19 August 2022).

Nobel Peace Prize. (2021) 'The Nobel Peace Prize 2021 announcement'. Available at: www.nobelprize.org/prizes/peace/2021/press-release/ (Accessed: 15 January 2022).

Nobel Prize. (2021) 'Dmitry Muratov Nobel lecture', 10 December. Available at: www.nobelprize.org/prizes/peace/2021/muratov/lecture/ (Accessed: 15 January 2022).

O'Neill, O. (2012) 'So, what is a free press?' *The Guardian*, 23 November. Available at: www.theguardian.com/commentisfree/2012/nov/23/what-is-a-free-press (Accessed: 8 January 2022).

Rappler. (2011) 'The Social News Network. Uncompromised journalism that inspires smart conversations and a thirst for change', July. Available at: https://twitter.com/rapplerdotcom (Accessed: 15 January 2022).

Ratcliffe, R. (2021) 'Journalists Maria Ressa and Dmitry Muratov receive Nobel peace prize', 10 December. Available at: www.theguardian.com/world/2021/dec/10/journalists-maria-ressa-and-dmitry-muratov-receive-nobel-peace-prize (Accessed: 15 January 2022).

Reed, K., Walsh-Childers, K., Fischer, K. and Davie, B. (2020). 'Restoring trust in journalism: An education prescription', *Journalism & Mass Communication Educator*, 75(1), 40–45. doi: 10.1177/1077695820904192.

Robinson, J. (2011) 'Phone hacking: 58% of UK public say they have lost trust in papers', *The Guardian*, 14 November. Available at: www.theguardian.com/media/2011/nov/14/phone-hacking-public-trust (Accessed: 4 January 2022).

Robinson, S. (2019) 'Crisis of shared public discourses: Journalism and how it all begins and ends with trust', *Journalism*, 20(1), pp. 56–59. doi: 10.1177/1464884918808958

RSF Reporters without Borders. (2022) 'World Press Freedom Index 2021'. Available at: https://rsf.org/en/ranking (Accessed: 8 January 2022).

Sample, I. (2020) 'What are deepfakes—and how can you spot them', *The Guardian*, 13 January. Available at: www.theguardian.com/technology/2020/jan/13/what-are-deepfakes-and-how-can-you-spot-them (Accessed: 6 January 2022).

Schudson, M. (2000) *The good citizen: A history of American civic life*. New York: Free Press.

Siddique, H. (2021) 'UK government loses legal battle over transparency of "Orwellian" unit', *The Guardian*, 8 June. Available at: www.theguardian.com/politics/2021/jun/08/uk-government-loses-legal-battle-transparency-orwellian-unit (Accessed: 11 January 2022).

Sridhar, D. (2022) 'I've been lied about and others get death threats. Covid has shown the power of misinformation', *The Guardian*, 1 January. Available at: www.theguardian.com/commentisfree/2022/jan/01/death-threats-covid-disinformation-public-health-expert-pandemic (Accessed: 19 August 2022).

The Washington Post. (n.d.) '100 days of Trump claims'. Available at: www.washingtonpost.com/graphics/politics/trump-claims/ (Accessed: 4 January 2022).

Tobitt, C. (2020) 'Government gives "key worker" status to all journalists reporting on coronavirus pandemic to the public', *Press Gazette*, 20 March. Available at: https://pressgazette.co.uk/government-gives-key-worker-status-to-all-journalists-reporting-on-coronavirus-pandemic/ (Accessed: 4 January 2022).

Tobitt, C. (2021) 'Ofcom: In week 67 of pandemic public still hungry for coronavirus news but misinformation still widespread', *Press Gazette*, 11 August. Available at: https://pressgazette.co.uk/how-covid-19-news-consumption-and-misinformation-changed-week-1-to-67-of-pandemic/ (Accessed: 6 January 2022).

Tobitt, C. and Turvill, W. (2021) 'The future's bright: 22 news industry leaders share their tips for success in 2022', *Press Gazette*, 23 December. Available at: https://pressgazette.co.uk/media-predictions-2022/ (Accessed: 4 January 2022).

Toews, R. (2020) 'Deepfakes are going to wreak havoc on society. We are not prepared', *Forbes*, 25 May. Available at: www.forbes.com/sites/robtoews/2020/05/25/deepfakes-are-going-to-wreak-havoc-on-society-we-are-not-prepared/?sh=18b3415c7494 (Accessed: 6 January 2022).

United Nations. (n.d.) 'Universal declaration of human rights', *Article 19*. Available at: www.un.org/en/about-us/universal-declaration-of-human-rights (Accessed: 7 January 2022).

Usher, N. (2014) *Making news at The New York Times*. Ann Arbor, MI: University of Michigan Press.

Usher, N. (2018) 'Re-thinking trust in the news: A material approach through "Objects of Journalism"', *Journalism Studies*, 19(4), pp. 564–578. doi: 10.1080/1461670X.2017.1375391

Wardle, C. (2017) 'Fake news: it's complicated', 16 February. Available at: https://firstdraftnews.org/articles/fake-news-complicated/ (Accessed: 6 January 2022).

Wardle, C. (2019) 'First Draft's essential guide to understanding information disorder', October. Available at: https://firstdraftnews.org/wp-content/uploads/2019/10/Information_Disorder_Digital_AW.pdf?x76701 (Accessed: 6 January 2022).

White, A. (2015) 'The five core values of journalism'. 19 February. Available at: www.youtube.com/watch?v=uNidQHk5SZs (Accessed: 6 January 2022).

2
Regulating the mainstream media
Who guards the guardians?

Sallyanne Duncan

Codes of conduct and the regulatory bodies associated with them are considered by most mainstream media organisations to be the fundamental tools for ensuring their work is ethical. This chapter describes the main UK regulators, their codes and systems for maintaining professional standards and other means of promoting responsible reporting including readers' editors, professional networks, monitoring groups and public pressure via social media. It also discusses issues with codes of conduct and the importance of the public interest. In the *Ethics in Action* section, Aidan White, founder and honorary president of the Ethical Journalism Network (EJN), explores the effectiveness of current regulatory systems and codes, the role of the EJN in maintaining standards and the challenges for journalists after the COVID-19 pandemic.

Who are the key regulatory bodies in the UK?

Despite print media now offering video, audio and other multimedia content, and broadcasters providing online text and photographs alongside their TV and radio content, regulatory systems split down traditional lines. Newspapers, magazines and their online editions, as well as hyperlocal sites and independent publishers, adhere to voluntary self-regulation overseen by standards organisations that also deal with complaints from the public. Broadcasters, like the BBC, Channel 4 and Sky News, and their online versions and on-demand systems are accountable via statutory regulation under the Communications Act 2003 and the regulator it provides.

Two regulators are responsible for maintaining standards in the print media. These are the Independent Press Standards Organisation (IPSO), of which most regional and national newspapers are members, a non-Royal Charter system set up by the national and regional press after the Leveson Inquiry, and the Independent Monitor for the Press (IMPRESS), which has Royal Charter

DOI: 10.4324/9780429505386-3

recognition and whose members are mostly independent micro-publishers, hyperlocals or local news sites.

Regarding broadcasting, the Office of Communications, the UK's broadcasting, telecommunications and postal regulatory body, known as Ofcom, regulates BBC news and current affairs content, as well as Sky News, ITN who produce ITV news, Channel 4 News and Channel 5 News and various radio stations, through its Broadcasting Code. Additionally, BBC journalists adhere to their company's Editorial Guidelines, which set out their values and standards.

Freelance journalists are expected to adhere to the regulatory system that applies to the sector that has hired them. All journalists, including freelancers, should familiarise themselves with the relevant codes.

What do they do?

Independent Press Standards Organisation

IPSO is the largest independent press regulator in the UK. It deals with complaints from the public about actions by their member publications that appear to have breached their ethical code, the Editors' Code of Practice. It investigates any complaints about printed or online editorial content or journalists' behaviour by the newspapers and magazines that have signed up to its terms and can force publications to publish corrections or adjudications if they breach the code, including on the front page (see IPSO, 2020).

Since its inception in 2012, IPSO has faced controversy. Fearing that the government would impose a statutory regulator on the press following the Leveson Inquiry, various major news publishers endorsed the Hunt/Black plan to establish a new press regulator to replace the discredited Press Complaints Commission. However, not all prominent publications supported the plan and several like *The Guardian/Observer, Independent, Financial Times, Evening Standard, Private Eye, Yahoo.com* and the *Huffington Post* opted out because of IPSO's apparent lack of independence. IPSO is funded by a Regulatory Funding Company (RFC), set up by the major publishers and industry employer associations, that raises a levy on the news and magazine industries. Nine directors sit on the RFC's board, all of them executives from the major publishers and their views are expected to be considered when appointments from the industry are made to the IPSO board of directors, which is composed of five industry members and seven independent, lay members. The RFC also convenes the Editors Code of Practice Committee, which oversees the operation and revision of the code. One critic,

Steven Barnett, professor of communication at the University of Westminster, described the RFC as "shadowy". He added: "IPSO's rules are therefore written and controlled by the very newspapers it purports to regulate 'independently'" (2016). Concerns about IPSO's independence persist, although it has taken on board several Leveson recommendations over the years to address this.

Today, more than 90% of national and local newspapers, most magazines and several digital-only publications are members of IPSO. This means they have agreed to comply with the Editors' Code of Practice, to accept IPSO's rulings on complaints and to submit annual reports on how they safeguard editorial standards including how they follow the Editors' Code and handle any serious complaints.

Unlike its predecessor, the PCC, it can investigate members and issue fines up to £1 million, although in reality it has never done so. It can act accordingly if there has been serious, systemic breaches of the Editors' Code; failure to comply with the requirements of IPSO's Board who are responsible for IPSO's vision and strategic direction; and crucially, if significant issues of concern are identified in a publication's annual statement.

In addition to the Editors' Code, it offers further protection to the public through a 24-hour anti-harassment advice line where people who have concerns about potential media intrusion or harassment can ask IPSO to intervene. The regulator may use a private advisory note to inform the newspaper or magazine publishers that through their actions they may have breached the Editors' Code. However, because it operates a self-regulatory system, IPSO does not have the formal power to stop publication or to prevent journalists asking questions. It also provides a low-cost arbitration scheme that gives victims of press abuse an alternative to legal action. A senior barrister, appointed as arbitrator, rules on the case and can require publishers to pay damages of up to £60,000 including aggravated damages. All 16 national newspapers are required to participate in arbitration when anyone with a "valid legal claim" against them contacts IPSO and pays a maximum fee of £100. However, other media groups like Conde Nast Publications Limited and the Press Association are part of a voluntary scheme where a complainant can request arbitration but the media outlet does not have to oblige. In doing so, the regulator has moved closer to the Leveson Inquiry recommendations for an affordable arbitration scheme that offers redress to those who cannot take a publication to court. Individuals can use the scheme to make legal claims about the publication of statements that may have caused them harm, the use of confidential or private information and unacceptable behaviour by reporters or photographers. These claims can be about defamation, malicious falsehood, misuse of private information and harassment, amongst others.

Assistance is also available to editors and journalists. They can seek pre-publication advice on how to interpret the Editors' Code or the public interest clause in relation to certain articles. They can access further guidance on reporting certain controversial topics, for example, deaths and inquests, major incidents, sexual offences, suicide, transgender issues and social media use. They can also consult the Editors' Codebook, a document designed to provide context to the code via examples of past cases. It aims to help journalists make difficult decisions on stories and to assist the public in determining whether their situation is a contravention of the code. For journalists who feel they have been pressured into acting in a way that contravenes the Editors' Code, they provide a whistleblowing hotline. Through its work with certain charities, NGOs and other organisations, it can provide advice for journalists on specific areas with a view to improving press standards.

Independent Monitor for the Press

IMPRESS plays an important role in the digital news industry. Although membership is open to all UK publications, its members are mainly small, independent organisations. More than 140 micro-publishers, investigative and specialist outlets have signed up to the regulator that sees itself as "building understanding and trust between journalists and the public", although no major news organisations are part of it (IMPRESS, n.d.a). Established in 2015, it is fully compliant with the Leveson Inquiry recommendations and the only one to be recognised by the Press Recognition Panel ([PRP]; in 2016), which ensures press regulators are independent, properly funded and able to protect the public. IPSO is not recognised by the PRP, so is essentially an unrecognised regulator, even though it complies with several Leveson recommendations. Despite its PRP recognition, it has attracted controversy over its funding, which comes from donations from the Independent Press Regulation Trust (IPRT). This charity is itself funded by the Alexander Mosely Charitable Trust, which was established by Max Mosely, a victim of press abuse, who was seen by some news organisations as having a vested interest in regulating the press. The IPRT initially provided £3.8m over the first four years of the new regulator's existence, and in 2018, IPRT agreed further funding of £2.85m until 2022. Funding also comes from an annual fee from its member publishers (IMPRESS, n.d.b).

IMPRESS has its own Standards Code, low-cost arbitration system and whistleblowing hotline. It operates a complaints service dealing with breaches of its Standards Code where complainants must raise their dispute with the member publication first, who have 21 days to respond to it. Thus, member publications must have their own compliance systems in place. For example, the investigative journalism network, *The Ferret*'s complaints system refers its audience to check the Standards Code; then it outlines a three-stage process of making a complaint; recording, investigating and resolving the complaint; and escalating the complaint to IMPRESS (see Ferret, n.d.). Thereafter, if the complainant is still dissatisfied, they can take their complaint to IMPRESS who will investigate and will ask both parties to explain their position. It can appoint an independent expert where issues relating to the complaint are complex or require specialist knowledge. It can also start its own investigations without a complaint, such as into a specific news story or media outlet's conduct where a breach is severe or where there is a pattern of behaviour by a publication.

Complaints are adjudicated by the IMPRESS Board, and where a complaint is upheld, it can require a news outlet to publish its determination. Additionally, it can impose sanctions including fines of up to 1% of a publishers' annual turnover, up to a maximum of £1million, and can direct the nature, extent and placement of corrections and apologies (see IMPRESS, n.d.c).

Separately and unrelated to complaints arising from breaches of its code, it offers an arbitration scheme to settle legal disputes involving its members, similar to IPSO, that is free to the complainant. Arbitrators are appointed by the Chartered Institute of Arbitrators, whose fee is paid by IMPRESS. It covers legal claims about defamation, breach of confidence, malicious falsehood, misuse of private information, harassment and breach of data protection, and aims to provide a quick, effective form of justice without going to court.

Prior to publication, the public can contact IMPRESS if they are experiencing harassment from the media. They can request IMPRESS to issue an advisory notice to warn its members about unwelcome press intrusion. It will also consider requests about news outlets it does not regulate or will ask other regulators to issue advisory notices.

As for helping journalists, IMPRESS runs a disclosure service operated by the whistleblowing charity, Protect. Anyone who works for a news outlet—whether they are staff members, freelance journalists, agency workers or working to contract – can use its hotline. It can raise the alarm on wrongdoing that is an offence or breaks the law, that breaches the Standards Code, that encourages others to breach the code, or any other unethical conduct that undermines the code's principles and spirit (see IMPRESS, n.d.d).

Office of Communications

Ofcom has wide-ranging responsibilities for regulating the UK's broadcasting, telecommunications and postal industries. It has a statutory duty to promote competition amongst the companies it regulates and to maintain standards for most TV and radio output including commercial stations, community services, temporary stations with restricted service licences and the BBC. However, it does not regulate radio stations that only broadcast over the internet and complainants should seek redress from the radio service provider.

In December 2003, Ofcom took over the regulatory responsibilities of five bodies:

- The Broadcasting Standards Commission, which regulated all radio and television—both BBC and commercial—as well as text, cable, satellite and digital services and could order broadcasters to publish the verdicts of complaints on-air at the same time as the original programme
- The Independent Television Commission, which licensed and regulated all commercial television in the UK, including teletext, terrestrial, cable, digital and satellite services, and could fine offending companies up to 3% of their annual revenue for serious breaches of their licences
- The Office of Telecommunications (oftel), which was responsible for promoting competition and looking after consumers' interests in the UK telecommunications market
- The Radio Authority, a watchdog for all national and local, cable, digital, satellite, hospital, community and student radio services which had similar powers to the ITC, including sanctions such as on-air apologies and corrections, fines and the shortening or withdrawal of licences
- The Radiocommunications Agency, which was responsible for managing the radio spectrum including licensing and enforcement

Since Ofcom draws on the work of five regulatory bodies, it is not surprising that its remit covers a wide range of areas such as licensing, the issuing of codes, conducting research, addressing complaints and overseeing competition issues. Amongst other responsibilities, Ofcom polices news and current affairs content for the major broadcasters and their on-demand services through its Broadcasting Code. Introduced in July 2005 with a new version instituted in January 2019, the code is a weighty document—its 10 sections have as many as 30 rules in some cases, along with guidance notes, a cross-promotion code and on-demand programme service rules (Ofcom, , 2021). Among the issues, the code covers are: protecting under-18s; harm and offence; crime, disorder, hatred and abuse; religion; elections and referenda; fairness, informed consent and deception; privacy including suffering and distress; and commercial references on TV and radio. Ofcom ensures that broadcasters address diversity in their programme making, protect audiences from harmful and offensive material and safeguard people from unfair treatment and invasions of privacy.

Complaints about privacy or fairness can be brought by those affected or someone they authorise to make the complaint. Regarding the BBC, someone complaining about privacy infringement or unfairness can contact the BBC or Ofcom, but not both. Other complaints can be brought by anyone and investigations can be launched by Ofcom itself. Overall, Ofcom dealt with 6,206 cases, which consisted of 55,801 complaints from April 2018 to March 2019. Of these, 132 cases raised substantive issues that they investigated further and 6,074 cases did not require further investigation or fell outside Ofcom's remit (Ofcom, 2019a). Where Ofcom decides that a breach of its code has been "serious, deliberate, repeated and/or reckless" (Ofcom, 2019a), it can forbid a repeat of the programme; direct them to broadcast a correction or statement of the regulator's findings; impose a fine or shorten, suspend or revoke a licence (with the exception of the BBC, S4C or Channel 4). For example, between April 2018 and March 2019, Ofcom imposed the following statutory sanctions: on Ausaf UK Limited by revoking the licence of its service, *Ausaf TV*; on JML Media Limited by levying a financial penalty of £7,500 on them in respect of its service, JML Direct; and on Radio Ikhlas Limited by enforcing a financial penalty of £10,000 and a direction to broadcast a statement of Ofcom's findings regarding their station Radio Ikhlas.

Ofcom does not deal initially with complaints about BBC programmes or its on-demand service, iPlayer, and people are expected to complain to the BBC first. However, it will review complaints in areas it regulates where a person has gone through the BBC's complaints process, has received a final response from them but wishes to take it further.

BBC complaints process

As noted in the Ofcom section, complaints about BBC content must be made to them firstly. Its Royal Charter and Agreement with the Secretary of State requires the BBC to have a framework for handling and resolving complaints (BBC Complaints Framework and Procedures, 2020). It also gives Ofcom the responsibility to regulate the BBC according to the standards in its Broadcasting Code.

The framework outlines five procedures for complaints relating to editorial content; general issues; television licensing; party election, party political and referendum campaigns; and regulatory matters. Editorial complaints are deemed to be those that fail to meet the values and standards set out in the BBC's Editorial Guidelines (see BBC Editorial Guidelines, 2020) such as accuracy, impartiality and avoiding offence.

Complaints are dealt with in three stages: 1) the complaint and initial response from a BBC manager or producer; 2) if the complainant is dissatisfied with the reply, the BBC's Executive Complaints Unit (ECU) will make a final response; 3) complainants who are still dissatisfied will be advised to contact Ofcom, who will investigate editorial complaints that appear to breach their Broadcasting Code. Ofcom considers that the BBC complaints system works effectively with many complainants being satisfied with the BBC's final response (Ofcom, 2019b). Of the 218,352 complaints received in 2018–2019, 549 editorial complaints progressed to the ECU, and of these 236 were referred to Ofcom. Only two of these complaints raised "a substantive issue under the Broadcasting Code which warranted further investigation" (Ofcom, 2019b). One concerned the factual programme *Sunday Politics*, BBC One, 30 April 2017 when presenter Andrew Neil was deemed to have materially misled the audience when he asked former Scottish First Minister Alex Salmond (Scottish National Party) about the SNP's record on education.

> In one of his questions ("Why, after a decade of SNP rule, do one in five Scots pupils leave primary school functionally illiterate?"), Andrew Neil appeared to quote data from an official statistical source to criticise literacy levels among Scottish primary school leavers in 2017. The interview took place during the election period for the 2017 Scottish local elections. In November that year, the BBC's Executive Complaints Unit upheld a complaint about this interview and a complainant subsequently referred their complaint to Ofcom
>
> Ofcom, 2019b, p. 50

If Ofcom finds in favour of the complainant, it can require the BBC to remedy the failure including broadcast an on-air correction or apology and/or publish its response on its complaints page; prevent it recurring, and in serious and repeated breaches of its code, can fine the BBC up to £250,000. (For recent complaints, see BBC Complaints, 2020.)

Are there any other forms of regulation?

Yes, after the Leveson Inquiry, some publications like *The Guardian* and the *Financial Times* chose to regulate themselves using their own codes and complaints procedures, such as appointing a readers' editor, ombudsman or complaints commissioner, instead of joining IPSO or IMPRESS. These internal processes aim to bring greater transparency and accountability to their news organisation in order to build trust between the audience and the news outlet. And US research suggests that journalists on newspapers with ombudsmen are more likely to exercise "ethical caution" in their work (Wilkins and Coleman, 2005, p. 112).

The Guardian has had a readers' editor, or internal ombudsman, since 1997, the first in the UK to do so, when Alan Rusbridger, the editor at the time, appointed Ian Mayes as the publication's readers' representative. Virtually every week, Mayes commented on the issues raised and supervised a daily 'Corrections and Clarifications' column. The system had been pioneered in the United States where, for many decades, the top newspapers had appointed internal ombudsmen (*The Washington Post*, e.g., since 1970). Elizabeth Ribbans, who was appointed in 2019, is *The Guardian*'s fifth incumbent. However, her remit has expanded considerably in two decades. As global readers' editor, she is responsible for *The Guardian*'s international editions, online content, print, their apps, podcasts and social media feeds. On her appointment she said: "I start from a position that all complaints are made in good faith—and equally that no journalist comes to work to mislead or mistreat readers" (Ribbans, 2020).

A readers' editor mediates between the audience and the publication's editorial team regarding complaints, concerns and corrections. Their task is to ensure that the publication's content is accurate and truthful; that it upholds ethical standards, usually set out in a code of conduct; and that it is balanced and fair. For their role to be credible, they should meet three conditions. The readers' editor should be independent of the publication's editorial staff through a structured process where they report to a board of trustees or executives (for *The Guardian*, Ribbans reports directly to the Scott Trust). They should have no involvement in the publication's editorial content as their role is to act as an independent appraiser of complaints about content. The readers' editor should have a prominent, public, independent forum, such as a regular column where they can explain their assessment of any issues that the audience has raised and where relevant be critical of the publication's coverage (*The Guardian* has the Open Door column where Ribbans writes about audience complaints, concerns, suggestions and other issues.) However, the effectiveness of their rulings depends on the editorial team's willingness to accept them and on the newsroom culture. Also, as their judgements are made public, they are under scrutiny from the wider audience including journalists from other news outlets who can judge how impartial they are.

The *Financial Times* operates a slightly different system in that complaints are handled firstly by senior editors, then are referred to an independent complaints commissioner appointed by the publication if their seriousness warrants such action. After examining the complaint, they can recommend redress such as corrections and clarifications. Other news outlets like the *Independent* and the *Huffington Post* run similar internal processes. (For more information see The Guardian, 2014; Financial Times, 2017; Independent, n.d.; HuffPost, 2020.)

New media accountability initiatives, such as journalism blogs that comment on current practices and media watch websites run by news consumers, also contribute to press regulation, albeit indirectly, especially if they have participatory features. Additionally, critical posts on social media platforms can influence public opinion and potentially damage the reputations of news outlets and individual journalists. Research shows that even though new online and participatory accountability systems do not supersede the more traditional self-regulatory methods, they have gained relevance as a source of criticism or influence (Fengler et al., 2015). The Ethical Journalism Network and the Poynter Institute promote and advance education in ethical standards. Generally, they consist of networks of media professionals, former journalists and journalism academics. As well as offering training for journalists, they raise awareness of ethical issues where the media's actions are a cause for concern. By offering advice on responsible reporting, they provide journalists with opportunities to monitor and regulate their own work thus offering them a constructive way forward through any dilemmas they may encounter. The media are also monitored by organisations like Hacked Off and iMediaEthics, who campaign for more accountable media, although their influence on news outlets is limited. Hacked Off was set up in 2011 in response to the phone hacking scandal that led to the Leveson Inquiry in 2012. They work with people who have experienced media abuse and are often asked to comment when such situations arise. Their potential to influence news outlets' ethical standards may be limited but the celebrity status of members like actor Hugh Grant does get them public attention. IMediaEthics similarly investigates lapses in ethical standards but they also cover news about journalism ethics and highlight good ethical examples as well as bad.

What issues arise with codes of conduct?

Media self-regulation is built around the promotion of ethical codes. Most democratic societies throughout the world require their media outlets to adhere to a set of ethical standards that are upheld by regulators. As Frost notes, they are "a list of dos and don'ts to guide journalists through the maze of moral problems they face from day to day" (2015, p. 322). Journalists who follow these rules do not need to consider the consequences of their actions in order to behave morally because they are following universal laws based on their duties and obligations that have been agreed by their profession. However, that does not mean that journalists should follow codes blindly without an appreciation of the culture in which they work. The Accountable Journalism project, run by The Reynolds Journalism Institute at Missouri School of Journalism and the Ethical Journalism Network, states on their website:

> There is a greater need to know and understand ethics in an increasingly global world and the nuances between different cultures. While media policies may differ between news organizations and certain ethical topics are colored in shades of grey, the core concepts of accuracy, independence, impartiality, accountability, and showing humanity are international baselines for journalistic work.
>
> *Accountable Journalism, n.d.*

The project maintains a searchable database of more than 400 codes from around the world. Through this crowdsourcing initiative, it invites media professionals to submit their codes to update the database.

What are the advantages?

Codes provoke a range of responses from journalists (Hafez, 2002; Limor and Himelboim, 2006). Some regard them as vehicles of professionalisation, as a means of professional education, as instruments of consciousness-raising and as deliberate attempts by journalists to regulate the media and ward off legislation restricting their activities. They can be perceived as mere rhetorical devices to preserve special privileges such as access to the powerful and camouflage hypocrisy (Keeble, 2009, pp. 67–68). Codes can also fulfil important public relations functions for professionals. As Frost suggests (2015, p. 323):

> They are often introduced to reassure the public that a profession has standards of practice and to imply, at least, that professionals who transgress those standards will be disciplined. Many professions and trades have raced to introduce codes of practice over the past few years in the light of rising consumer consciousness.

What are the disadvantages?

Some critics argue that codes inherently restrict press freedom by encouraging certain patterns of behaviour and condemning others, while some suggest the media are more effectively regulated by the market, anyway. Pragmatically, because codes are rules-based, they are believed to save journalists time in making ethical decisions. However, that requires journalists to know what they cover and be able to apply them to specific situations. Critics claim that few journalists are aware of the content of codes, particularly when they are regularly changed. IPSO frequently update their Editors' Code of Practice, having invited public consultation in 2020, whilst IMPRESS seeks suggestions for revisions on an ongoing basis. Therefore, interpretation of how a clause in the code might apply to a given situation is a concern for some journalists, particularly inexperienced ones. To alleviate this concern, IPSO produced the Editors Codebook, a guide that explains its thinking on recent cases that breached the Editors' Code. Others suggest that this flexibility and reflection of changing cultural norms is a strength. Some journalists claim that codes are there simply to be broken. Wilkins and Coleman see value in this journalistic scepticism:

> Genuine moral development can occur only when people go beyond a stage of being other-directed by rules to an inner-directed stage of internalised rules ... Perhaps the rejection of written codes of ethics is a reflection of this growth.
>
> *2005, p. 112*

What principal underlying values appear in the codes?

Some values are evident in codes throughout the world and generally are based on the ethical principles of truth-telling, minimizing harm, humanity, fairness, independence and impartiality and accountability (Hafez, 2002; Laitila, 1995; Roberts, 2012). They include:

- Respecting and seeking after truth
- The separation of fact and opinion
- The need for accuracy linked with the responsibility to correct errors
- The deliberate distortion and suppression of information are condemned
- Maintaining confidentiality of sources
- Upholding journalists' responsibility to guard citizens' right to freedom of expression
- Fairness
- Protecting people's right to privacy
- Minimizing harm to vulnerable people
- Avoiding discrimination on grounds of race, sexual orientation, gender, language, religion or political opinions
- Struggling against censorship
- Recognising a duty to defend the dignity and independence of the profession
- Avoiding conflicts of interests (particularly with respect to political and financial journalists/editors holding shares in companies they report on) (Keeble, 2009, p. 69).

According to Frost (2015), codes contain two main types of clauses: rights-based and function-based. Rights-based clauses are concerned with the rights of both journalists and the public. They acknowledge the rights journalists have to do their jobs and they identify what people can expect of them as a result. These rights include freedom of expression, accuracy, privacy, respect and avoiding discrimination. Function-based rights state how journalists should behave if they are to be ethical. A key right for journalists is to provide the public with truthful, impartial information that is honestly presented. Others include minimizing harm to vulnerable people, protecting sources and avoiding conflicts of interest.

What is the public interest and what does it have to do with codes?

The public interest is often cited by journalists as the reason for them taking certain actions in their reporting. It is a key aspect of most codes and provides them with the moral authority for apparent transgressions, situations where they seem to act against the clauses in codes that are there to protect the public from unethical journalism. However, there are situations where it is right for journalists to breach these clauses in order to tell the truth or to reveal some serious wrongdoing. The public interest "tests the limits of ethical practice in order to discover the truth" (Ethical Journalism Network (Public Interest), n.d.).

But what is the public interest? Its interpretation can be nebulous, although mostly journalists and editors claim to know what it is. This issue around its definition leaves room for liberal interpretation and some dubious ethical application. We often hear the phrase "the public's right to know" in reference to the public interest, but this can be used by unethical news outlets as an excuse for bad behaviour such as intrusion into the private lives of celebrities.

Ideally, it is about matters that affect everyone and that are important to them. It goes to the heart of journalism's public service function of pursuing the truth for the common good. Therefore, it is more than just a claim by journalists or about fulfilling the desires of their audiences. It is about them executing their public obligation and duty to the community they serve. And on some occasions, the public may have a legitimate need for certain information that might potentially harm others. But such decisions should not be taken without due consideration. Codes of conduct that include a definition of the public interest offer a starting point for that consideration.

Regulators such as IPSO and IMPRESS include a definition in their codes. These are founded on the notion that the public has a legitimate stake in a story because of its contribution to an important matter to society (IMPRESS). IPSO also considers the extent to which the material is already in the public domain, or will be. Claiming there is no exhaustive definition, they suggest the public interest applies to proper administration of government; open, fair and effective justice; public health and safety; disclosing or exposing crime; incidents where the public are being misled or affected by incompetent or unethical behaviour; and raising a matter of public debate. The IPSO code also states there is a public interest in freedom of expression itself (see IMPRESS and IPSO for further details). Some news outlets, particularly broadcasters, explain their meaning of public interest in their company guidelines. For example, in its producers' handbook, Channel 4 (2020) specifies the various occasions when the public interest can be justified as a reason for compromising standards, for example, withholding information, payment in connection with criminal activities, misrepresentation or deception. In line with the Ofcom Broadcasting Code, they emphasise that it should be proportionate.

What are the major differences between the National Union of Journalists' code and the other industry codes?

Some trades unions and professional bodies, such as the National Union of Journalists (NUJ) and the Chartered Institute of Journalists (CIoJ), also have codes of conduct. However, their ability to regulate is limited because their codes only apply to their members and not to specific news outlets.

The NUJ's Code, first adopted in 1936, now incorporates 12 general principles (2011). It contains clauses on freedom of the press, accuracy, news-gathering conduct, intrusion, protection of sources, bribes, suppression of the truth and product endorsement. It also has a conscience clause that enables journalists who believe they are being asked by their employers to act unethically to refuse to undertake that work. However, in the current climate of precarious employment, it could prove difficult for a journalist to challenge their employer in this way. That said, it does establish the moral right to do so.

Other codes tend to contain detailed specifications of what is deemed either ethical or unethical. But as Harris (1992, p. 67) points out:

> One of the consequences of bringing out detailed sets of regulations is that it fosters a loophole-seeking attitude of mind. The result could be that journalists will come to treat as permissible anything that does not fit the precise specifications of unethical behaviour. Furthermore, short codes consisting of broad principles can often be applied to new types of situation, which could not have been envisaged by those drawing them up.

Frost (2015, p. 325) argues:

> A short code has the advantage of being easier for journalists to remember and use. They are able to measure directly their performance against the principles contained in the code and quickly realise when they are straying from the straight and narrow.

As an enforcement measure, the NUJ set up an Ethics Council in 1979 to promote higher ethical standards and hear complaints against members alleged to have breached the Code of Conduct. But after a number of extremely controversial attempts to discipline its own members, important changes were made in the early 1990s. Now only members can complain about another member: complaints from members of the public are no longer permitted (Frost 2015, pp. 351–352). Former NUJ press officer, Tim Gopsill, described the code as a "positive thing, a beacon for journalists to aim for rather than a means to punish" (2008).

The Chartered Institute of Journalists, the oldest professional body for journalists in the world, does discipline its members who breach its code. Its 12-clause code (2020) covers similar ground to the NUJ code but also expects its members to adhere to the Editors' Code of Practice except where that will compromise a member's sources or is contrary to any legal advice they have been given.

Codes endorsed by industry regulators such as IPSO, IMPRESS and Ofcom are less concerned with issues that primarily affect the individual journalist and their credibility as opposed to the news outlet and its reputation. Although they advise news outlets on how their employees should act, they are also focussed on protecting the public from unethical journalism. Their codes generally cover accuracy, transparency, reporting crime, paying witnesses and criminals, reporting suicide, children and vulnerable people, intrusion and privacy.

In a worldwide context, the International Federation of Journalists (IFJ), which is the world's largest journalists' organisation representing 600,000 media professionals from more than 140 countries, has its own code, the Global Charter of Ethics for Journalists, which was adopted in 2019. It completes the IFJ Declaration of Principles on the Conduct of Journalists (1954), known as the Bordeaux Declaration. It is based on international law, specifically the Universal Declaration of Human Rights, and contains 16 clauses that define journalists' ethical duties and rights (IFJ, 2021).

Do current codes adequately address ethical issues in digital journalism?

Digital journalism throws up distinct ethical problems alongside the more standard issues, like use of technology, participating with their audiences, and how to use text and images generated by citizens. Díaz-Campo and Segado-Boj (2015) observe that the fact that codes are updated or recently adopted does not mean that they will include rules for digital activity. Few codes written or revised since 2000 mention digital journalism and the tiny minority that do tend to do so in the context that online journalism is subject to the same principles as traditional journalism. The core ethical principles of truth-telling, minimizing harm, humanity, fairness, independence and impartiality and accountability are relevant to digital journalism, but many codes do not take account of the specific issues raised by new journalism forms. Díaz-Campo and Segado-Boj state:

> The point is that, even though many of these countries have written specific documents or guidelines to address digital journalism or some particular aspect of it (blogging, social media, etc.), the codes themselves also should be reformulated—for they are, after all, self-regulation's benchmark documents.
>
> 2015, p. 741

Ethics in action: Aidan White, founder of the Ethical Journalism Network: "Journalism is needed more than ever, but to survive it must be ethical to its core."

Aidan White is the founder and honorary president of the Ethical Journalism Network, an international coalition of more than 70 groups of journalism professionals who share the belief that the principles of ethical journalism are universal and are a valuable resource in building respect for democracy and human rights. He set up the EJN in 2012 after he left the IFJ where he worked as general secretary for 25 years. During his tenure, the IFJ became the world's largest journalism organisation with members in 126 countries. Before he stepped down as EJN director in 2018, Aidan edited several reports on journalism ethics, media issues and human rights. These include *Censorship in the Park* (2014) on press freedom in Turkey, *The Trust Factor* (2015) on self-regulation in journalism, *Untold Stories* (2015) on corruption in journalism, *Moving Stories* (2015) on media reporting of migration, *Journalism Ethics: An inspiration for free expression and media literacy* (2016), *Ethics in the News* (2017) on challenges for journalism in the post-truth era and *The Key to Media Futures* (2018) on trust in ethical journalism.

He was also heavily involved in setting up the global free expression network, the International Freedom of Expression Exchange (IFEX) in 1993 and the International News Safety Institute, which campaigns internationally for news safety, in 2003. As a journalist, he worked for several major UK newspapers, including the *Birmingham Evening Mail*, the *Financial Times* and *The Guardian*.

How effective do you think the current regulatory systems in the UK are? What are your thoughts on statutory regulation of the press? Should there be one system for all news organisations in the UK?

When I first thought of launching the Ethical Journalism Network 10 years ago, I was motivated by the conviction that journalists and news media who presume to speak in the name of the people and fight wrongdoing in public life have a duty to act professionally and with moral purpose.

But how do journalists maintain standards when their industry is failing? And how can the public hold media to account when the news business, in the midst of an information revolution, is faster, more pressurised and infinitely more complex?

Thousands of news outlets (mainly newspapers) have closed. Tens of thousands of journalists have lost their jobs. Access to reliable and trusted information has narrowed as traditional news sources, particularly at local and regional level, have contracted, even though the space for free speech has expanded dramatically.

With less money to pay for public interest journalism, newsrooms struggle to maintain their ethical base. Problems that have always been there – political bias, undue corporate influence, stereotypes and conflicts of interest – are magnified. And new threats abound, from social networks and unregulated online communications.

The Ethical Journalism Network was launched in the teeth of this crisis. It is the world's first independent group of reporters, editors and media support groups dedicated to ethics, good-governance and self-regulation.

It aims to counter the downward drift in ethical standards inside journalism and to help news media confront public antagonism and mistrust of what journalists do (Ethical Journalism Network, 2021).

The crisis of failing public trust was highlighted in the UK by the Leveson Inquiry into media ethics after the scandals of phone hacking and press bribery at News International, which saw the closure of the *News of the World*, Europe's biggest-selling newspaper, and journalists sent to jail.

That inquiry made lacerating criticism of Britain's Press Complaints Commission over its ineffectiveness and called for stronger press regulation – if necessary, within a legal framework – and more systematic application of ethical norms across the media landscape.

It recommended the creation of a unified, credible system of self-regulation that could command public trust, but this is a challenge that the press industry and policymakers have been wrestling with for almost 70 years.

In Britain, journalism works under two regulating umbrellas – one for the press and another for broadcasting, the platform that provides most people with their news and information, where journalists are monitored by a regulator underpinned by law and set up by the government, Ofcom, but which is independent and paid for by the companies it regulates.

The failure of press self-regulation free of specific statutory controls has been evident since the newspaper industry created the first General Council of the Press in 1953 (under threat of government intervention). What followed was a pattern of public scandal followed by promises to do better and new council launches, first in 1962, then in 1991 and, most recently, in 2014 at Leveson's insistence with the creation of the Independent Press Standards Organisation .

But this latest attempt, which commends little public confidence, also looks fragile, not least because of divisions within the press itself. Some national newspapers – *The Guardian*, *Financial Times* and *Independent* – have refused to join IPSO or its new rival IMPRESS, an independent regulator recognised under a Royal Charter created to facilitate press regulation after the Leveson Inquiry.

With two competing press regulators and some heavyweight absentees from the industry's preferred option, it's not surprising that people are confused, and public confidence in the notion of self-regulation is at an all-time low.

Surprisingly, news media, particularly the press, have shown little or no imagination about how to set up a credible system for regulating journalism in the digital age.

They fail to recognise that revolutionary changes in how journalism works and is delivered to the public renders obsolete the traditional divide between broadcast and print journalism and introduces a whole new sector of online journalism.

Today, journalists in the digital newsroom produce video, print and audio at much the same time, but there is confusion about which regulator has jurisdiction over their work.

There are strong arguments in favour of a single, unified and independent body to deal with public complaints and to monitor media performance across all platforms of journalism.

In some countries, such arrangements are already in place. In Norway, the Netherlands and Belgium, for example, the work of all journalists on all platforms, including state broadcasting, comes under the jurisdiction of a single press or media council. And in many countries, including Britain, judicious use of law is already used to reassure the public that media are being held to account.

Do codes of conduct help journalists to work through ethical problems?

Industry codes have been around for almost 100 years, but the first notion of codified standards to protect journalism emerged in the 1850s when UK newspapers – particularly *The Times* – campaigned for recognition of "fourth estate" journalism and the right to criticise government – even in times of war.

Today, there are around 400 different codes governing journalistic work worldwide. These can be found on the EJN website (see also https://accountablejournalism.org/).

Most journalists know the ethics of their craft, even if they can't recite the precise wording from their national codes – and there are three industry codes in play in the UK: the National Union of Journalists, IMPRESS and IPSO. Many major newspapers also have developed their own internal codes.

The EJN does not support any single code, but broadly endorses five core values, which in one form or another are reflected in them all:

- Accuracy and fact-based communication
- Independence
- Impartiality
- Humanity
- Transparency and accountability

To help journalists in their daily work, codes need to be translated into working rules and guidelines. The EJN has produced model editorial guidelines for an international project – the *Journalism Trust Initiative* – which promotes self-auditing by media houses to meet basic standards of transparency and accountability (see www.journalismtrustinitiative.org/). Such guidelines help journalists resolve tricky dilemmas, including conflicts of interest, paying sources of information, interviewing children or vulnerable groups and eliminating hate speech.

The editorial guidelines of major news media like *The Guardian*, BBC and *The Associated Press* are usually available to the public through their websites.

Post Leveson, these codes are further supported by the emergence of more in-house ombudsmen or readers' editors and the use of "corrections and clarifications" columns.

In terms of regulation, besides promoting debate on the issue, the EJN supports and promotes self-regulation at all levels within the media pyramid – from the owner's chair down to newsroom.

The EJN argues strongly that with structures for credible and independent regulation in place, ethical journalism can be protected speech, its public purpose underpinned by law if necessary and, above all, its editorial independence ring-fenced from political or other interference.

What is the work of the Ethical Journalism Network in maintaining standards? How do you see the EJN's role in terms of journalism regulation?

The EJN works nationally and internationally. The issues facing journalists in Britain are multiplied in countries and regions where there is political and social conflict and poverty. These journalists face many pressures – not least the threat to their own safety.

We have worked in countries like Syria and Palestine, China and Turkey, Rwanda and Egypt, and most recently helping journalists in Bulgaria, Poland, Hungary and Slovakia – countries of Europe where media are at particular risk from political interference.

In all of these areas, we promote the importance of ethical journalism, we organise education and training for reporters, editors and owners and help journalists and news media create structures for self-regulation and help them defend their professional rights.

We've helped publish glossaries against hate speech in Cyprus, Egypt and Palestine and we've promoted ethical auditing of news media in Albania, Montenegro, Turkey and Serbia. We've helped local media establish national networks for ethical journalism.

The demand for such support is strong, even in the most difficult circumstances. In 2019 and 2020, the EJN helped Syrian journalists in exile prepare a new association for self-regulation and ethical journalism.

The EJN has also developed guidelines and practical tips in specific areas of work. These include: a five-point test for hate speech, which has been produced in an infographic and is available in 30 languages; how to protect sources and whistle-blowers; interviewing guidelines; glossaries of terms to avoid discrimination; and guidance on reporting suicide, dealing with gender rights and covering migration.

In Britain, the EJN, through its national UK committee, is promoting debates on critical issues such as migration, reporting the COVID-19 pandemic, structural racism in newsrooms, misinformation in mainstream media and the challenge of regulating social media while protecting free speech.

In all of this, the aim is to improve ethical awareness and moral reasoning inside journalism, and to build public confidence in news media.

If you were writing a code for journalists working in today's digital world, what would you include in it?

The most significant ethical challenge facing journalists these days is to ensure the accuracy of information and the veracity of their sources.

Journalists know there's nothing new about fake news. Deceptive, unverified and error-filled reporting has always been with us, but the scourge has grown in the wake of technology that has shaped a new world of click bait, viral communications and confirmation bias.

All of us are surrounded by websites that peddle disinformation or online sources that are deceptive in the handling of facts and that show misleading or illegal content. The EJN suggests some simple guidelines for reporters and editors to make sure they don't become victims of slippery stories published online.

One of the fundamental rules for ethical behaviour today is avoid a rush to publish. Journalism has always been competitive and news media have always enjoyed the race to be first, but in today's information environment, journalism will always be slower than social networks and online providers.

Ethical journalism is thinking journalism. It takes time. We need to reflect and make choices about headlines or pictures or footage; we need to ask ourselves – have we done good work? Have we asked all the right questions? Have we included all the relevant voices in the story?

Modern journalism will always be slower than the internet, but it will always be more reliable. That's why, particularly in times of crisis, people seek out known media brands that give them information they can trust.

What do you think of social media comments as a form of regulation?

Many people believe that social media can be an ally for regulation of media. By calling out falsehoods, bias and dishonesty, social media users on Twitter or Facebook, for example, can provide an instant response to errors or malicious falsehoods.

Opening up media and journalism to public comments on individual stories was welcomed as a fresh opportunity for community engagement and a way of adding context and clarity.

But experience has shown that these positive expectations may have been a mite optimistic. Twitter and others do a good job of instant response, but the internet has become a battleground for polarised opinions. In a world of "alternative facts" and "post-truth", there are constant, unresolved disputes over what is accurate and reliable.

Comments under online stories are often an excuse for different interest groups to provoke their opponents and to make mischief. Newspapers like *The*

Guardian rarely open the door to readers' comments on stories linked to the Israeli-Palestinian conflict because it will only encourage angry exchanges with vested interest groups.

Use of social media has been diminished by abusive users who voice their frustrations often in unpleasant and unacceptable ways, as shown by the online racism that followed the penalty misses of three black footballers in England's defeat at the European Cup Final in 2021.

A major problem is social media companies are unregulated without any formal or convincing attachment to ethics or regard for public protection from the owners of major technology companies.

Not surprisingly, there is growing criticism over the role of social networks and big technology companies over secrecy, lack of transparency and wilful disregard for the impact of abusive postings.

In 2021, policymakers in Europe and the United States targeted these companies with threats of new laws. Britain had its own Online Harms Bill trundling through Parliament to address internet threats facing the public – particularly young people and children.

Despite empty promises of reform and change, the revealing testimony in September 2021 of Facebook whistle-blower Frances Haugen, who claimed that Facebook wilfully puts profits before people, and exposed the lack of moral leadership of this company and its neglect of a duty of care (Clayton, 2021).

She claimed Facebook deliberately suppressed research showing that Facebook's social media company Instagram was damaging the mental health of teenagers. She said it covered-up findings that suggested the platform was a "toxic" place for many youngsters (Clayton, 2021).

Although the company predictably denied the claims, Haugen also said Facebook helped fuel the violence during the deadly Capitol Hill riots in January 2021 (Clayton, 2021).

Surprisingly, Mark Zuckerberg, the chief executive of Facebook, is on record as saying that his company and others in the industry need more government interference and regulation. He says this would preserve the freedom for people to express themselves while also protecting society from broader harms (Zuckerberg, 2019).

In particular, he calls for new laws to protect democratic elections, to deal with harmful content and hate speech, to provide privacy and data protection and to give people the right to shift data from one service to another on the internet (Zuckerberg, 2019).

These sentiments are welcome, but the evidence is that Facebook and other big technology companies are not ready to adopt and implement ethically based rules, particularly if they undermine a business model that has created trillion-dollar companies and delivered billions of dollars in profits.

It would be absurd, of course, to expect these companies to adopt the EJN's five-core values to monitor all content, given that two of them call for independence and impartiality, and when the rules of free expression defend the rights of everyone to be biased, opinionated and as robust in their views as they want.

But there is no doubt that social media companies could learn a lot from journalism and its regulatory efforts to be led by public interests rather than the accumulation of unfathomable amounts of money.

What are the challenges for journalism after the COVID-19 pandemic and what are the EJN's plans for the future?

Although traditional news media played a critical role during the global health emergency, providing vital information to the public with spikes in audience share as a result, the pandemic brought new threats to journalism and reinforced existing global pressures:

- Human Rights Watch reported that 83 governments used the pandemic as cover for new laws undermining human rights and press freedom (Human Rights Watch, 2021)
- Social media opened the door to a new wave of disinformation surrounding COVID-19, which the World Health Organization (WHO) declared an "infodemic" causing mass anxiety and uncertainty. In the UK, for example, some 5G masts were set on fire after circulation of an absurd conspiracy theory linking 5G to COVID-19.

Changes in working arrangements – particularly working from home – have added to the strains caused by cuts in newsroom capacity. Isolating journalists reduces the scope for ethical debate and reflection.

These problems add to the range of issues the EJN will be tackling in the coming years. The Network is focused on building its presence in the UK, searching for new and sustainable models for news media as well as building on international work where the media crisis is intensifying under the weight of political populism and disinformation.

Fresh work is planned in Central Europe, the Western Balkans and Turkey and, further afield, there are plans to reconnect with media and journalists striving for professional freedom in China and across the Arab world.

The major themes of EJN work remain, including hate speech, migration reporting and the challenge of race and gender equality, as well as reinforcing the importance of the five core principles of ethical journalism.

As always, the emphasis will be on developing practical tools and resources to help those journalists in the vanguard of the fight for media freedom.

The challenge is to confront a crisis of trust in media and in the wider public information sphere.

The EJN will also work with academic institutions, journalism schools and media literacy groups to raise awareness of the importance of ethical news media to the cause of truth-telling, transparency and democracy. Journalism is needed more than ever, but to survive, it must be ethical to the core.

Ethical workout

- What do you think is the best way to regulate the media today? Statutory or self-regulation?
- Where do you stand on the public interest – a useful and noble defence for journalists to act for society's benefit or an excuse for ethically dubious journalism?
- If you were to write a new code of conduct for 21st-century journalists, what would you include in it?

Five takeaways from this chapter

- Regulation in the UK is built on the ethical principles of truth-telling and accuracy, independence, fairness and impartiality, humanity and minimizing harm and accountability: the five core principles of journalism.
- Several regulators operate in the UK, but essentially, they promote and uphold similar ethical standards and behaviours.
- Adherence to a code of conduct is the main form of regulation for UK journalists, whether these are voluntary (e.g. IPSO, IMPRESS); statutory (e.g. Ofcom, BBC); internal (e.g. *The Guardian*, *Financial Times*, *Huffington Post*); or the instrument of a trade union or professional body (e.g. NUJ, CIoJ, IFJ).
- News outlets and their journalists are subject to complaints procedures that enable members of the public to complain about actions by the media that breach ethical codes.

- Journalists' reputations can be affected by comment or criticism by online accountability initiatives like journalism blogs, media watch websites and public commentary on social media.

Ethics toolbox

- Accountable Journalism – Codes of Ethics. See: https://accountablejournalism.org/ethics-codes
- Ethical Journalism Network: https://ethicaljournalismnetwork.org/
- Foreman, Gene (2015) *The Ethical Journalist: Making responsible decisions in the pursuit of news* 2nd edition, Wiley
- Frost, Chris (2015) *Journalism Ethics and Regulation* Abingdon: Routledge
- Frost, Chris (2019) *Privacy and the News Media*, Chapter 12 Abingdon: Routledge
- International Federation of Journalists – Ethics. See: www.ifj.org/what/press-freedom/ethics.html
- Leveson Inquiry: Culture, Practice and Ethics of the Press (2012). See www.discoverleveson.com
- Poynter Institute, a non-profit journalism school and research organisation that champions ethical journalism, freedom of expression and civil dialogue. See: www.poynter.org/

References

Accountable Journalism. (n.d.) 'Codes of ethics'. Available at: https://accountablejournalism.org/ethics-codes (Accessed: 9 July 2020).

Barnett, S. (2016) 'IMPRESS vs IPSO: A chasm not a cigarette paper', *Press Gazette*, 28 October. Available at: https://pressgazette.co.uk/impress-vs-ipso-a-chasm-not-a-cigarette-paper/ (Accessed: 10 February 2022).

BBC Complaints. (2020) 'Contact the BBC'. Available at: www.bbc.co.uk/contact/complaints (Accessed: 9 February 2021).

BBC Complaints Framework and Procedures. (2020) Available at: www.bbc.co.uk/contact/sites/default/files/2020-06/BBC_Complaints_Framework.pdf (Accessed: 9 February 2021).

BBC Editorial Guidelines. (2020) 'Guidelines'. Available at: www.bbc.co.uk/editorialguidelines/guidelines (Accessed: 9 February 2021).

Channel 4. (2020) 'Producers' handbook'. Available at: www.channel4.com/producers-handbook/ (Accessed: 9 February 2021).

Chartered Institute of Journalists. (2020) 'What we expect of our members: CIoJ code of conduct'. Available at: https://cioj.org/the-cioj-code-of-conduct-for-our-members/ (Accessed: 9 February 2021).

Clayton, J. (2021) 'Frances Haugen: Facebook whistleblower reveals identity'. *BBC News*, 4 October. Available at: www.bbc.co.uk/news/technology-58784615 (Accessed: 18 October 2021).

Díaz-Campo, J. and Segado-Boj, F. (2015). 'Journalism ethics in a digital environment: How journalistic codes of ethics have been adapted to the Internet and ICTs in countries around the world', *Telematics and Informatics*, 32 (4), pp. 735–744.

Ethical Journalism Network. (2021) 'About EJN'. Available at: https://ethicaljournalismnetwork.org/who-we-are. (Accessed: 18 October 2021).

Ethical Journalism Network. (n.d.) 'The public interest: Is it in the public interest?' Available at: https://ethicaljournalismnetwork.org/the-public-interest (Accessed: 28 August 2020).

Fengler, S., Eberwein, T., Alsius, S., Baisnee, O., et al. (2015) 'How effective is media self-regulation? Results from a comparative survey of European journalists', *European Journal of Communication*, 30(3), pp. 249–266. https://doi.org/10.1177/0267323114561009

Ferret. (n.d.) 'Complaints: Complaints policy and procedures of The Ferret'. Available at: https://theferret.scot/complaints/ (Accessed: 28 August 2020).

Financial Times. (2017) 'FT editorial code'. Available at: https://aboutus.ft.com/en-gb/ft-editorial-code/ (Accessed: 28 August 2020).

Frost, C. (2015) *Journalism Ethics and Regulation*. 4th ed. Abingdon: Routledge.

Gopsill, T. (2008) 'Life on flat Earth', *Free Press*, March–April, pp. 4–5.

Hafez, K. (2002) 'Journalism ethics revisited: A comparison of ethics codes in Europe, North Africa, the Middle East, and Muslim Asia', *Political Communication*, 19(2), pp. 225–250. https://doi.org/10.1080/10584600252907461

Harris, N. (1992) 'Codes of conduct for journalists', in Belsey, A. and Chadwick, R. (eds.), *Ethical Issues in Journalism and the Media*. London: Routledge, pp. 62–76.

HuffPost. (2020) 'Standards and corrections'. Available at: www.huffingtonpost.co.uk/p/corrections (Accessed: 14 February 2021).

Human Rights Watch. (2021) 'Covid-19 triggers a wave of free speech abuse', 11 February. Available at: www.hrw.org/news/2021/02/11/covid-19-triggers-wave-free-speech-abuse (Accessed: 18 October 2021).

Independent. (n.d.) 'Code of conduct'. Available at: www.independent.co.uk/service/code-of-conduct-a6184241.html (Accessed: 9 February 2021).

International Federation of Journalists (IFJ). (2021) 'IFJ global charter of ethics for journalists'. Available at: www.ifj.org/who/rules-and-policy/global-charter-of-ethics-for-journalists.html (Accessed: 11 February 2021).

IMPRESS. (n.d.a) 'About us'. Available at: www.impress.press/about-us/ (Accessed: 19 December 2020).

IMPRESS. (n.d.b) 'About us: Funding – How are we funded?' Available at: https://impress.press/about-us/funding.html#:~:text=IMPRESS%20also%20receives%20funding%20from,develops%20a%20sustainable%20business%20model (Accessed: 10 February 2022).

IMPRESS. (n.d.c) 'Complaints FAQ'. Available at: www.impress.press/complaints/complaints-faq.html (Accessed: 19 December 2020).

IMPRESS. (n.d.d) 'Whistleblowing'. Available at: www.impress.press/regulation/whistleblowing.html (Accessed: 19 December 2020).

IPSO. (2020) 'FAQ editors code'. Available at: www.ipso.co.uk/faqs/editors-code/ (Accessed: 19 December 2020).

Keeble, R.L. (2009) *Ethics for Journalists.* 2nd ed. Abingdon: Routledge.

Laitila, T. (1995) 'Codes of ethics in Europe', in Nordenstreng, K. (ed.), *Reports on Media Ethics in Europe.* Tampere: University of Tampere, Department of Journalism and Mass Communication, pp. 23–79.

Limor, Y. and Himelboim, I. (2006) 'Journalism and moonlighting: An international comparison of 242 codes of ethics', *Journal of Mass Media Ethics*, 21(4), pp. 265–285. https://doi.org/10.1207/s15327728jmme2104_4

National Union of Journalists. (2011) 'NUJ code of conduct'. Available at: www.nuj.org.uk/about/nuj-code/ (Accessed: 27 October 2020).

Ofcom. (2019a) 'The Office of Communications annual report and accounts for the period 1 April 2018 to 31 March 2019'. Available at: www.ofcom.org.uk/__data/assets/pdf_file/0024/156156/annual-report-18-19.pdf (Accessed: 27 December 2020).

Ofcom. (2019b) 'Ofcom annual report on the BBC', 24 October 2019. Available at: www.ofcom.org.uk/__data/assets/pdf_file/0026/173735/second-bbc-annual-report.pdf (Accessed: 27 December 2020).

Ofcom. (2021) 'The Ofcom broadcasting code (with the cross-promotion code and on-demand programme service rules)'. Available at: www.ofcom.org.uk/tv-radio-and-on-demand/broadcast-codes/broadcast-code (Accessed: 27 June 2021).

Ribbans, E. (2020) 'I'm *The* Guardian's new readers' editor, and I welcome your views'. Available at: www.theguardian.com/commentisfree/2020/feb/02/guardian-new-readers-editor-journalism-fairness-accountability (Accessed: 30 December 2020).

Roberts, C. (2012) 'Identifying and defining values in media codes of ethics', *Journal of Mass Media Ethics*, 27(2), pp. 115–129. https://doi.org/10.1080/08900 523.2012.669289

The Guardian. (2014) 'How to make a complaint about Guardian or Observer content', *The Guardian*. 22 September, 2014. Available at: www.theguardian.com/info/ 2014/sep/12/-sp-how-to-make-a-complaint-about-guardian-or-observer-content (Accessed: 28 August 2020).

Wilkins, L. and Coleman, R. (2005) *The Moral Media: How Journalists Reason About Ethics*. Mahwah, NJ: Lawrence Erlbaum Associates.

Zuckerberg, M. (2019) 'Opinion: Mark Zuckerberg: The internet needs new rules. Let's start in these four areas', *The Washington Post*, 30 March. Available at: www.was hingtonpost.com/opinions/mark-zuckerberg-the-internet-needs-new-rules-lets-start-in-these-four-areas/2019/03/29/9e6f0504-521a-11e9-a3f7-78b7525a8d5f_st ory.html?utm_source=CJR+Daily+News&utm_campaign=76d06575f6-EMAIL_ CAMPAIGN_2020_11_11_06_33_COPY_01&utm_medium=email&mc_cid= 76d06575f6&mc_eid=5e8478bb33 (Accessed: 18 October 2021).

3
Journalists and social media
Entering an 'ethical vacuum'?

Frances Yeoman

The rise of a digital era in which the average citizen can post information or commentary without the need to pass through the 'gate-keepers' of the big media outlets has been hailed as a great democratising shift for journalism. Self-evidently, social media and the wider internet have revolutionised both news gathering and news publishing, creating powerful new tools for journalists to reach sources and audiences alike. But this has also generated huge and novel ethical challenges, for the news media industry and also for citizens. How do journalists uphold ethical practices—and how do professional news outlets compete and survive—in a digital informational landscape crowded with unregulated, ethically unconstrained actors? And what should be the relationship between journalists and the sea of online content in which they now swim?

Media ethics has been described by the prominent scholar Stephen J.A. Ward as the responsible use of the freedom to publish (cited in Auman et al., 2020). This chapter aims to explore what that can mean in practice, in an era when the regulated 'mainstream' media has comprehensively lost its monopoly over that freedom, and a multiplicity of other actors can quickly and cheaply reach mass audiences without the need to consider professional values, regulation, codes or—in many cases—legal comeback. Jim Waterson, media editor at *The Guardian*, reflects on the profound effect that social media has had on journalism, and how ethical journalists navigate their way through it in the *Ethics in Action* section.

Is journalism actually any different from other online content?

In an age when every citizen with an internet connection can publish 'news', some have suggested that the distinctions between professional journalists, citizen journalists and the myriad creators of user-generated content (UGC) might no longer be relevant. This enthusiasm about popular participation in information sharing—a form of democratised journalism—was particularly

DOI: 10.4324/9780429505386-4

prevalent in the early years of the new millennium (Roberts, 2019), forcing professional news organisations to reassess their function now that possession of the means for mass communication is no longer sufficient to set them apart. After initially adopting a model of free content in exchange for clicks in the hope of advertising revenue, many have more recently decided that only by reassigning value to their products and distinguishing them from the morass of digital material, via paywalls, subscriptions or donation models, can they hope to survive financially or as an identifiable and distinct industry.

Journalists and academics have meanwhile made the case that professionally produced journalistic content remains distinct from other content. Elvestad and Phillips argue that mobile technology has transformed 'witnessing'—citizens can now film and publish the news event they see, rather than simply recount it to a reporter—but that this sort of UGC content is the digital equivalent of the eyewitness quote rather than journalism in itself (Elvestad and Phillips, 2018, p. 46). Just as with quotes and other evidence, the professional journalist brings the ability to sift, contextualise, verify and curate, none of which has been usurped. An example of this is the death of May Day protestor Ian Tomlinson in 2009. The raw footage of him being struck by police was captured by a member of the public, but it took an investigation by *The Guardian* to combine that footage with other evidence and help secure a prosecution.

The journalist Kristine Lowe argues that UGC and "proper citizen journalism" are often lumped together incorrectly. The former, she argues, is blogging and raw material generated by members of the public, which is often opinion-driven and lacking facts or evidence. The latter should be "people from the community gathering evidence from different sources and writing a balanced and fair interpretation of that research", and predates the internet. "Once you make that distinction then actually the range and extent of proper citizen journalism appears to be fairly small" (quoted in Keeble, 2009, p. 38). As Alan Knight put it:

> The internet promises everyone can be a publisher. But not everyone has the skills or training to be a journalist…Anyone applying professional practices within recognised codes of ethics will be different from most bloggers as well as from our friends at Fox News.
> *quoted in Harcup, 2015, pp. 231–232*

Other important features continue to set the professional news media apart from the rest, even in a time of increased challenge and competition. One is the renewed attention paid of late to the notion of 'public interest journalism' as somehow distinct and more vital to society than other forms of journalistic and pseudo-journalistic content. This notion was evident in the government-commissioned Cairncross Review into the future of journalism, and is implicit in the BBC's Local Democracy and Facebook's Community Reporter schemes.

It was highlighted by the inclusion of some journalists, who produced 'public service' reporting, on the list of key workers during the 2020 coronavirus pandemic. During that time, journalists provided a public service by filling an information gap as well as contributing to debates about issues of common concern. Professional journalists continue then to represent a distinct group within the digital information ecosystem. Indeed, as of 2019, the so-called 'legacy' brands that began life offline continued to dominate UK online news consumption compared even with other professional but digitally native news outlets (Newman et al., 2020, p. 62). Of the top 10 online news sources cited by UK respondents to the Reuters Institute's Digital News Report 2020, only two were digital native sites (Huffpost in seventh place and Buzzfeed in ninth). The BBC was by a long way the most popular source. It has been argued that the mainstream media also provide an important social linking function, a shared set of basic facts around which different opinions and interpretations can orbit. Last but by no means least, journalism is distinguished by some degree of professional, legal and social accountability, and by its declared adherence to ethical values and codes. Lord Justice Leveson argued in his 2012 report that a claim to ethical standards was a distinguishing feature of the professional press in the digital era. Of the internet, he wrote:

> Some have called it a Wild West but I would prefer to use the term 'ethical vacuum' … That is not to say for one moment that everything on the internet is therefore unethical … The point I am making is a more modest one, namely that the internet does not claim to operate by ethical standards, so that bloggers and others may, if they choose, act with impunity.
> *quoted in Frost, 2016, p. 215*

For all of the limitations and flaws of journalistic self-regulation in reality, it is still worth considering whether a citizen would have more chance of redress from a tabloid newspaper, a fringe website, a (potentially anonymous) blogger or a social media poster? Yet the tabloid newspaper, like all professional, regulated media outlets, must compete to be heard with such unconstrained rivals. The financial temptation can be to ditch traditional journalistic norms in order to survive in the digital era. However, with the limitations of a click-based advertising model for journalism becoming increasingly evident, and research suggesting that 'distinctiveness and quality' is the key driver of paid-for news subscriptions, continued adherence to ethical and professional standards might prove to be good business sense as well as good practice. The question is what those standards should be and whether, as Ward contends, we need "a new ethics for a digital media era" (Ward, 2014, p. 459). If traditional journalism ethics "has little to say about how journalists should use content from social media" or "about what norms are appropriate for citizen journalists", as he contends, and a new ethical norms around these topics are still developing, then today's journalists must make some complex and often nuanced decisions about their work. In many instances, they have little by way of precedent or code to help them.

Is it ever ethical to report on online rumours?

Accuracy and the minimization of harm are at the heart of professional journalistic codes of ethics across the democratic world (Knowlton and McKinley, 2016, p. 133). While one can query the extent to which individual media outlets conform to these ideals, these concepts remain part of the regulatory frameworks for journalism in many countries. Fact-checking before publication and sourcing of information are seen as ethical and desirable behaviours, and negative consequences in the form of regulatory censure, legal action or public opprobrium can follow for journalists and outlets who do not engage in them. Yet to maintain both professional authority and market share, professional journalists must appear to be across the news agenda; aware of and ready to report on stories in the public eye. In the digital era, these can and often do include unsubstantiated but widely circulating online rumours.

This throws up a number of interrelated ethical questions. Firstly, should a responsible news outlet report on information or rumours that are 'out there' in the digital space, in order to show that they are aware of the story, even if it has not yet been properly substantiated? Such information, in the predigital age of gatekeeper media, could often be kept safely away from the public eye until it had been verified. Now, a source—authoritative and well-meaning or otherwise—can take their claim or 'fact' straight to the masses via a Twitter feed. An example is the death of British 'ISIS bride' Shamima Begum's baby in a Syrian displacement camp in March 2019. Initial news reports were based on a Tweet by the Begum family lawyer, Tasnime Akunjee. This was a credible source but one who conceivably had an agenda to get his client back to the UK and who himself, in the words of his own post, was not sure about the truth of the situation. Mr Akunjee (2019) wrote: "We have strong but as yet unconfirmed reports that Shamima Begum's son has died. He was a British citizen." News outlets could not ignore this incendiary development in what was at the time a high profile story. But should they have verified Mr Akunjee's claim, which was initially disputed by forces running the camp, rather than repeating it with caveated headlines like: "Baby of ISIS bridge Shamima Begum 'may have died'—according to family's lawyer" (Blewett and Raven, 2019)? In this *Liverpool Echo* article, the reporters state that the Foreign Office had been contacted for confirmation of the death; was it right to publish before receiving that confirmation?

There are a host of digital techniques that can be used to verify the authenticity of online content before publication. Here, the issue was not about Mr Akunjee's real identity or the veracity of his belief in the baby's death, but about substantiating that belief before repeating it. Should traditional journalistic practices such as seeking corroborating sources, photographic or documentary evidence have been deployed here? The detail of how this could have been done is beyond the scope of this chapter. The question is not whether and how information circulating online *can* be fully verified, but whether the ethical imperative of prepublication fact-checking is removed or diminished if the information or assertion is already in the public domain.

In the context of reporting matters as serious as terrorism, Emily Bell, director of the Tow Center, has written in the context of the Christchurch shooting in New Zealand in 2019 that it absolutely is not. "Responsible reporters ought to have the basics imprinted on their subconscious: Do not report facts until they are verified," she writes. However, she also notes:

> While the ambition is always to have the best possible reporting in difficult situations, there is inevitably debate about where the line should be drawn in terms of coverage and focus—now, that balance must also take into account the fact that the press no longer controls what information is available.
>
> Bell, 2019

Reporting unverified facts might be unethical in a situation as grave as a terrorist attack, but if the stakes are lower and the story is circulating online anyway, is there any ethical wriggle room? "Sometimes, the impact of publishing an online rumour is not world shaking—a false report that a hockey coach has been fired," reflects Ward (n.d.). Journalists must inevitably take each unsubstantiated story as its own particular case, and make appropriate decisions in that context.

The journalistic format also has a bearing. Live-blogging, for example, which is more conversational and informal in tone than a traditional inverted pyramid-style news story, provokes different attitudes to verification and the publication of rumour, even within the same newsroom. *The Guardian's* US blogs and network editor have suggested that live blogs might be used to "flag up" leads for the audience to help verify (Thurman, 2018, p. 109). Many major publications similarly now 'put things out there' online in a way that they might not have done in print or on TV or radio. Is this a smart way to crowd-source the truth, or could it be considered an abdication of responsibility for a prominent newsroom to put unsubstantiated leads before its large audience and under its trusted masthead, even with clear health warnings? Paul Lewis, an investigative reporter for *The Guardian*, has argued that nothing should be posted before authentication. "Our job is to find out whether it's true," he is quoted as saying, "not to put it out and ask people to decide for us" (quoted in Thurman, 2018, p. 110).

For those journalists who are tasked with rapid-fire activities such as live-blogging and tweeting, which often occur with less editorial oversight than traditional reporting, these can be big judgment calls. It is incumbent on their editors and managers, therefore, to make it clear what their fact-checking standards are. "The ethical challenge," as Ward notes, "is to articulate guidelines for dealing with rumours and corrections in an online world that are consistent with the principles of accuracy, verification, and transparency" (n.d.).

In setting and following these guidelines, journalists might usefully ask themselves the questions:

- What am I, as a professional reporter, adding here?
- Whose voices are not being heard in this story that should be?

Anyone with an internet connection can recirculate the rumour about the hockey coach. But neither the hockey club nor the coach is likely to offer interviews or distribute press releases to that average internet user, and it takes journalistic skill and contacts to write a complete (and legally safe) version of the story. Reporters can differentiate themselves and their employers by resisting the temptation to build their own rumour mill, and instead offer investigation and substantiation of the rumours being churned out by others.

Unfortunately, the economics of digital journalism and the perceived imperative in many newsrooms to attract a large volume of 'clicks' can generate a willingness to repeat claims without performing even rudimentary checks, particularly if they relate to a story that has good potential to go viral. This was seen in late October 2020, when many mainstream news websites ran stories about the potential return of Woolworths shops to the UK high street. These articles were based entirely on a tweet from an unverified Twitter account, @WoolworthsUK, which had fewer than 1,000 followers and linked to a non-existent website. It was set up by a 17-year-old from York, who later said it was part of an experiment related to their business A-level (Waterson, 2020). Checking this story would not have been difficult. In fact, a single phone call to the press office of Woolworths' owner, Very, would have quickly debunked it, raising questions about how much some newsrooms really wanted to fact-check this nostalgia-driven, click-driving tale rather than rapidly publish it. The subject matter here was relatively inconsequential, but the episode raised more serious questions about fact-checking standards and led the BBC's heavyweight *Newsnight* programme to run a segment on how audiences had been duped. Katie Grant, consumer affairs correspondent for the *i newspaper*, reflected on the potential cumulative effects of such practices in the industry:

Nobody likes to wait for their news (it's called yesterday's news for a reason) but rush to be first/get a chunk of the traffic surely has to slow down if news orgs/journalists hope to retain what public trust there is?

Grant, 2020.

How do you responsibly cover online/social media conspiracy theories?

In the Begum case, those shaky early stories proved to be true. The Woolworths example shows us that this is not always the case. A second key question is about whether journalists should acknowledge and report on unsubstantiated information because it is already in the public domain, even if they know or suspect it to be false, or steer clear to avoid any risk of amplifying or oxygenating the story. One case in point is the false conspiracy theory that the 2020 coronavirus pandemic was linked to 5G wireless technology. In the UK, the mainstream media largely kept away from this subject until it reached the point of 5G infrastructure coming under attack. At this point, the story was widely reported, and ITV presenter Eamonn Holmes was widely criticised for suggesting that a possible 5G link was being prematurely shut down by the mainstream media during a televised discussion on 'fake news' (Tobitt, 2020c).

The outcry that his comment provoked is an indication of the impact that pickup by major news outlets can have on the reach and credibility of a false story, even one that already has a substantial presence elsewhere online. This reflects a useful concept known as the 'trumpet of amplification', whereby inaccurate claims that begin life in the niche recesses of the anonymous web travel through stages of progressively greater amplification—closed networks, conspiracy communities and social media—before being blasted out at maximum volume by the professional media (Wardle, 2018). Ethically minded journalists should bear in mind that, even in the digital age, their 'trumpets' can generally blow far louder and with more authority than other sources of information.

How then does a journalist square the competitive and commercial imperative to cover the stories that people are talking about with the ethical imperative to avoid oxygenising dangerous conspiracy theories or spreading inaccurate rumours, even if the coverage is an attempt to debunk those inaccuracies?

First Draft, a project that seeks to combat online misinformation and disinformation, suggests that the ethical moment to act is at the 'tipping point' in such a story's digital life. This is the stage at which a conspiracy theory or falsehood already has sufficient traction that a journalist's coverage will not markedly inflame the situation, but before it becomes so commonplace that views on its veracity are entrenched. First Draft suggests that a reporter could consider five questions in reflecting whether the tipping point has been reached (First Draft, 2020). These are:

1. Has the story jumped between several platforms?
2. Has it travelled outside a niche online community, for example, the anti-vax movement, into general circulation?
3. Are other mainstream outlets covering it?
4. Are celebrities or influencers promoting it?
5. How big are digital engagement numbers for the story where it already appears?

Claire Wardle, First Draft's executive director, argues that journalists have a legitimate role in debunking dangerous misinformation on the web. This can be done most effectively, she argues, if newsrooms work together:

> We need newsrooms to work collectively to push out consistent messages around false and misleading information. We need responsible headlines that don't use SEO for clicks that can then reinforce the rumours.
> Wardle, 2020

In the case of 5G and COVID-19, it could be argued that most of the mainstream UK news media acted ethically and attempted to debunk the theory only when it reached the tipping point of phone masts coming under attack. At this point, the 5G conspiracy had clearly reached general circulation, and was attracting attention from high-profile figures.

This is not always the case. Consider, as a counterpoint, the non-existent 'Momo' suicide challenge of 2019. This began with misinformation circulating online that a ghoulish character was exhorting children to kill themselves via videos on platforms like WhatsApp. The story gained massive traction once picked up by the mainstream media, and ultimately, news reporting of a non-existent problem became something of a self-fulfilling prophecy. As schools and police forces issued warnings in response to news reports about fears of the challenge, data showed that search interest in Momo increased dramatically (Waterson, 2019).

Momo demonstrated the power of professional journalism to amplify inaccurate stories far more powerfully than other conduits of information. Journalists should be mindful of this and note that even if attempting to expose a story as false, the very act of covering it can give a falsehood powerful oxygen simply by affording it familiarity through repetition. If a debunk is done poorly, studies have shown, audiences might be more likely to remember the lie than the evidence that contradicts it (Swire and Ecker, 2018, p. 200).

Headlines, intros or news leads and associated social media posts must be carefully worded and avoid the temptation of clickbait, as readers often do not get past them. Research has also suggested that explaining why a conspiracy theory might be attractive, rather than simply attacking its content or using derogatory language about its adherents, is also more effective (First Draft, 2020). In the cases of future conspiracy theories, and particularly those that have grave implications in areas such as public health, newsrooms might consider working together as Wardle's suggests to cover and debunk in a coordinated fashion.

What are the ethical challenges around using content from social media accounts and online groups?

Earlier sections of this chapter looked at the ethics of covering stories or rumours that are already circulating online. There are also important ethical issues to consider in how journalists deploy social media content within their own stories. These are in addition to legal questions around copyright, privacy and defamation that might be relevant depending on the nature and format of the material.

Firstly, journalists would be wise to remember that crowdsourcing or fact-checking stories online has problems just as it does offline. Those who respond to requests for information or opinion put out via social media channels are likely to be as self-selecting as an unscientific street vox pop, while it is difficult to be sure that contributors are who they purport to be (Frost, 2016, p. 151). A post asking for help with a story can be an efficient and effective way of newsgathering, but any results need to be carefully verified.

Often, the reporter goes looking for content rather than inviting contributions. In this case, the responsible journalist owes some duty of care to 'civilian' social media users who might be unprepared for the implications of a post becoming the centre of a news story. An example here is Mary Matthews, the widow of an early UK coronavirus victim Nick Matthews. Mrs Matthews posted on Facebook advising friends to get tested if they had been in recent contact with her late husband, who she described as her "soul mate", and the tribute quickly became part of news stories about his death. Alerted by the attention, scammers then set up a fake crowdfunding page in Mr Matthews' name and his widow was forced to post again warning: "This is not me! Please do not send any money" (Pickstock, 2020).

The journalists who took extracts from Mrs Matthews' original post were likely acting in good faith, wishing to humanise a tragic story with the words of a grieving widow. What this example illustrates, though, is that non-journalists posting on platforms like Facebook do not necessarily realise that their content could be accessible to everyone including the world's media. Nor is everybody an expert in the various privacy settings they can deploy to limit access. What journalists *can* see and what they ethically *should* publish—particularly without even alerting the poster to the fact that their content is about to gain potentially huge profile—are not necessarily the same thing. The National Union of Journalists (NUJ) uses the useful analogy of eavesdropping on a group of friends who do not expect others to listen in or repeat it in a news story in its social media guidance to members. Ruth Palmer's study *Becoming the News* shows that even contributors who are expecting to feature in a story, having spoken to a journalist, can be unprepared for the impact that can have in terms of reach and feedback—positive and otherwise—from digital audiences, or for the story's lasting footprint on their online identity (Palmer, 2017, pp. 172–193). The potential for shock is only magnified if a story subject wasn't aware that the material they had put online would be used in that way.

Journalists need to approach UGC online on a case-by-case basis, and indeed platform-by-platform. It is legitimate to follow anyone who is publishing on a public forum like Twitter in the hope of gathering leads, tip-offs and quotes, although the issue of verifying information found there still applies, as discussed above. For politicians, celebrities, journalists and others in the public eye, it can safely be assumed that a tweet is expected to secure widespread consumption. If the person posting is not a public figure of some form, however, it might be wise to consider their intent (as well as any legal questions such as copyright) before embedding or scraping their content. If a post or picture is clearly intended to attract attention—for example, if news organisations or public figures are tagged or there are encouragements to share—then concerns about privacy might be diminished. A journalist might still want to consider notifying the poster that they intend to use their material, particularly if the subject matter is controversial, so that the individual in question is at least braced for the attention. If it is less clear that the poster intended to attract attention, or was even aware of the potential for doing so, then the ethical imperative to get in touch is arguably greater.

On platforms like Facebook that have privacy settings, these must be respected, although as discussed above it is ethically problematic to rely on all 'civilians' having a detailed understanding of their privacy options. The press regulator IPSO recommends taking a screen shot of an account's privacy settings before using material found there, as well as "a contemporaneous note of any discussion around the public interest in publishing information, where relevant" (IPSO, n.d.). Only if there is an overwhelming public interest should private pages be accessed, and it would be wise for individual journalists to consult with their editors and legal teams before doing so. In the case of stories about private individuals who have died in newsworthy circumstances, it would be judicious to consider the impact of reusing their social media content on surviving friends and family, whether the individual's privacy settings offer you access or not.

Should journalists clearly identify themselves when they join closed social media groups?

When it comes to closed groups on platforms such as Facebook and WhatsApp, journalists need to consider the ethics as well as legal perils of joining without clearly identifying themselves as a journalist. This could be likened to subterfuge—something that needs a good public interest justification—offline. Indeed, it should be noted that IPSO has previously ruled, in the case of the 2014 'sexting' scandal that led to the resignation of minister Brooks Newmark after he sent sexually explicit photographs to a *Sunday Mirror* journalist posing as a Conservative activist, that setting up a fake social media account constitutes misrepresentation and requires a public interest defence (Frost, 2016, pp. 145–146). A journalist who identifies themselves as such when joining a closed group should also make it clear if they intend to publish material gleaned from within the group.

In general, it is worth remembering that obtaining access to a closed digital space—perhaps someone has shared a link or invitation, or a journalist has joined under a different identity—does not make that access ethical. *Financial Times* journalist Mark di Stefano found this out to his cost when he lost his job after eavesdropping on a Zoom call among staff at the *Independent* in May 2020 (Joy, 2020; Ponsford, 2020). Access details had been shared with him, but di Stefano would presumably not have sneaked into the *Independent's* newsroom to listen to the equivalent in-person meeting if someone had left the door open. Conference and video meetings bring a different set of issues to closed online groups, but the principle of respecting an expectation of privacy online, as you would offline, is comparable. For a journalist exposing corruption, illegality or other wrongdoing, the calculations are different but still relevant.

In interacting with closed groups on social media platforms, a journalist should furthermore bear in mind their own safety, just as they would if going undercover offline. Again, context is key: a group for primary school teachers is less likely to generate risk than one for far-right activists. Editors and managers should be consulted if there is any realistic prospect of risk. Journalists whose work leads them to report on controversial topics or engage with problematic and fringe groups should think about how to minimize the personal information about themselves that is available online to be misused by disgruntled story subjects or trolls. *The New York Times*' Information Security team offers a package of advice, originally developed for the newspaper's own journalists, on how to clean up your digital footprint. This includes recommendations for social media account settings and tips on how to opt out of people search websites, which can be carried out regularly or before publishing a controversial story (Kozinski and Kapur, 2020).

How should we handle content from 'witness contributors' and 'citizen journalists'?

Many people who become embroiled in a news event, whether by witnessing something happening, receiving information or otherwise, still choose to contact established media outlets as a means to tell their stories. However, witness contributors and so-called citizen journalists can alternatively now choose to gather, record and publish content directly on to the internet. This kind of material, that is deliberately and self-consciously relevant to news stories, can be thought of as different to the general mass of social media content discussed above that is usually newsworthy only inadvertently or in retrospect. Text, images and raw video footage from witnesses and citizen journalists can add vital evidence that brings a completely new story to light or fills gaps in a journalist's knowledge of an existing one. Witness videos proved a vital, graphic element in raising the profile of the May 2020 killing of George Floyd by police in Minneapolis, which sparked that year's wave of Black Lives Matter protests in the USA and elsewhere (Kansara, 2020). Citizen reporters played a key role in reporting on parts of the Syrian civil war between President Assad's forces and various opposition groups, after foreign news outlets deemed them too risky. Their material was widely used in the mainstream media. This kind of content can enable the telling of stories that would otherwise go unnoticed.

However, journalists and news organisations should consider the ethics of if and how they use citizen journalism in their own reporting. Questions that could usefully be asked, in addition to checking the veracity of any content and the identity of its creator, might include:

- the expectations of the creator in terms of attribution and/or payment,
- what their perspective or agenda might be (whose voices the content does *not* include), and
- whether they have put themselves or others in danger to obtain it.

Reporters Without Borders recorded six deaths among citizen journalists in Syria in 2019, compared with half of that among professional journalists (Reporters Without Borders, 2019). Much closer to home, Frost cites the example of some amateur footage of a fire sent to a newsroom in which the person filming could be heard commenting that they hoped the burning depot didn't explode (Frost, 2016, p. 211). By using the footage, would the newsroom be condoning the risk taken in obtaining it, or encouraging others to take similar risks? What is an editor's duty of care to citizen contributors, or to others who might see the publication of one piece of material as tacit invitation to gather more? In short, journalists who make use of material offered up by citizen journalists or witness contributors should consider both the limits and the cost, as well as the merits, of what they are getting. If such material has been gathered in ways that would breach ethical codes—or laws—if employed by a professional journalist, news organisations risk sanction or reputational damage by making use of it.

How does a journalist keep their own social media accounts ethical?

From receiving a first tip-off to promoting the finished story, social media has become a part of everyday newsroom life. Even back in 2013, a survey suggested that 96% of UK journalists use social media every day (Bartlett, 2013). Platforms such as Twitter have also generated unprecedented opportunities for audiences to engage with journalists. It has also created a new imperative for journalists to engage back. All this generates ethical questions that in many countries are not addressed in detail by national regulatory frameworks such as the IPSO Editors' Code of Practice (Díaz-Campo and Segado-Boj, 2015). There is often an expectation from employers that individual journalists will have a personal online brand and profile, in order to boost traffic or viewing figures. Yet there are also normative—albeit contested—expectations that those who work in news in particular will remain 'objective' or impartial about those stories. What, given those potentially contradictory demands, are the ethics of social media use—public and private—for journalists?

Some news media organisations have their own internal policies governing their employees' use of social media. Channel 4 News policy states that news and current affairs journalists "do not as a rule agree or disagree with a political party or politician, or take a fixed stance on politically contentious issues" (Channel 4, 2020).

Amid bubbling controversy around use of social media by its staff and contributors, the BBC released tougher new social media guidance in October 2020 (BBC, 2020). Among its stipulations was a renewed call for the traditional journalistic position of impartiality: "If your work requires you to maintain your impartiality, don't express a personal opinion on matters of public policy, politics, or 'controversial subjects'." It clearly placed the BBC's corporate reputation above the need for individual profile: "Remember that your personal brand on social media is always secondary to your responsibility to the BBC" and, perhaps more controversially, urged against "virtue signalling" online. A month before it was issued, the corporation's incoming director general, Tim Davie, signalled a shift in attitude when he told staff to work elsewhere if they wanted to share opinions online or in columns and urged the need to "champion and recommit" to impartiality (Tobitt, 2020b).

BBC journalists are perhaps inevitably under particular scrutiny when it comes to any hint of political leaning, but many others working elsewhere continued at the time of Davie's clampdown to comment freely on the news agenda in a way that sits uncomfortably with notions of objectivity and impartiality. Norms and rules are in flux, it seems. Perhaps we are moving to an era when 'transparency'—being clear about one's affiliations and standpoint rather than pretending to have none—usurps impartiality as a core journalistic principle. But young and trainee journalists should be mindful that at least some news organisations still expect their staff to avoid overt bias, and as the NUJ advises its members, when journalists identify themselves with a particular news outlet they should adhere to that organisation's social media rules.

However, it is also worth remembering that an individual journalist's social media brand, once established, carries over from job to job (quoted in Fincham, 2018, p. 176), and unguarded or partisan comments that went down well in one context might damage professional credibility or even employment prospects in another.

Aside from commenting directly on news events, a journalist's social media activity—even if ostensibly carried out in a private capacity—can affect perceptions of their reporting. Social media has made individual journalists into public figures. While some seek to maintain separate personal and professional accounts, research suggests that most either use social media for professional purposes only or blend their personal and professional identities within the same accounts (Bossio and Sacco, 2017, p. 527). In any case, it would be unlikely to make much difference to the ensuing controversy if a reporter were found to have admitted to inappropriate behaviour, whether far-right campaigning; anti-vax lobbying or drunken loutishness, on a profile they considered to be private. Guidelines for staff at America's National Public Radio caution that "nothing on the web is truly private" (quoted in Fincham, 2018, p. 182), and urges caution even in joining groups on platforms like Facebook if membership might be taken as endorsement of that group's views. It is an inadvisably high-risk strategy for a journalist to post inappropriate material to private or even pseudonymous social media accounts assuming that nobody will join the dots to their professional identity.

Likewise, disclaimers such as "All views are my own" in Twitter profiles and elsewhere are useful, but not a license to post unguardedly. Indeed, the BBC rules warn staff: "Disclaimers written in biographies such as 'my views not the BBC's' provide no defence against personal expressions of opinion on social media that may conflict with BBC guidelines" (BBC, 2020). Readers often do not read biographies and profiles. Even where they do, they might lack faith in a cast-iron separation between a personal view and any news content produced by the same person. Further, social media trainer Sue Llewellyn advises that journalists should think of each post being read in isolation (Hewett, 2018, p. 122); there is no guarantee that a reader will note that a particular message is part of a longer, more balanced chain or sits within an archive of nuanced commentary. One thing that readers will almost always see next to each tweet, however, is a reporter's byline picture: for that reason, it is wise to choose a professional and sober image, particularly if you are likely to be posting about sombre or sensitive subjects.

Journalists need also to be mindful of what they like, re-post and share on social media. A tendency to circulate material critical of one political party, for example, might over time give the impression of bias even if none were intended. Such behaviour can even have legal ramifications, giving a complainant ammunition to suggest malign intent if a negative article about them appears. Reuters cautions its staff: "Everything we say can be used against us in a court of law" (Fincham, 2018, p. 179). American lecturer Kelly Fincham suggests a useful classroom exercise for a journalism student is to download their Twitter archive into a spreadsheet and analyse it for inappropriate content or signs of partiality (Fincham, 2018, pp. 179–180).

How should journalists engage with comments from audiences?

Journalists using social media should also consider to what extent it is ethical and constructive to engage with comments from audiences. Should one engage with or block offensive posters, for example? Research by *The Guardian* found that its female and ethnic minority staff were the prime targets of abusive comments on its website (Gardiner et al., 2016). In extreme cases such as that of Newquest's chief reporter for South Cumbria, Amy Fenton, who was forced to flee her home in 2020 after receiving death threats amid false claims that she had helped to cover up sexual abuse of young women in Barrow, online abuse reaches the point where police intervention is required (Tobitt, 2020a). Journalists who feel able to engage or spar with so-called 'trolls' should perhaps consider whether doing so might lead to more harassment of those who already bear the brunt. The better course of action might be to ignore them. *The Guardian's* guidelines for freelancers take that approach: "Ignore those who are abusive or offensive, and avoid public arguments on social media, with colleagues, contributors or others. If in doubt, do not respond" (The Guardian, 2020).

When that abuse becomes threatening, the same guidelines are clear:

> Make sure you are safe. If someone is in immediate danger dial 999 … Report abuse to social media platforms but do not respond or escalate—block or mute troublemakers so you do not see their posts. If you feel threatened, tell your editor. We have guidelines and support in place to help you.

It should not be forgotten, however, that there can be a positive dimension to engaging with audiences via social media. As a reporter, it can boost the morale, vindicate hard work and of course provide fresh evidence. For audiences, particularly people whose lives are impacted by or reflected in a piece of reporting, interaction with the relevant journalist can evidently feel worthwhile.

In the midst of the storm over prime ministerial adviser Dominic Cummings' controversial trip to his parents' home in County Durham at the height of the COVID-19 lockdown in May 2020 when the UK was under severe travel restrictions and families and friends were unable to be together, *Daily Mirror* political editor Pippa Crerar, who broke the story, tweeted:

> Thank you to everybody who has got in touch the last few days—especially those who have shared your personal experience of the lockdown. Some of you have endure terrible hardship and loss. Your bravery in the midst of this horror absolutely floors me. Stay strong. X.
>
> *Crerar, 2020*

The tweet received thousands of likes. Whatever one's views on Cummings, in this instance, social media provided a means for a journalist and her audience to interact in a way that was meaningful for both sides.

Finally, the ethically minded journalist must also bear in mind the responsibility that comes with their status as a provider of trustworthy information. They should of course make sure that any factual reporting they do via social media is accurate—particularly now that this is often the way that important stories such as trial verdicts are broken. But they should also think about how their wider online behaviour might impact on their journalistic authority. The UK code for non-broadcast advertising governs the labelling of advertising and sponsored content on social media, including posts that result from having received a 'freebie'. But even if such a post is clearly labelled, is it ethical for a journalist to promote products and companies in this way? The National Union of Journalists thinks not. Its code of conduct states that a journalist:

> Does not by way of statement, voice or appearance endorse by advertisement any commercial product or service save for the promotion of her/his own work or of the medium by which she is employed.
>
> NUJ, 2011

Ethics in action: Jim Waterson, *The Guardian*: "The internet has upended everything about the industry"

Jim Waterson is media editor of *The Guardian*, where he leads on all media coverage across print and digital. He joined the news outlet in 2018, and prior to that, he was political editor of Buzzfeed UK from 2013. There, he helped to establish the site's UK news coverage. Prior to that, he was a politics and business journalist at City AM. He has more than 252,000 followers on Twitter.

Has the advent of social media changed the ethics of journalism? If so, in what ways?

Abandon the idea there was ever a golden age for journalism ethics. Journalism is a messy, imperfect, constantly changing industry that revolves around bringing people information they don't know. As a result, over the centuries it has always attracted individuals trying to score political points, people looking to make a quick buck or push the limits of the truth in the search for a dramatic headline. What we now consider 'media ethics' is really a culmination of decades of best practice on how decisions should be made in an ideal world. In reality, a lot relies on the moral compass of an individual journalist and their publication.

What's changed is that until the internet arrived the media used to consist of a limited number of well-resourced news outlets, who controlled access to audiences. This also meant that if one of those news outlets lied or conducted journalism in a deeply immoral manner, the public would rarely find out due to an attitude of 'honour amongst thieves'.

It was often only when another major news outlet or the government got involved that the public would learn of these mistakes—such as when Piers Morgan was forced to resign as *Daily Mirror* editor after he printed faked photos of supposed war crimes. Even in the 2000s, when hacking of celebrities' voicemail accounts was widespread at UK tabloid newspapers, it was largely left to *The Guardian* and *Private Eye* to expose such widespread and widely known criminal activity.

The internet has upended everything about the industry.

At the reputable end of journalism, news outlets that care about their reputations have never been more accountable. Readers will dissect every sentence of an online article, call out aspects of TV news reports they find objectionable, and run campaigns on Twitter demanding advertisers stop paying for promotions. It's hard for a tabloid newspaper to run negative stories about relatively innocent members of the public if that individual can then go viral with their side of the story.

But at the less reputable end of journalism, social media has helped create a series of widely read outlets that will do almost anything in the hunt for clicks if they don't care about ethical consideration. The financial collapse of the industry has also led to outlets that have cut back on original reporting and fact-checking—meaning they're more liable to repeat falsehoods. Unfortunately, many online readers are more than happy to lap up sensational fact-free news articles rather than more sober fact-based equivalents.

Is all online content (e.g. photographs/Tweets) ethically fair game for use within reporting if there are no legal barriers such as privacy settings or copyright?

Until the 2000s, almost all the power lay with the news outlet—if they wanted to use a photograph or a video in their output, then there was little the individual could do about it. But most material was still created by professional reporters, photographers or filmmakers. At the same time, if an individual wanted to get attention for a campaign they were running, then they'd have to approach a mainstream news outlet.

There are basic questions to ask yourself: What was the expectation of the person when they posted the material online? Would they be surprised to find it used in a news story without being contacted? Even if they would be shocked, can it still be justified? Just because something is public on one part of the internet doesn't mean that people want it covered by a news outlet. In most cases, simply contacting the individual allows you to check how they feel and perhaps get a better story in the process.

But even if someone does not want their material to be used it may well be ethical to push ahead regardless. For instance: If an Instagram picture is of an obviously newsworthy event, if the tweet was posted by an elected politician, or if you're using a Facebook post as evidence to expose wrongdoing, then it can easily be justified.

How—if at all—does an ethically minded journalist report on rumour and unsubstantiated stories that are circulating online?

Just because you're sourcing material from the internet doesn't mean that you don't have to apply the old traditional standards to journalism. Take the time to contact the person making a claim, try to double source their accusations and check with any relevant authorities to make sure it's correct. Never be afraid to ping a message to an individual and ask for a quick chat—you can pretty quickly pick up whether someone is lying or not if you actually engage with them.

Sadly, the financial state of the news industry means there's increasing pressure at a lot of news outlets to publish stories as fast as possible. This leads to headlines quoting unverified online accusations—often in quote marks with words such as 'claims' or 'allegedly'—in a bid to get articles online as fast as possible. On countless occasions, it's later turned out that there's a lot more to the story and the original claim was wrong, or missing key facts.

It can be hard to stand up to editors, but it's going to be your name on the story if it turns out to be false—and you have to live with the hit to your credibility.

Should the ethically minded journalist attempt to debunk misinformation and disinformation online, or ignore it?

One of the most exhausting roles of a credible journalist in the 2010s is debunking falsehoods that spread online. Standing up for the truth matters immensely, but you've also got to be careful that you're picking your battles wisely and not inadvertently amplifying disinformation.

As such, it's worth assessing the scale of online disinformation before getting involved in debunking it. Has that fake Facebook post had a real-world impact or is it just being shared by a few hundred conspiracy theorists? How do you engage with the content without accidentally promoting the original conspiracy to a new audience? And how do you write a debunk story that can actually change people's minds? Simply asserting that something is false won't necessarily convince people who have already bought into a fake interpretation of events.

However, if a false claim has already reached millions of people, then there is a public service to debunking it and explaining how it came to be. Showing people exactly how they were duped into believing a falsehood is often more helpful then just declaring it be wrong. What was the original source? Why was it misleading?

But a problem with limited resources in a newsroom is you may be attempting to play whack-a-mole with falsehoods. It could be that you're better off focussing on exposing new, true stories rather than obsessing over yesterday's lies.

What are the main ethical issues for journalists who want to build a profile on social media?

The general public—and your potential employers—won't see any difference between what you put on social media and write in a professional capacity. As such, you should broadly treat them the same. This might seem unfair, but in a world with ever-increasing scrutiny of journalists and their biases—alleged or real—then you should be careful.

This is reflected in the changing attitude of major news outlets. The likes of the BBC spent years trying to get their journalists to engage on social media but have become increasingly concerned that the enormous followings of some of their reporters can undermine the carefully edited version of the news that goes out through official channels. This is a particular issue at a time of immense pressure on the media from politicians, who will seize on every badly phrased tweet and attempt to make it into a scandal.

Has your use of social media as an individual reporter changed with your change of jobs? Are there any examples of particularly good or bad ethical practice among journalists on social media that you'd cite?

Social media—and especially Twitter—used to be a fun place for a small group of tech-savvy journalists to hang out and trade gossip with their colleagues and a tiny audience of news obsessives. As a result, it was often a fun place for reporters to spend their time, with little impact on their day jobs.

Now that audiences have migrated to social media platforms, with audiences measured in the hundreds of millions of views, that old informality has been lost.

In place of the old media's self-written ethics guidelines has come a whole new group of ethical considerations for the modern journalist: is it fair to retweet someone with a few hundred followers if they aren't expecting the attention? How can you convince a politician to talk to you if they find your tweet criticising them, even if it was posted when you were a student? What would a source think if the top Google result for your name is your personal Instagram ranting about the state of the world?

However, there's also the risk of being 'edited by Twitter', with journalists pulling their punches for fear of offending a particular group of activists online. The best rule of thumb is always this: how would I feel if a tweet or an Instagram post or a Facebook post went viral? If you'd be happy to defend the ethics and the thought process that went into it, then push ahead. If not, then consider whether you're doing the right thing.

Ethical workout

- Are journalists entitled to offer opinions about the news through their personal social media channels?
- Is it acceptable to embed content from a social media account in your work without telling the account holder, as long as their privacy settings allow you to access it?
- Should there be an industry-wide code of practice for journalists on how to use social media in their work?
- Would it be better if the professional news media ignored conspiracy theories altogether rather than reporting on them?

Five takeaways from this chapter

- Resist the temptation to republish rumours; think instead about what you can add to the story as a journalist, for example, by corroborating or debunking the rumour.
- Don't assume that it is ethically safe to publish material from social media accounts just because you're able to access it; consider the expectations of and impact on the individual and their contacts.
- Before you republish content from witness contributors or citizen journalists, think about the strengths and limitations of the material and the manner in which it was gathered.
- Consider the reach and impact of a conspiracy theory or false story before covering it in order to debunk, and take care with language, tone and headlines if and when you go ahead.
- Remember that your social media accounts shape perceptions of your reporting and professionalism, whether or not you choose to post directly about news stories. Over time, they will build into a public picture of your likes, interests and attitudes that could affect your reputation and job prospects.

Ethics toolbox

- BBC, Guidance: Social media, BBC. See www.bbc.com/editorialguidelines/guidance/social-media#expressionsofopiniononsocialmedia
- Channel 4, Social Media Guidelines, channel4.com. See www.channel4.com/producers-handbook/c4-guidelines/social-media-guidelines

- *The Guardian*, Social media best practice: Guidelines for freelance contributors, *The Guardian*, 29 May. See www.theguardian.com/info/2020/may/29/social-media-best-practice-guidelines-for-freelance-contributors?fbclid=IwAR2RHQGK0PbRjDoAsxgxkFIAVgJiOcjXwubZuRRvs-mpqW2yOVHyFaP0Mts
- IPSO, Social media guidance. See www.ipso.co.uk/member-publishers/guidance-for-journalists-and-editors/social-media-guidance/
- Online Journalism Blog (Paul Bradshaw). The blog publishes interviews, analysis, discussions of data journalism, interactive storytelling and the internet. See https://onlinejournalismblog.com/.

References

Akunjee, M. (2019) 'Strong but unconfirmed reports…He was a British citizen'. *Twitter*. Available at: https://twitter.com/mohammedakunjee/status/1104022748509155330?lang=en (Accessed: 15 September 2020).

Auman, A., Stos, S. and Burch E. (2020) 'Ethics without borders in a digital age', *Journalism & Mass Communication Educator*, 75(1), pp. 9–15.

Bartlett, R. (2013) 'Study: 96% of UK journalists use social media every day', *Journalism.co.uk*, 7 November. Available at: www.journalism.co.uk/news/study-96-of-uk-journalists-use-social-media-each-day/s2/a554687/ (Accessed: 15 September 2020).

BBC. (2020) 'Guidance: Social media', *BBC*. Available at: www.bbc.com/editorialguidelines/guidance/social-media#expressionsofopiniononsocialmedia (Accessed: 4 January 2021).

Bell, E. (2019) 'Terrorism bred online requires anticipatory, not reactionary coverage', *Colombia Journalism Review*, 20 March. Available at: www.cjr.org/tow_center/facebook-twitter-christchurch-emily-bell-terrorism.php?ct=t(Top_Stories_CJR_new_Jan_26_1_25_2017_COPY_01) (Accessed: 15 September 2019).

Blewett, S. and Raven, D. (2019) 'Baby of ISIS bride Shamima Begum "may have died" – according to family's lawyer', *Liverpool Echo*, 8 March. Available at: www.liverpoolecho.co.uk/news/liverpool-news/baby-isis-bride-shamima-begum-15944617 (Accessed: 15 September 2020).

Bossio, D. and Sacco, V. (2017) 'From "selfies" to breaking tweets: How journalists negotiate personal and professional identity on social media', *Journalism Practice*, 11(5), pp. 527–543.

Channel 4. (2020) 'Social media guidelines', *channel4.com*. Available at: www.channel4.com/producers-handbook/c4-guidelines/social-media-guidelines (Accessed: 15 September 2020).

Crerar, P. (2020) 'Thank you to everybody...Stay strong'. *X [Twitter]*. Available at: https://twitter.com/PippaCrerar/status/1265410595622453248 (Accessed: 23 September 2020).

Díaz-Campo, J. and Segado-Boj, F. (2015) 'Journalism ethics in a digital environment: How journalistic codes of ethics have been adapted to the Internet and ICTs in countries around the world', *Telematics and Informatics*, 32(4), pp. 735–744.

Elvestad, E. and Phillips, A. (2018) *Misunderstanding news audiences: Seven myths of the social media era*. Abingdon: Routledge.

Fincham, K. (2018) '"These views are my own": The private and public self in the digital media sphere', in Zion, L. and Craig, D. (eds.), *Ethics for digital journalists: Emerging best practices*. Abingdon: Routledge, pp. 174–186.

First Draft. (2020) 'Ethical questions around covering coronavirus [online video]'. Available at: www.youtube.com/watch?list=PL0n8am2uBRCBUZI5ftm2jQ63tl YrtY4_I&v=kwkKLOUGHqk (Accessed: 23 September 2020).

Frost, C. (2016) *Journalism ethics and regulation*, 4th ed. Abingdon: Routledge

Gardiner, B. et al. (2016) 'The dark side of *Guardian* comments', *The Guardian*, 12 April. Available at: www.theguardian.com/technology/2016/apr/12/the-dark-side-of-guardian-comments (Accessed: 23 September 2020).

Grant, K. (2020). 'Nobody likes … what public trust there is?' *Twitter*. Available at: https://twitter.com/kt_grant/status/1321063534546112512. (Accessed: 4 January 2021).

Harcup, T. (2015) *Journalism: Principles and practice*. 3rd ed. London: Sage.

Hewett, J. (2018) 'Live Tweeting: The rise of real-time reporting', in Zion, L. and Craig, D. (eds.), *Ethics for digital journalists: Emerging best practices*. Abingdon: Routledge, pp. 115–129.

IPSO. (n.d.) 'Social media guidance.' Available at: www.ipso.co.uk/member-publishers/guidance-for-journalists-and-editors/social-media-guidance/ (Accessed: 4 January 2021).

Joy, I. (2020) 'Mark Di Stefano: The right kind of hack', *Spiked*. Available at: www.spiked-online.com/2020/05/04/mark-di-stefano-the-right-kind-of-hack/ (Accessed: 5 August 2020).

Kansara, R. (2020) 'Black lives matter: Can viral videos stop police brutality?' *BBC*, 6 July. Available at: www.bbc.co.uk/news/blogs-trending-53239123 (Accessed: 15 September 2020).

Keeble, R. (2009) *Ethics for journalists*. 2nd ed. Abingdon: Routledge.

Knowlton, S. and McKinley, J.C. (2016) 'There's more to ethics than justice and harm: Teaching a broader understanding of journalism ethics', *Journalism & Mass Communication Educator*, 71(2), pp. 133–145.

Kozinski, K. and Kapur, N. (2020) 'How to dox yourself on the internet', *open.mytimes.com*, 27 February. Available at: https://open.nytimes.com/how-to-dox-yourself-on-the-internet-d2892b4c5954 (Accessed: 15 September 2020).

National Union of Journalists. (2011) 'NUJ code of conduct', *nuj.org.uk*. Available at: www.nuj.org.uk/about/nuj-code/ (Accessed: 23 September 2020).

Newman, N., Fletcher, R., Schulz, A., Andi, S. and Nielsen, R.K. (2020) 'Reuters Institute digital news report 2020', *Reuters Institute for the Study of Journalism*. Available at: www.digitalnewsreport.org/ (Accessed: 23 September 2020).

Palmer, R. (2017) *Becoming the news: How ordinary people respond to the media spotlight*. New York: Columbia University Press.

Pickstock, H. (2020) '"Low-life" set up fake fundraiser for man who died with coronavirus', *Bristol Post*, 18 March. Available at: www.bristolpost.co.uk/news/bristol-news/coronavirus-death-north-somerset-fundraiser-3961485 (Accessed: 15 September 2020).

Ponsford, D. (2020) 'FT reporter resigns after eavesdropping at conference calls at Independent and Standard', *Press Gazette*, 1 May. Available at: www.pressgazette.co.uk/ft-reporter-eavesdropped-on-independent-zoom-call-informing-staff-of-cutbacks/ (Accessed: 15 September 2020).

Reporters Without Borders. (2019) 'Violations of press freedom barometer', *Reporters Without Borders*. Available at: https://rsf.org/en/barometer?year=2019&type_id=240#list-barometre (Accessed: 15 September 2020).

Roberts, J. (2019) 'The erosion of ethics: From citizen journalism to social media', *Journal of Information, Communication and Ethics in Society*, 17(4), pp. 409–421.

Swire, B. and Ecker, U.K. (2018) 'Misinformation and its correction: Cognitive mechanisms and recommendations for mass communication', in Southwell, B.G., Thorson, E.A. and Sheble, L. (eds.), *Misinformation and mass audiences*. Austin: University of Texas Press, pp. 195–211.

The Guardian. (2020) 'Social media best practice: Guidelines for freelance contributors', *The Guardian*, 29 May. Available at: www.theguardian.com/info/2020/may/29/social-media-best-practice-guidelines-for-freelance-contributors?fbclid=IwAR2RHQGK0PbRjDoAsxgxkFIAVgJiOcjXwubZuRRvs-mpqW2yOVHyFaP0Mts (Accessed: 23 September 2020).

Thurman, N. (2018) 'Real-time online reporting: Best practices for live blogging', in Zion, L. and Craig, D. (eds.), *Ethics for digital journalists: Emerging best practices*. Abingdon: Routledge, pp. 103–114.

Tobitt, C. (2020a) 'Local journalist forced to flee home with young daughter says she will carry on reporting', *Press Gazette*, May 27. Available at: www.pressgazette.co.uk/local-journalist-forced-to-flee-home-with-young-daughter-says-she-will-carry-on-reporting/ (Accessed: 23 September 2020).

Tobitt, C. (2020b) 'New BBC director-general tells staff to work elsewhere if they want to share opinions online or in columns', *Press Gazette*, 3 September. Available at: https://pressgazette.co.uk/new-bbc-director-general-tells-staff-to-work-elsewhere-if-they-want-to-share-opinions-online-or-in-columns/ (Accessed: 23 September 2020).

Tobitt, C. (2020c) 'Ofcom assessing Eamonn Holmes' comments on 5G after 419 complaints', *Press Gazette*, 14 April. Available at: www.pressgazette.co.uk/ofcom-assessing-eamonn-holmes-comments-on-5g-coronavirus-conspiracy-after-419-complaints/ (Accessed: 15 September 2020).

Ward, S.J. (2014) 'Radical media ethics', *Digital Journalism*, 2(4), pp. 455–471.

Ward, S.J. (n.d.) 'Digital journalism ethics', *Center for Journalism Ethics*. Available at: https://ethics.journalism.wisc.edu/resources/digital-media-ethics/ (Accessed: 15 September 2020).

Wardle, C. (2018) '5 lessons for reporting in an age of disinformation', *First Draft*, 27 December. Available at: https://firstdraftnews.org/latest/5-lessons-for-reporting-in-an-age-of-disinformation/ (Accessed: 15 September 2020).

Wardle, C. (2020) 'What role should newsrooms play in debunking Covid 19 misinformation?' *Neiman Reports*, 8 April. Available at: https://niemanreports.org/articles/what-role-should-newsrooms-play-in-debunking-covid-19-misinformation/?mc_cid=79b29abf9e&mc_eid=8531780769 (Accessed: 15 September2020).

Waterson, J. (2019) 'Momo hoax: Schools, police and media told to stop promoting viral challenge', *The Guardian*, 1 March. Available at: www.theguardian.com/technology/2019/feb/28/schools-police-and-media-told-to-stop-promoting-momo-hoax (Accessed: 15 September2020).

Waterson, J. (2020) 'Sixth-form student revealed to be behind "Woolworths reopening" fake news', *The Guardian*, 28 October. Available at: www.theguardian.com/business/2020/oct/28/sixth-form-student-revealed-behind-woolworths-reopening-fake-news (Accessed: 4 January 2021).

4
Sources
The lifeblood of journalism

Jackie Newton

Interaction with others, whether in person, online or by means of document exchange, poses a wealth of ethical challenges for journalists. As with all such dilemmas, there are issues of fairness, honesty, transparency and power at the heart of source relationships. This chapter examines how sources, or the choice of sources, can shape news and influence the news agenda, sometimes to the detriment of wider society. How do we make contacts? Whom do we believe? Whom do we rely on to tell us what is happening in areas of politics, business and other organisations that we can't personally witness? When people risk all to tell us of wrongdoing, how can we protect them? In the *Ethics in Action* section, Gerard Ryle, who led the worldwide teams of journalists working on the Panama Papers, Paradise Papers and Pandora Papers investigations, discusses using anonymous sources, protection of sources and the ethics of handling large-scale data sets involving news outlets and journalists from all over the world.

How should journalists choose their sources?

> They are the lifeblood of quality journalism. Reporters may be stylish writers or polished presenters, but what counts most to the public is the reliability of the stories they tell, and that depends on the quality of our sources. These may be people with their own stories to tell, or who are experts and insiders. They may give us testimony or written reports or confidential documents, even pictures or recordings–all potentially vital in exposing corruption or wrong-doing in public life.
>
> White, 2020

The answer to this fundamental question is that we should choose our sources liberally but carefully. The more people who have a voice, the more democratic, balanced and ethical the news is and the wider it will be appreciated and acknowledged. News audiences are changing and journalists must become more responsive to changing preferences. Yet in a competitive industry with

DOI: 10.4324/9780429505386-5

fewer journalists and more demands on their time, it is easy to see why tried and trusted sources are consistently relied upon. The legalities are important too. Statements from the police carry qualified privilege. Statements from a witness in the street who has a different version of events are open to legal challenge and therefore a risk to the journalist's credibility.

Traditional journalistic divisions of sources into primary and secondary sources tend to underline the dependence on authority. Primary sources include MPs, local government officers and councillors, the emergency services, hospitals and other official bodies. Hall et al.'s classic work (1978) on journalistic sources suggests a hierarchical approach to news sources in which establishment and authority figures are not just primary sources but "primary definers" of the news, causing structural problems with a news agenda that favours the elite. Yet others claim that mainstream journalists use a remarkably limited range of sources. Johan Galtung and Mari Ruge (1965, 1973), in their seminal analysis of news values, highlighted the bias in the Western media towards reporting elite, First World nations and elite people. The elements of the hierarchy were different within and across different media. Television soap stars and showbiz personalities feature far more in the tabloid media than in the broadsheets. Joseph and Keeble (2016) argue that there is a distinct consensus over sourcing routines in the mainstream media. Some sources are always prominent, others will be marginalised, eliminated or covered generally in a negative way. Harcup and O'Neill's reflection on their previous work found that power elites were more likely to influence the news content and agendas of broadsheet/quality press than tabloids, "possibly because these papers report 'serious' news more prominently" (2017, p. 1478).

Other classic studies have suggested that journalists stick to a narrow range of sources because of the need for efficiency (Gans, 1980) when writing multiple stories to deadline. Gans also suggested that journalists apply a number of "source considerations" when choosing people or organisations to deal with regularly. These include past suitability, that is, sources who have come up with credible stories previously, productivity, reliability, trustworthiness, authoritativeness and articulateness. Journalists seek to protect themselves from unreliable information by adopting a number of strategies, according to Reich (2011). The first is "typecasting" in which a reporter will surround themselves with a coterie of regular, dependable sources. In the news-gathering phase, "practical scepticism" is applied to those whose information requires further verification and cross-checking. A further conclusion was that "less credible" sources were subject to "distancing by attribution" (Reich, 2011, p. 32).

Much of this may seem obvious. Journalists have always relied on sources for stories and will trust those who have proved reliable in the past, thoroughly checking out any new source for accuracy. The problem comes when the time for checking is limited, and the range of sources diminished by the tendency for journalists to come from a certain section of society, that is, the white and middle class. The ethical argument about greater diversity in the employment of journalists is not just about the makeup of newsrooms; it is also about the experiences and contacts those reporters would bring with them.

> Indeed, a core part of journalism is developing sources, and the more a journalist knows about the inner workings of a community, the better equipped they are to know who to ask, what questions to ask, and how to frame those questions in a way that gets to the heart of the story. If a journalist is from a community they are reporting on, they're more likely to know the history of that community and be able to put it into proper context for their audience.
>
> *Childers, 2020*

Much work is going on to create a more inclusive news environment, concentrating on widening sources and content as well as diversifying recruitment. The BBC's 50:50 project is an example of how monitoring output for fairness can improve representation in news and current affairs. Originally set up to encourage more accurate gender representation in output, it has gone on to monitor race and disability. In the United States, Melba Newsome, working with the Donald W. Reynolds Journalism Institute, has developed teaching materials to aid novice journalists in their search for wider sources in the wake of the George Floyd killing. She says that reporters who "parachute" into a community when a news story arises are likely to encounter indifference at best and hostility at worst. Her advice for developing wider sources includes:

1. Redefine who is an expert. Don't rely on CVs, credentials and formal training in a particular area to determine who's an expert. If we broaden our definition of who qualifies as an expert to include lived experience and people who are involved in the issues, this greatly expands the number and kinds of voices we can include.
2. Lay the groundwork first. If possible, try to recruit new sources before you actually need them in a story to avoid making a cold approach when you're on deadline.
3. Explain the process. Whether they are real people sharing their experiences or subject matter experts, few non-media people know what to expect when they agree to be.
4. Practice cultural competence. The notion of cultural competence is not just for white journalists, says inclusive media consultant Linda Miller, who helped create the Public Insight Network of diverse sources for American Public Media. "Understanding that different communities have different histories and experiences with the press should be the starting point for every journalist," says Miller (Newsome, 2021).

Of course, the changes in news audience and the moves to online first production have resulted in many challenges to the journalist. The traditional relationship in which sources speak to reporters and then the journalist fashions the story is unlikely to exist in quite the same way in contemporary media. Matthews (2015) believes the relationship is "out of kilter", with under-pressure journalists serving multi-media platforms more likely to be passive receivers of information from sources than verifiers of truth and accuracy. It leaves newsrooms prey to proactive sources (O'Neill and O'Connor, 2008). Having said that, journalists must tread carefully when dealing with sources for many reasons, not least their ability to misinform and, increasingly in the social media world, deliberately mislead.

Should journalists be concerned about the growing industry of news management and their reliance on "embedded" journalists?

Public relations (PR) professionals are thought to outnumber journalists by 6:1 in the United States according to figures extracted from the US Census (Tanzi and Hagan, 2019). While this figure fluctuates and has been exacerbated by a wave of redundancies in the news media in recent years, it has risen drastically since 2000 when the ratio was more like 2:1. In the UK, it is difficult to calculate a comparison from employment figures because of differences in the reporting, but anecdotal evidence over recent years tells us that there has been a shift in employment from traditional newsrooms into corporate communications and news production and management. Along with the ills and issues of the news media, the introduction of the internet and social media means that all organisations and companies have an increased need to communicate directly with the public. Large organisations have upped their game. They can and do employ journalists to provide a professional news service and many, such as Starbucks, have created their own newsrooms. Sports organisations, charities, businesses, government and emergency services among others have their own dedicated news and communications teams. For journalists, this "comms" boom has provided work while traditional newsrooms have shrunk. The opportunities on offer are very different from the strategic PR roles and more akin to the reporting and content generation roles they are trained for—until, that is, there is criticism of their organisation.

The worry for those believers in the free press is that the content generated by "commercially embedded" journalists is not free of obligation to their employer. They cannot fulfil the traditional role of the journalist because they have a publicity role rather than a watchdog function on behalf of the public. The ethical challenges to freedom of information are dire and obvious. It is a situation that concerns those involved in the new boom as much as it does journalists themselves, as they see the lack of a robust news media as danger, both democratically and commercially.

> ... several PR practitioners interviewed said they have a vested interest in the preservation of independent media, claiming that having information about their organization positively reported in respected independent media was more credible and more impactful than publicity in partisan media or saying it themselves through "owned" media.
>
> *Macnamara, 2014, p. 743*

There are a number of issues here. The most obvious is that the need for robust checking and verification remains the same, whether your information is delivered from a previously unknown member of the public or a former colleague now working in PR. Everyone expects this, including the PRs themselves, but with the decline of traditional newsrooms and expectation that journalists will work across multiple platforms, the basic tasks are time-consuming and difficult to keep up. Another is that "easy" PR content tends to further limit access to the media by those who do not have the skills and means or professional communicators (O'Neill and O'Connor, 2008). Various studies have looked at the amount of pre-packaged content published by news media outlets with estimates of between 40% and 75% of stories having some PR input (Macnamara, 2014). However, journalists perceive that only around a third of their work is influenced by PR (Obermaier, Koch and Riesmeyer, 2018).

Not all of these figures are as alarming as they sound. The issue of source dependence has become more obvious since the professionalisation of communications, but it has always existed to some degree, particularly on specialist issues. For instance, reporters tend to go to "experts" when the issue is complex and information requires interpretation. Anderson (2017) observes that peaks in climate change coverage are driven by international events such as climate summits and the production of reports by the Intergovernmental Panel on Climate Change (IPCC). Painter (2014) found that almost three-quarters of those featured on screen in TV news reports were IPCC authors or other scientists, no doubt organised and driven by the organisation's communications team.

Can I use anonymous sources? What are the concerns?

As with many dilemmas in journalism, it very much depends on the circumstances. In many cases, unattributable information is inadequate and should only be used with care. Audiences need to know who is speaking so that they can judge the veracity of their comments or the worth of their evidence. After all, information that a river has been polluted by a chemical company will be judged according to who is making the claim—a local green campaign group, a governmental organisation or the chemical company themselves.

Some sources cannot and should not be identified because of the risk to their person, their emotions or their position. Often, these people are whistleblowers, drawing the attention of the media to some failing or other in their organisation, which has consequences for the public. Some whistleblowers eventually "out" themselves, such as Frances Haugen, a Facebook employee who, in 2021, accused the company of putting profit before online safety. She released documents known as the "Facebook Files" to the *Wall Street Journal* (2021), but later revealed her identity to give evidence to the US Senate and the UK Parliament. Most sources prefer to remain anonymous and journalists have a duty to ensure this is the case. The UK's Independent Press Standards Organisation (IPSO, 2021) says in its Editors' Code of Practice that journalists have a "moral obligation to protect confidential sources of information", a sentiment shared in the National Union of Journalists' Code of Conduct.

That obligation continues even when faced with legal pressure to disclose, and many journalists consider the threat of imprisonment an occupational hazard. The main protection under UK law comes under the Contempt of Court Act 1981, section 10, which states that in a free and democratic society there is a need to protect journalists' sources and presumes in favour of those journalists wishing to do so. The European Court of Human Rights goes further.

> Protection of journalistic sources is one of the basic conditions for press freedom. … Without such protection, sources may be deterred from assisting the press in informing the public on matters of public interest. As a result the vital public-watchdog role of the press may be undermined, and the ability of the press to provide accurate and reliable information be adversely affected. … [A]n order of source disclosure … cannot be compatible with Article 10 of the Convention unless it is justified by an overriding requirement in the public interest.
>
> ECHR, 2020, p. 1

This judgement from the ECHR comes after careful consideration of many cases throughout the EU in which journalists were pressured to reveal sources. Among those cases was that of Bill Goodwin, a trainee journalist on *The Engineer* magazine who was subjected to a disclosure order requiring him to reveal the identity of his source of information on a company's confidential corporate plan. There was not, in the European Court of Human Rights' view, "a reasonable relationship of proportionality between the legitimate aim pursued by the disclosure order and the means deployed to achieve that aim" (ECHR,

2020, p. 1). The court found that both the order requiring the applicant to reveal his source and the fine imposed upon him for having refused to do so gave rise to a violation of his right to freedom of expression under Article 10 of the European Convention on Human Rights.

A more recent violation of journalists' rights came in 2018, when investigative journalists Trevor Birney and Barry McCaffrey were arrested for allegedly "stealing" a confidential report from the office of the Police Ombudsman for Northern Ireland. The document had actually been leaked by an anonymous source, and it contained investigative material about the killing of six men in Loughinisland, Northern Ireland, in 1994, including proof of an existing connection between the gunmen and the police. The homes of the two journalists were raided and they were questioned for 14 hours. However, the High Court in Belfast quashed the warrants against them in 2019. The court found that that the journalists were only rightfully protecting their sources, and concluded: "We see no overriding requirement in the public interest which could have justified an interference with the protection of journalistic sources in this case" (PSNI and Durham Constabulary v Fine Point Films, Birney T. and McCaffrey, B., 2020, p. 19). Birney and McCaffrey were supported in their case by the National Union of Journalists, which celebrated the release of this judgement as a victory for the union's ethical code of conduct and for all journalists who protect their sources against pressures. Another notable case from Northern Ireland was that of journalist Suzanne Breen, who won the right to withhold information on the Real IRA from the state in 2009. Seen as a landmark ruling for press freedom, the case concerned an application by the Police Service of Northern Ireland (PSNI) to the courts to force Breen to hand over her interview notes and other material on the republican dissident group regarding their killing of two British soldiers at the Massereene Barracks in March 2009. Despite the extremely serious ethical dilemma she found herself in, Breen refused to do so, stating that it would "breach journalistic confidentiality and would put her family's lives at risk" (McDonald, 2009). Had the judge found in favour of the PSNI, Breen faced five years in jail, but the Real IRA had also been warned that she would be killed if she co-operated with the police. Recognising the continuing danger to herself and her family if she was forced to disclose the information, the judge, Mr Tom Burgess, said it would be "close to inconceivable as to how she and potentially her family could be protected for what could well be many years to come". After the trial, Breen said: "This is a landmark case decision. I think Judge Burgess has gone further than any judge in recognising the confidentiality of sources, in terms of respecting journalism and it couldn't have been better." She added that she hoped as a result of her ruling that no other journalist would find themselves before the courts or facing five years in prison. Sadly, that proved not to be the case as the previous example shows.

While whistleblowers deserve protection, there is another form of anonymous sourcing that is more controversial, particularly when it is used to convey official information, such as government intentions or issues of public interest. Peter Oborne, a former chief political commentator at *The Telegraph* and *Daily Mail* columnist, is dismayed by the practice of identifying political actors only as "a Number 10 source". He argues that this practice facilitates a government "fake news machine" (2019) by allowing the then UK Prime Minister Boris Johnson's team to float damaging attack lines against opponents while making it impossible to hold ministers accountable for such attacks. Other journalists argue that without the ability to remain anonymous very few people would risk leaking to the public, whether from Westminster or elsewhere, but it is a truism that the less readers know about the source of information in political stories the harder it is for them to evaluate the content.

In everyday practice, anything presented anonymously should be explained and the information should be corroborated by at least one other source. These journalistic standards, though, can soon be overwritten by commercial concerns. The former executive editor of Sky Sports News, Andy Cairns, has admitted that, "Sky sources" used in the breaking news ticker sometimes refers to information from just one source rather than at least two sources, which might have been best practice in the past. Cairns said the growing phenomenon of "unnamed sources" was not ideal, but was in part the result of the heightened competition to be the first with the news. "We've had to respond. I think for a while, most news organisations followed the two sources rule for any story. With the pace of news and increased competition, that's not workable now for every story" (Byrne, 2017).

Can I protect my sources from public disclosure in the digital age?

So much of our communication now takes place online and the information journalists gather is recorded in digital form. This very fact poses challenges to traditional legal protections for journalists' sources, many of which were created in an analogue past. One of the biggest dangers is that of mass surveillance by governments and other parties, although retention of data is another weakness. The threat of terrorism has given governments a dilemma between freedom of communication and mass surveillance, with law enforcement concentrating on prevention of threats rather than detecting crimes already committed. It is an understandable stance, given the consequences of security agencies missing a terror plot that is then enacted, but the consequences of digital surveillance are worrying. Anyone can be subject to surveillance by the simple act of using certain modes of communication—such as mobile technology, email, social networks and the internet. Journalists and their confidential sources can be swept up in this surveillance despite offering no threat to the nation. In the UK, the Investigatory Powers Act 2016 (IPA, 2016), also known as the Snoopers' Charter, provides the main legal framework governing the use of covert surveillance. Previously, this area had been governed by the Regulation of Investigatory Powers Act 2000 (RIPA, 2000).

The UK' journalism industry news site, *Press Gazette*, launched an award-winning campaign called Save Our Sources after public authorities made more than 500,000 requests for telecommunications data under RIPA in 2013. Editor Dominic Ponsford said the requests appeared "to drive a cart and horses" through the protection of confidential journalistic sources established by European Court of Human Rights (Ponsford, 2014). In perhaps the most egregious case of trampling on public interest under RIPA, the Metropolitan Police secretly obtained the phone records of *The Sun's* political editor Tom Newton Dunn and of calls to *The Sun* news desk. The Met then used the information to track down and dismiss three police constables accused of leaking information about the 'Plebgate' incident of September 2012, in which the then Government chief whip Andrew Mitchell swore at a police officer outside 10 Downing Street, the Prime Minister's residence. This was despite the fact that the Crown Prosecution Service ruled that no charges should be brought against the officers because a jury would judge that they acted in the public interest (Ponsford, 2014). While some safeguards have been introduced to protect journalists' phone records, concerns about surveillance of online data through IPA continue to grow. Both the campaign group Liberty and the National Union of Journalists continue to challenge the government on the consequences of mass electronic surveillance. Investigative journalist and academic Paul Lashmar is pessimistic about future protection for confidential sources.

> Despite some improvements, when it comes to whistle-blowing in the private sector, the balance between government – which now often has a huge surveillance capacity and draconian laws – and the fourth estate has been tipped askew.
>
> *Lashmar, 2022*, p. 199

The United Nations Educational, Scientific and Cultural Organization (UNESCO) states that a robust and comprehensive source protection framework would encompass the need to "recognise the value to the public interest of source protection, with its legal foundation in the right to freedom of expression (including press freedom), and to privacy" (Posetti, 2017, p. 9). The organisation suggests that such protections be embedded in national law and should extend to all acts of journalism and across all platforms, services and mediums. They should:

- Recognise the potential detrimental impact on public interest journalism, and on society, of source-related information being caught up in bulk data recording, tracking, storage and collection.
- Affirm that State and corporate actors (including third-party intermediaries) who capture journalistic digital data must treat it confidentially (also acknowledging the desirability of the storage and use of such data being consistent with the general right to privacy).
- Shield acts of journalism from targeted surveillance, data retention and handover of material connected to confidential sources.

How can I be sure I'm dealing fairly with interviewees?

Interviewees come from many backgrounds with all sorts of life experiences and differing levels of media literacy and engagement. They also come in person, via the telephone, video call or through email and social media. Levels of engagement with the journalist vary according to mode of communication and purpose, informational for background, performative for broadcast or the many shades in between. This cornucopia of interaction means journalists must have a variety of strategies and checks to ensure compliance with ethical standards and codes of conduct. Honesty and transparency are crucial if sources are to receive fair treatment.

While it is fraught with challenges for both parties, the interview has become a crucial and central method of news-gathering, and is often the main means by which reporters and feature writers gather their material (Adams and Hicks, 2009). In many cases, it could be described as a business transaction between relatively equal partners, for example, a council press officer answering queries from a local radio journalist. When the terms of engagement are clear and the roles are established by convention, there is an element of safety for both interviewer and interviewee. Both understand the routine and the likely outcomes. Arguably, the professionalisation of news management and growth in communications teams has made dealing with organisations less problematic for journalists, although the responses and stories arising are undoubtedly more predictable and less illuminating for the public.

Dealing with individuals who are less media-savvy is still fraught with ethical issues. Unless you are investigating wrongdoing and have a solid public interest reason for subterfuge, you should be as honest as possible with your interviewee and always make your identity as a reporter plain. As far as possible, explain how their information will be used and be as clear as possible about how much control you have over their story. Novice journalists should look to the clarity and control aspect of Duncan and Newton's (2017) model of ethical participation for guidance (see Chapter 6). Some excellent advice also comes from the late *Independent* journalist David Randall who reminds us that journalism "is quite a lot like real life".

> From this flows the devastating truth that if you want sources to help you, then being friendly, honest and treating them fairly works a lot better than bullying, trickery or intimidation. Being fair is especially vital. If they are being criticised or accused of wrongdoing, you should not only put these claims to them, but also give them time to reply. Ten minutes before deadline is not good enough.
>
> Randall with Crew (2021, p. 85)

A growing practice among sources is to ask for copy approval, meaning the interviewee will see and sanction the story before it is published or broadcast. With the rise in news management, PRs sometimes demand this as a condition before celebrities agree to an interview. The only ethical answer is no, unless you want your story to be a piece of promotion rather than journalism. Of course, situations occur when you want to check quotes for accuracy, and in this case, you would be foolish not to run them past the source. This is particularly important in the case of marginalised groups or media novices—or when your own expertise in a complex area is minimal. Accuracy is vital and sensible checks do not constitute copy approval (Randall with Crew, 2021).

In her classic attack on her profession, Malcolm describes the journalist as a "kind of confidence man, preying on people's vanity, ignorance or loneliness" (1994, p. 3). Although she undoubtedly dramatises the relationship between interviewer and subject, and "over-generalises from her own experience" (Jack, 2004), we should take her somewhat jaundiced position as an extreme to be noted and avoided. It is probably sensible, though, to take into account the views of those interviewed when we talk about source relationships. Both Newton (2011), who interviewed bereaved relatives in the UK, and Palmer (2017), who revisited Malcolm's stance by interviewing people named in New York news stories, found that the majority of interviewees reported positive aspects of speaking to the news media. Their reasons varied from being part of the narrative to receiving recognition of their experience and raising awareness of issues. Both studies also found that the most negative reactions to stories came from people who had not been interviewed by journalists. It underlines the fact that the most ethical way to cover issues is to approach people involved in the story even when you fear they may not be welcoming, to listen to them carefully and fairly represent what they say. Palmer (2017) also found that journalists may over-dramatise their long-term role in the emotions of sources who have been interviewed as witnesses or participants in major events. It is the news events themselves (the triggers) that such interviewees return to when asked to recall their experience, not the interview or news story.

In the most extreme cases, the trigger completely dominated their narratives when I asked them to describe their experiences 'making the news'; some had to be prompted repeatedly to discuss their interactions with journalists or the resulting coverage at all.

Palmer, 2017, p. 586

Ethics in action: Gerard Ryle, director of the International Consortium of Investigative Journalists : "We only publish in the public interest."

Gerard Ryle is the director of the International Consortium of Investigative Journalists (ICIJ). He led the worldwide teams of journalists working on the Panama Papers, Paradise Papers and Pandora Papers investigations, the biggest in journalism history. Under his leadership, ICIJ has become one of the best-known journalism brands in the world.

Before joining as ICIJ's first non-American director in September 2011, Ryle spent more than 20 years working as an investigative reporter and editor in Australia. His work as a journalist began in his native Ireland. He was later a Knight-Wallace Journalism Fellow at the University of Michigan, and in 2013, he accepted an honorary doctorate from the University of Liege, on behalf of ICIJ.

Reporters Without Borders has described Ryle's work with ICIJ as "the future of investigative journalism worldwide" when naming him as one of "100 information heroes" of worldwide significance. Ryle is a book author and TED speaker, and he has won or shared in more than 50 journalism awards from seven different countries, including the 2017 Pulitzer Prize, three George Polk Awards, and honours from the Society of Professional Journalists, Overseas Press Club of America, the New York Press Club, the Barlett and Steele Awards, Investigative Reporters and Editors and Harvard University. He and his ICIJ colleagues also shared an Emmy Award with the US television program *60 Minutes*.

The majority, if not all, of your sources will contact you online. Does this bring its own set of challenges? Is there a new set of rules online?

You still have to use old-fashioned methods when checking your sources. All that's changed is that people have more ways of finding you online. It's a bit like fishing. You rely on people to come to you, so the more readers you have the better. You publish stories about things that will interest them and hope that they respond and engage with you.

I see it as offering more opportunities to get sources and reach an audience you wouldn't necessarily expect to be involved with. These are more exciting times for journalism in my view, although not without challenges. Mainly financial!

Your sources are often anonymous. Does this and the document "dumps" you have encountered give you ethical headaches?

I know all my sources. I wouldn't use anonymous sources but I will look at anonymous information. Then you have to go out of your way to check. There is an enormous obligation to verify that information and it leads to better journalism in the long run.

It's my cardinal rule to never turn down anonymous information, but you know that every source has their reasons and an inherent bias. For example, with the Panama Papers, the German journalists didn't know John Doe (leaker of 11.5 million documents from the law firm Mossack Fonseca to the German newspaper *Süddeutsche Zeitung*). There is more onus these days to check out the information because there's a chance they are not being straight or telling you everything. For instance, you have to be careful that they haven't inserted 10 false documents among the 100 or more they have released to you. It's a matter of cross-checking against known information such as court records and making sure they match. In this case, they did.

In complex financial investigations, there is a huge amount of personal information, some of it relevant and some tangential to the story. How do you decide which aspects to release?

If you have a massive leak of documents, such as with the Panama Papers, there will be a lot of personal information involved such as passwords. An organisation like WikiLeaks believes all information should be made public, but we step back from that. We only publish in the public interest.

Obviously, there's a decision to be made about what is personal and what is public interest, but when property deals relate to the leader of Pakistan or, in the case of Iceland, where the crisis crashed the banks and the economy and the leader of the country had a personal interest, then that sort of information should be made public.

It's difficult because you always get this criticism that if you don't make everything public you are part of the cover-up—but if you do, you'll be embroiled in legal wrangles probably for the rest of your life.

Protection of sources is at the heart of investigative journalism. How can journalists ensure confidentiality?

Encryption should be a basic part of a journalist's skills nowadays. It's not that difficult to learn and there's plenty of help and advice out there. I don't see it as learning to encrypt or secure messages and information; I see it as learning to protect your sources and that is fundamental to journalism practice. The other thing you need is safe and secure storage for information. That's a must.

Most good stories involve a whistleblower, but they take enormous risks. The story and the leak often defines the rest of their lives if they decide to out themselves. There is some protection in Europe, but in general, they risk everything. I would always encourage sources not to go public!

Do your international collaborators sign up to a code of ethics for your investigations?

Ethics are seen differently in every country. For instance, hidden cameras are generally seen as okay in the UK as long as there is a public interest reason but they're a big no-no in the United States. In many countries, paying for information is frowned upon, yet it is quite normal to pay for government documents in India, particularly things like court documents because it's the only way to get hold of them. When we're managing collaborations, we ask journalists to do what they would normally do in their practice.

Often, our international collaborations can give us an advantage. For instance, the Icelandic PM wouldn't talk to the journalist working on the Panama Papers, so our response was to get a Swedish camera crew to ask the questions.

The internet has disrupted the financial model for journalism in general and in-depth investigative journalism in particular. How do you survive? Are there any lessons journalism could learn from your experience?

I spend more of my time raising funds than anything else. We need £5m a year to keep going. I'm in the middle of a six-week tour of the world to raise money because it's really hard to raise money for the type of work we do.

Rich people don't like what we do. Most of our money comes from foundations and lotteries. We rely on charity, yet when we're reporting on offshore issues, we're really reporting on iniquity. This offshore secrecy is the biggest driver of iniquity and the biggest undermining of democracy ever.

The issues we report on are more and more transnational as giant corporations operate on a global level. I think journalism is late to cover stories in a truly global way, and it also seems staggering that journalism has been so slow to wake up to the possibilities that technology brings, rather than being frightened of it.

To work on a global level, we have to share information and that is something investigative reporters are often loath to do. The Pandora Papers involved

100 media organisations in 76 countries. That's an unprecedented level of collaboration—and ultimately trust.

Ethical workout

- There are obvious advantages of using pre-packaged PR material in your journalistic work, but what are the dangers?
- How can you mitigate this "news management" in your practice and choice of sources?
- How can you make sure you have a representative range of sources?
- When is it appropriate for a source to remain anonymous?
- Should a journalist ever reveal the identities of confidential sources?

Five takeaways from this chapter

- For the news media to provide adequate and ethical news coverage, sources need to come from all walks of life, not just the official or authoritative.
- Sources are not all media-savvy. Those without media experience should be treated sensitively and with absolute clarity in terms of your role as a reporter and their part in the story.
- Checking information is vital no matter how "trusted" your source is. The more sources and evidence you have in a story, the better it is for transparency and credibility.
- There are times when sources should be confidential—and others when the public need to know where the information is coming from.
- Protecting anonymous sources who have much at risk is a prime journalistic duty. All journalists should be using encryption and other means of technical security.

Ethics toolbox

- The International Consortium of Investigative Journalists, for advice on protection of sources. Available at: www.icij.org/
- *Press Gazette*, particularly the Save our Sources campaign. See: https://pressgazette.co.uk/
- Nieman Lab, US research site looking at journalism in the digital age. Available at: www.niemanlab.org/
- BBC 50:50, the equality project. See: www.bbc.co.uk/5050

- The Ethical Journalism Network, for ground rules when dealing with sources. Available at: https://ethicaljournalismnetwork.org/handling-sources

References

Adams, S. and Hicks, W. (2009) *Interviewing for journalists*. London: Routledge.

Anderson, A.G. (2017) 'Source influence on journalistic decisions and news coverage of climate change', *Oxford Research Encyclopedia of Climate Science*. Available at: https://pearl.plymouth.ac.uk/bitstream/handle/10026.1/9777/acrefore-9780190228620-e-356.pdf?sequence=3 (Accessed: 9 September 2021).

Byrne, L. (2017) 'Sky Sports News executive editor says "Sky sources" ticker can refer to information from one source', *Press Gazette*, 30 October. Available at: https://pressgazette.co.uk/sky-sports-news-executive-editor-says-sky-sources-ticker-can-refer-to-information-from-one-source/ (Accessed: 4 October 2021).

Childers, N.A. (2020) 'The moral argument for diversity in newsrooms is also a business argument—and you need both', *Nieman Lab*. Available at: www.niemanlab.org/2020/11/the-moral-case-for-diversity-in-newsrooms-also-makes-good-business-sense/ (Accessed: 9 September 2021).

Duncan, S. and Newton, J. (2017) *Reporting bad news: Negotiating the boundaries between intrusion and fair representation*. New York: Peter Lang.

European Court of Human Rights. (2020) 'Protection of journalistic sources'. Available at: www.echr.coe.int/Documents/FS_Journalistic_sources_ENG.pdf (Accessed: 6 July 2020).

Galtung, J. and Ruge, M.H. (1965) 'The structure of foreign news', *Journal of Peace Research*, 2(1), pp. 64–91. Available at: www.jstor.org/stable/423011 (Accessed: 6 July 2020).

Galtung, J. and Ruge, M.H. (1973) 'Structuring and selecting news'. In Cohen, S. and Young, J. (eds.), *The manufacture of news*. London: Constable, pp. 62–72.

Gans, H. (1980) *Deciding what's news: A study of CBS Evening News, NBC Nightly News, Newsweek, and Time*. London: Constable.

Hall, S., Clarke, T., Critcher, C., Jefferson, T. and Roberts, B. (1978) *Policing the crisis: Mugging, the State, and law and order*. London: Macmillan.

Harcup, T. and O'Neill, D. (2017) 'What is news?' *Journalism Studies*, 18(12), pp. 1470–1488. doi: 10.1080/1461670X.2016.115019

IPSO. (2021) 'Editors' code of practice'. Available at: www.ipso.co.uk/editors-code-of-practice/ (Accessed: 20 May 2020).

Investigatory Powers Act 2016. Available at: www.legislation.gov.uk/ukpga/2016/25/contents/enacted (Accessed: 18 August 2022).

Jack, I. (2004) 'The flash of the knife: Ian Jack on The Journalist and the Murderer', *The Guardian*, 7 February. Available at: www.theguardian.com/books/2004/feb/07/society1 (Accessed: 5 July 2021).

Joseph, S. and Keeble, R.L. (2016) *Profile pieces: Journalism and the 'human interest' bias*. Abingdon: Routledge.

Lashmar, P. (2022) '"Ventriloquists' dummies" or truth bringers? The journalist's role in giving whistle-blowers a voice'. In Trifonova Price, L., Sanders, K., and Wyatt, W. N. (eds.), *The Routledge companion to journalism ethics*. London: Routledge, pp. 192–200.

Macnamara, J. (2014) 'Journalism–PR relations revisited: The good news, the bad news, and insights into tomorrow's news', *Public Relations Review*, 40(5), December, pp. 739–750.

Malcolm, J. (1994) *The journalist and the murderer*. New York: Vintage Books.

Matthews, J. (2015) 'Journalists and their sources: The twin challenges of diversity and verification'. In Fowler-Watts, K. and Allan, S. (eds.), *Journalism: New challenges*. Bournemouth: Centre for Journalism & Communication Research, Bournemouth University.

McDonald, H. (2009) 'Judge upholds journalist Suzanne Breen's right to withhold IRA details', *The Guardian*, 18 June. Available at: www.theguardian.com/media/2009/jun/18/suzanne-breen-ira (Accessed: 9 September 2021).

Newsome, M. (2021) 'Diverse sources, inclusive reporting: Four ways to increase the diversity of your sources', *Redrawing the Line, Nieman Reports*, Spring 2021, 72(2), pp. 32–33.

Newton, J. (2011) 'The knock at the door: Considering bereaved relatives' varying responses to news media intrusion', *Ethical Space: The International Journal of Communication Ethics*, 8(3/4), pp. 7–13.

Obermaier, M., Koch, T. and Riesmeyer, C. (2018) 'Deep impact? How journalists perceive the influence of public relations on their news coverage and which variables determine this impact', *Communication Research*, 45(7), pp. 1031–1053.

Oborne, P. (2019) 'British journalists have become part of Johnson's fake news machine', *Open Democracy*. Available at: www.opendemocracy.net/en/opendemocracyuk/british-journalists-have-become-part-of-johnsons-fake-news-machine/ (Accessed: 9 October 2021).

O'Neill, D. and O'Connor, C. (2008) 'The passive journalist: How sources dominate local news', *Journalism Practice*, 2(3), pp. 487–500.

Painter, J. (2014) 'Disaster averted? Television coverage of 2013/14 IPCC's climate change reports', *Reuters Institute for the Study of Journalism*. Available at: https://reutersinstitute.politics.ox.ac.uk/sites/default/files/2017-11/Disaster%20Averted%20Television%20Coverage%20of%20the%202013-14%20IPCC%E2%80%99s%20Climate%20Change%20Reports_0.pdf (Accessed: 9 September 2021).

Palmer, R.A. (2017) 'The journalist and the murderer revisited: What interviews with journalism subjects reveal about a modern classic', *Journalism*, 18(5), pp. 575–591. doi:10.1177/1464884916636125

Ponsford, D. (2014) 'Save our sources: Press Gazette campaign to stop public authorities spying on journalists' phone records', *Press Gazette*, 11 September. Available at: https://pressgazette.co.uk/save-our-sources-press-gazette-campaign-stop-uk-public-authorities-secretly-obtaining-journalists/ (Accessed: 9 September 2021).

Posetti, J. (2017) *Protecting journalistic sources in the digital age*. Paris: UNESCO publishing.

PSNI and Durham Constabulary v Fine Point Films, Birney T. and McCaffrey, B. (2020) No. (2020) NICA 35, Ref: MOR11288, Judicial Review, Available at: judiciaryni.uk (Accessed: 9 September 2021).

Randall, D. and Crew, J. (2021) *The universal journalist*. 6th ed. London: Pluto.

Regulation of Investigatory Powers Act 2000. Available at: www.legislation.gov.uk/ukpga/2000/23/contents (Accessed: 18 August 2022).

Reich, Z.V.I. (2011) 'Source credibility as a journalistic work tool'. In Franklin, B. and Carlson, M. (eds.), *Journalists, sources and credibility: New perspectives*. London: Routledge, pp. 37–48.

Tanzi, A. and Hagan, S. (2019) 'Public relations jobs boom as Buffet sees newspapers dying', *Bloomberg Quint*. Available at: www.bloombergquint.com/onweb/public-relations-jobs-boom-as-buffett-sees-newspapers-dying (Accessed: 18 October 2021).

Wall Street Journal. (2021) 'The Facebook files: A Wall Street Journal investigation'. Available at: www.wsj.com/articles/the-facebook-files-11631713039 (Accessed: 10 October 2021).

White, A. (2020) 'Protecting the sources who keep journalism alive', *Mediacenter*. Available at: www.media.ba/en/magazin-novinarstvo/protecting-sources-who-keep-journalism-alive (Accessed: 10 September 2021).

5
Privacy and intrusion
Navigating the muddy waters of conflicting rights

Sallyanne Duncan, with additional research by Anna Bryan

This chapter explores some of the ethical issues that arise when the media intrude on people's private lives. It examines particular tensions between people's right to privacy and the media's right to freedom of expression to report news. These include justification in the public interest and its potential for abuse, conflicts between reporting that is in the public interest and that which is merely of interest to the public and consideration of when individuals in the news spotlight have a reasonable expectation of privacy. The chapter starts by discussing rights and regulation, then explores intrusion into celebrities' private lives, particularly the Duchess of Sussex's call for a basic right to privacy, as well as the influential Sir Cliff Richard case. Intrusion into ordinary people's privacy is also explored before concluding with a discussion of taking care over children's privacy. In the *Ethics in Action* section, head of digital engagement and development at the *Scotsman*, Joshua King, outlines some key considerations for journalists weighing up privacy and intrusion.

What are privacy rights and why should journalists respect them?

To a certain degree, journalists have a legal obligation—and an ethical responsibility—to respect the privacy of the subjects of their stories. In Europe, every individual has a right to privacy protected by Article 8 for the European Convention on Human Rights. This article is also incorporated into the UK Human Rights Act 1998, which states:

> Everyone has the right to respect for his private and family life, his home and his correspondence. There shall be no interference by a public authority

DOI: 10.4324/9780429505386-6

with the exercise of this right except such as is in accordance with the law and is necessary in a democratic society in the interests of national security, public safety or the economic well-being of the country, for the prevention of disorder or crime, for the protection of health or morals, or for the protection of the rights and freedoms of others.

This right is further strengthened by being enshrined in Article 12 of the United Nations Universal Declaration on Human Rights. Thus, every individual has a right to privacy as it is necessary for human dignity and individuality, and is essential to our quest for happiness (Barrett-Maitland and Lynch, 2020). Privacy International, a charity that defends and promotes privacy rights throughout the world, stresses its importance. They state:

> Privacy is essential to who we are as human beings, and we make decisions about it every single day. It gives us a space to be ourselves without judgement, allows us to think freely without discrimination, and is an important element of giving us control over who knows what about us.
>
> *2017*

However, journalists also have a right to inform the public about occurrences in their communities, and sometimes, this is in conflict with others' right to privacy. For example, a news outlet may have to intrude on a business person's privacy in order to investigate corruption allegations. Thus, the right to free expression sometimes clashes with the right to privacy. Free expression is also incorporated into the European Convention on Human Rights (Article 10) and the United Nations Universal Declaration on Human Rights (Article 19), thus giving journalists a right to undertake their legitimate work.

The right to privacy does not mean that it should become a protective cover for secrecy when matters of public interest are at stake. Generally, privacy should be understood as the right to be let alone (Warren and Brandeis, 1890) and "the right not to reveal information about oneself" whereas secrecy refers to "blocking or hiding any type of information" (Debatin, 2011, p. 47). Ethical journalists, therefore, should be "less concerned about state or corporate confidentiality, where claims to 'a private life' is often about limiting accountability and disguising hypocrisy" (Hammarberg, 2011, p. 12).

Theoretically, the right to privacy should be applied equally across all people (Steel, 2012). However, in current journalistic practice, the reasonable expectation of privacy of an individual varies depending on their age and circumstances. For example, children's rights to a private life are generally considered to be greater than those of celebrities or indeed ordinary citizens in some situations. This right is also evident in some media codes of conduct in the UK, which make clear that while everyone is entitled to respect for their private life, it is reasonable for journalists to intrude upon people's privacy as long as they can prove that this invasion was outweighed by the public interest (see Chapter 2 for more on the public interest). Thus, the right to privacy needs to be weighed with the right to free expression, and one must prevail. Journalists must assess which is the greater right in given circumstances in order to overcome this conflict. Also, when considering rights, it is important to remember journalistic values like reliability, trust, honesty, fairness and accuracy. They are "hard-won values and we must protect these", according to Brewer (2007), and if we don't, news outlets may lose their audience's trust.

What do regulatory bodies have to say about privacy?

Regulatory bodies in the UK recognise the importance of privacy and make clear that "everyone is entitled to respect for his or her private and family life, home, health and correspondence, including digital communications" (Independent Press Standards Organisation [IPSO], 2021). The National Union of Journalists Code of Conduct's Clause 6 states: "A journalist shall do nothing which entails intrusion into anybody's private life, grief or distress, subject to justification by overriding considerations of the public interest" (2011).

A substantial section of the Ofcom Broadcasting Code focuses on privacy issues. It says, for instance, that wherever broadcasters wish to justify an infringement of privacy, they should be able to demonstrate why in the particular circumstances of the case it is in the public interest to do so. Examples of public interest would include revealing or detecting crime, protecting public health or safety, exposing misleading claims made by individuals or by organisations or disclosing incompetence that affects the public.

So the public interest looms large in codes and regulatory guidelines as a justification for breaching a person's privacy. Ofcom states that privacy is a matter of protecting the individual or organisation that is directly affected rather than the wider public such that "any infringement of privacy in programmes [...] must be *warranted*" (author's emphasis; 2019, p. 44), meaning broadcasters must show why the public interest outweighs any right to privacy in that particular case. However, they recognise that this assessment can be complicated by emergency situations where on-the-spot judgements about whether privacy is unwarrantably infringed can be problematic. Thus, they take into account a potentially strong public interest in reporting an unfolding disaster or emergency that may make it difficult at the time to judge whether filming or recording is an unwarrantable infringement of privacy.

However, IPSO and IMPRESS note that people must take some responsibility for their own privacy in terms of their public disclosures about their own personal information or whether they courted publicity. For IMPRESS age, occupation and public profile should also be considered (IPSO, 2021; IMPRESS, 2017).

Generally, codes and guidelines stress that people have more of a right to privacy in private places than public spaces, and especially stress that journalists must be particularly sensitive to people's privacy when they are in extremely private locations such as "ambulances, hospitals, schools, prisons or police stations" (BBC, 2019, p. 125). The Editors' Code of Practice offers "a reasonable expectation of privacy as a test in its privacy clause (Clause 2), which states that it is "unacceptable to photograph individuals without their consent, in public or private places where there is a reasonable expectation of privacy" (IPSO, 2021) but what that means in reality can lead to lengthy debates in the news room.

IPSO has decided that people can have an expectation of privacy on some occasions when they are in view of the public—but not on others. For example, a private yacht off the coast in the Mediterranean might be considered a private place but a busy beach at the height of summer would not. Places like restaurants, nightclubs and theatres will depend on the circumstances and public interest value of the story, but others like residential gardens and places of worship would be deemed places where people could have a reasonable expectation of privacy. IPSO's Editors' Codebook makes this clear: "A sheltered part of a person's garden is very likely to be regarded as a private place–but the exterior of a home may not be regarded as such if it is in plain view of the public" (2021, p. 50). This is particularly true when the house, for example, features in a legitimate news coverage, such as a gas explosion at the property.

Material obtained surreptitiously should not be used except in the public interest. This includes material secured through using long lens photography or recording devices, by leaving a camera or recorder unattended on private property without the informed consent of the owner, by taping a telephone conversation without informing the other person or by continuing to record when the source believes the reporter has stopped. Distressed people should not be pressured to give interviews unless this is warranted (i.e. in the public interest). The location of a person's home or family should not be disclosed without their consent, unless warranted (Quinn, 2018).

IMPRESS warns that journalists should "not use covert means to gain or record" (2017, p. 10), whilst the BBC recommends transparency when recording or filming in public spaces, unless they have approval from their senior editors or producers for secret filming. Their guidelines state:

> We should operate openly where there is a risk of infringing people's privacy, unless we have approval for secret recording. This is important when using inconspicuous recording devices or live streaming. Where practicable we should use notices to make people aware that we are recording or live streaming and to allow them to avoid us.
>
> *2019, p. 125*

Ofcom states that

> Surreptitious filming or recording should only be used where it is warranted. Normally, it will only be warranted if: there is prima facie evidence of a story in the public interest; and there are reasonable grounds to suspect that further material evidence could be obtained; and it is necessary to the credibility and authenticity of the programme.
>
> 2019, p. 46

However, some choices are not so transparent. A reporter might record an interview for their own note-taking purposes, but the interviewee might unexpectedly say something that they are tempted to use as an audio clip to accompany their online story. Should the reporter use it? Could their audio note taking be regarded as a secret recording? Would they breach a code of conduct if they put it up online? Possibly, if the reporter uses it without the interviewee's knowledge. Here, seeking their consent for its use retrospectively would seem to be a suitable ethical solution.

Should journalists intrude on celebrities' private lives?

Most politicians and celebrities anticipate constant public exposure as an inevitable part of their lifestyles and can expect to have reduced privacy in certain areas of their lives as a result. Most crave publicity, many are remarkably open (and even confessional) about extremely intimate aspects of their private lives when interviewed. Thus, it can be argued that they can hardly complain when they fall victim to 'bad publicity' and accordingly can expect to have reduced privacy in certain areas of their lives.

Consequently, editors often justify intrusion into celebrities' private lives as being in the public interest, partly because they have chosen to step into the limelight, and therefore, their consensual "status as a self-promoted and voluntary public figure" (Hong, 2016, p. 6) is believed to somewhat surrender their right to privacy. However, journalists should not assume that a celebrity has zero right to privacy and that the media can publish anything about them. Publishing details of a celebrity's home without their consent, for example, could infringe the IPSO code, especially because of security concerns and the threat of stalkers. The key test is not whether the exact location has been disclosed but whether the published information provides sufficient detail for people to find the home (Editors' Codebook, 2021). David and Victoria Beckham had a complaint to IPSO dismissed regarding the publication of the location of their new home because the published details were insufficient to identify the precise location of their property.

Journalists could determine how much privacy a public figure should be given based on the amount of media attention they actively seek outside the necessities of their job. Commenting on entertainers, Ingram and Henshall advises that if they "deliberately merge their on-screen and off-screen personalities, the media and the public can be forgiven for confusing the two and taking an interest in their private lives" (2019, Celebrities). Actors who shun publicity off-screen or stage would "have more success in demanding a private life away from media attention" (ibid).

Those fuzzy boundaries between public and private should not be the journalist's only consideration. As with any source or subject, they must evaluate the vulnerability of the person and the potential for causing harm. In 2004, model Naomi Campbell won a privacy case against the Daily Mirror following the publication of a photo taken of her at a Narcotics Anonymous meeting. The judges ruled that "the need for treatment for drug addicts was more important than the right of the public to know about it" (Gibson, 2004). However, news outlets will draw the line at different points, sometimes with tragic results. The death by suicide of TV presenter Caroline Flack is one such case. Subject to intense media interest in her personal relationships and her mental health, she took her own life when heightened media attention focussed on her upcoming court trial for allegedly assaulting her boyfriend. The treatment she received from the press led to a public outcry for the media to take greater care when publishing stories around celebrities' private lives (Marshall, 2020). This strength of feeling resulted in her supporters setting up an online petition calling for a law to stop the media "invading privacy and sharing private information that is detrimental to the celebrity, their mental health and those around them" (Davis, 2020), which reached 820,037 signatures by October 2021. Another petition calling for the launch of a government inquiry into the conduct of UK tabloids following Ms Flack's death reached 270,062 signatures by October 2021 (Brandwood, n.d.). Given this case, journalists should consider the vulnerability of their subjects and "weigh the consequences of publishing or broadcasting personal information" if they want to minimize harm (Society of Professional Journalists, 2014).

When it comes to intruding on a celebrity's privacy, journalists should not assume that simply because the public would likely be interested then the story is soundly justified by the public interest. In a 2016 legal case—PJS v News Group Newspapers Ltd—an anonymous celebrity appealed the earlier lifting of their privacy injunction against the press who published a story alleging that the celebrity had taken part in extramarital sexual behaviour. The Supreme Court judges ruled in the anonymous claimant's favour and upheld their privacy injunction. In explaining the judgement, Lord Mance stated:

> There is no public interest, however much it may be of interest to some members of the public, in publishing kiss-and-tell stories or criticisms of private sexual conduct, simply because the persons involved are well-known; and so there is no right to invade privacy by publishing them. … It is different if the story has some bearing on the performance of a public office or the correction of a misleading public impression cultivated by the person involved. But … that does not apply here.
>
> quoted in Bowcott and O'Carroll, 2016

This ruling sets a precedent that may hold news outlets to greater account if they do not ensure that their celebrity stories are truly in the public interest. The judges were also concerned with the damage that publication could inflict on the celebrity's young children—conveying the message that journalists should take care not to intrude too far into celebrities' family lives even when they are not directly invading the privacy of a child (BBC, 2016).

How far can the media intrude into a celebrity's family life?

While celebrities in some respects consent to intrusion through their choice of career, journalists must consider the arguably higher right to privacy of their families, and particularly, of their children, as we have seen in the previous section (PJS v News Group Newspapers Ltd). IPSO, IMPRESS and Ofcom all state that children of public figures should not have their right to privacy compromised simply because of who their parents are. The Editor's Code states: "Editors must not use the fame, notoriety or position of a parent or guardian as sole justification for publishing details of a child's private life" (IPSO, 2021). The regulators and the courts emphasise that news outlets should make decisions about intrusion that are in the best interests of a child, that prioritise their welfare and well-being and that minimize potential harms to them, even when they are not directly the subject of the story. Minimizing harm should be done by seeking parental consent to interview, report and publish content about children or disguising their identity. When the *Daily Mail* published photographs of musician Paul Weller on a shopping trip with his wife and three children in Los Angeles in 2016, they appeared to ignore IPSO's advice. The pictures were taken without their consent and with no apparent public interest justification. Whilst they were taken in public places, such as a street and in cafes, the UK Court of Appeal found that there was a reasonable expectation of privacy since the parents and children were involved in a private family activity and not one related to Mr Weller's professional life. The court also stated regarding the children that the fact that they had famous parents should not result in them having a lower expectation of privacy. In weighing up the family's right to privacy versus the news outlet's freedom of expression, the court concluded that the photographs were of no public interest value and that the children's interests must be prioritised because of the likely adverse effect. Morris and Messenger Davies (2018) noted:

> ... the Weller case judgement proposes that, where there is no public interest in identifying children, (as there could be in a case of children being injured in a major accident or military action), a publication's right to freedom of expression is less important than the child's right to privacy.
>
> p. 104

Thus, it would seem that all children—not necessarily just those of public figures—have a heightened expectation of privacy because of their presumed vulnerability.

Even reporting on the lives of adult family is seen as morally dubious. In 2019, English cricketer Ben Stokes launched legal proceedings against *The Sun* following their publication of a story covering the murder of Stokes' half-siblings in 1988 by his mother's ex-partner. *The Sun* claimed that the information was given freely by a family member and that the information was public knowledge as the murder had been covered in a New Zealand newspaper at the time (Waterson, 2019). However, a spokesperson for Hacked Off described the story as "an appalling invasion of privacy with no public interest justification" (Hacked Off, 2019). Questions to be considered are whether Stokes had a reasonable expectation of privacy and whose rights prevail: Stokes' right to privacy regarding events involving his extended family or *The Sun's* right to free expression to report events that are already in the public domain, albeit in a limited and local manner. But it is also about whether the family members and friends of public figures have the same right to privacy as ordinary citizens, or whether their relationship to a celebrity justifies an invasion into their privacy. Moosavian asks:

> ... would Stokes have a reasonable expectation of privacy in relation to events that happened to other members of his family before his birth, particularly where another extended family member is willing to speak to the media about them? This case raises the problem of who (if anyone) can "own" or control shared family experiences–particularly when family members have different attitudes to the information.
>
> 2019

As we will see in a later section, this was also an issue in the case involving the Duchess of Sussex and the *Mail on Sunday's* decision to publish a private letter to her father. *The Sun* settled the claim brought by Ben Stokes and his mother, Deborah, on 30 August 2021. The news outlet apologised, paid substantial damages and the Stokes' legal costs and admitted they should not have published the article (Ponsford, 2021b).

What were the ethical issues in the Sir Cliff Richard case?

A landmark case that is particularly useful to help journalists understand the complexities surrounding celebrity privacy is the 2018 Sir Cliff Richard case. After receiving allegations of historic sexual abuse, South Yorkshire Police raided Richard's home in Sunningdale, Berkshire. The BBC were tipped off about the search, which involved a helicopter flying over the singer's apartment to film and broadcast the search. South Yorkshire Police did not find any evidence and Sir Cliff was never arrested. The police later apologised to him and he was never charged. Richard decided to sue both the BBC and South Yorkshire Police for invading his right to privacy. He received £400,000 in damages from South Yorkshire Police after settling a legal action. However, the BBC refused to apologise and to offer "reasonable damages". Instead, they chose to fight the privacy case brought by Sir Cliff and lost.

Under the Human Rights Act 1998, the court had to balance Richard's Article 8 rights to respect for his private and family life against the BBC's Article 10 rights to freedom of expression and opinion (Olsson, 2018). In July 2018, the court ruling on the matter decided that Richard's privacy rights were violated and did indeed supersede the BBC's freedom of expression. The judge, Mr Justice Mann, told the court that a suspect in a police investigation "has a reasonable expectation of privacy", adding that there was no genuine public interest in this case, despite it being of interest to the public (BBC, 2018).

The BBC was required to pay Richard considerable damages. The court ruling was perceived by many as "a chilling blow to press freedom" (Greenslade, 2018), with Mr Justice Mann acknowledging that the case would have a significant impact on press reporting but that did not mean the law was changing. Despite Mr Justice Mann's determination that there was no genuine public interest in this case, law academic Thomas Bennett argues that there is a public interest in naming an individual under suspicion, such as Richard, especially in cases of historic sex assault allegations, where charges often rely on corroboration by other victims (Heawood, 2018). Publicity in these cases often results in more victims coming forward, thus the potential silencing of the media due to the ruling on the Richard case on police investigations could hamper further corroboration and justice in other historic abuse cases. Frost offers another perspective:

> The law in the area of police investigation is complex. A person under suspicion need not be arrested and whether journalists can write about them is confusing. There is no protection against lawsuits for defamation and as Sir Cliff's case shows, no protection against suits for intrusion of privacy. Once someone has been arrested then reporting restrictions come into play, but journalists are able to report the fact of the arrest.
>
> *2020, p. 168*

Regulator IMPRESS emphasised the need for journalists to minimize harm in such cases, stating that the journalist should ask themselves "what is the most intrusive coverage I have to engage in in order to satisfy the public interest?" (Heawood, 2018).

Are the media denying Prince Harry and Meghan, Duchess of Sussex, a "basic right to privacy"?

Since 2016 when Prince Harry first met American actress Meghan Markle, the couple have faced a long struggle with sections of the UK and US media over their privacy. This culminated in 2020 in a High Court hearing in London when Meghan, Duchess of Sussex, sued Associated Newspapers, the publisher of the *Mail on Sunday* and *MailOnline* for publishing a letter she wrote to her father about her anguish at their estrangement, claiming it was a breach of her privacy and copyright. Around the time that Meghan's lawyers lodged papers with the court in 2019, Prince Harry made a robust statement criticizing the UK tabloid press. He described his wife as "one of the latest victims of a British tabloid press that wages campaigns against individuals with no thought to the consequences–a ruthless campaign that has escalated over the past year". He added: "Put simply, it is bullying, which scares and silences people" (Prince Harry, 2019). Before the case started journalist and media law expert, David Banks predicted it would be "the privacy case of the century" (PA Media Lawyer and Press Gazette, 2019) because members of the royal family do not normally give evidence in court cases. As it turned out, the duchess won her case at the hearing stage in February 2021, thus avoiding the need to give evidence at a trial and make further public revelations about her private life.

Timeline

This timeline details the media's interest in the duke and duchess and their numerous attempts to protect their privacy.

- 2016: On 30 October, the news breaks that Prince Harry is in a relationship with American actress, Meghan Markle. Nine days later, the Prince attacks the media over its "abuse and harassment" of his girlfriend.
- 2017: The couple announce their engagement on 27 November and pose for organised media pictures and a TV interview. In December, the Palace announces their wedding day, 19 May 2018.

Privacy and intrusion

2018: Staged paparazzi pictures of Thomas Markle, Meghan's father, appear in the press a few days before the wedding. Meghan appeals to the media for "understanding and respect" after reports that her father suffered a heart attack. Later he announces via American website TMZ that he will not attend the wedding and that he needs cardiac treatment. The couple try to contact him without success as Prince Harry warns Mr Markle via text that "going public" will make matters worse. Two days before the wedding, Meghan confirms her father will not attend the wedding due to ill health. The couple marry on 19 May, taking the titles Duke and Duchess of Sussex. In August, Meghan writes to her father about their relationship and about him giving interviews to the media. Then in November, Mr Markle sends a text to his daughter, claiming he wants to reconcile with her, but she will state later in the *Mail on Sunday* court documents that she never received the text message. Pregnant with her first child, Meghan is accused by the tabloids of "flaunting" her baby bump.

2019: On 10 February, the *Mail on Sunday* and the *MailOnline* publish the article, "Revealed: The letter showing true tragedy of Meghan's rift with a father she says has 'broken her heart into a million pieces'".

Three months later, the duchess gives birth to the couple's son, Archie, and shortly afterwards, they attend a press briefing with their son at Windsor Castle. In August, the couple come under attack from the media for using private jets to go to the south of France on holiday, with Prince Harry claiming it was to "ensure their safety".

In October, the duke and the duchess take on certain elements of the UK press regarding their intrusive coverage: Prince Harry criticises the media in a robust statement over their reporting of Meghan; the couple release a statement confirming they intend to take legal action against Associated Newspapers, owners of the *Mail on Sunday*, for publishing one of her private and confidential letters; and Prince Harry starts legal proceedings against the publishers of *The Sun*, the *Daily Mirror* and the defunct *News of the World*, for alleged phone hacking in the early 2000s.

In the same month, Thomas Markle claims he felt pressured into publicly revealing the contents of his daughter's private letter after he was "mis-characterised" in an article in the American celebrity magazine, *People*.

A few days later, court documents outlining details of the duchess's assertions are lodged at the High Court. They state that the letter was "obviously private correspondence" and contained "her intimate thoughts and feelings about her father's health and her relationship with him at that time". Her lawyers also claim that the *Mail on Sunday* "chose to deliberately omit or suppress" parts of the letter resulting in its meaning being "intentionally distorted or manipulated". Also in October, Meghan discloses in an ITV documentary that she struggles with life as a royal and Harry hints at a rift with his brother, William.

2020: At the start of the year, Buckingham Palace releases a statement from the duke and the duchess stating that they are stepping back as senior members of the Royal family, with a view to becoming financially independent and relocating to Canada. After then moving to California, they face further privacy issues over an American celebrity news agency taking pictures of their son using drones and zoom lenses. The paparazzi agency, X17, apologises, hands over the photographs and promises not to do so again, but not before the pictures are sold to a German magazine, which publishes them. However, the couple's lawyers do manage to stop publication in the UK and the USA.

Associated Newspapers also files its defence against the duchess's claims and her suit for damages for alleged misuse of private information, copyright infringement and a breach of the Data Protection Act. The publisher denies all allegations, particularly that the letter was edited in any way that changed its meaning, adding that the letter was not private or confidential.

Later in January, whilst making a speech at a private charity event, Prince Harry describes the media as a "powerful force" and refers to the impact of excessive media intrusion on the daily life of his mother, Diana, Princess of Wales, who died when, pursued by paparazzi, the chauffeur-driven car she was in crashed in Paris in 1997.

Meanwhile, Thomas Markle does an interview with Piers Morgan on ITV's *Good Morning Britain*, where he describes his estrangement from Meghan as "ridiculous" and seeks a reconciliation. However, he also tells *The Sun* that he will see his daughter in court.

On 20 April, the couple write a forceful letter to the UK tabloids, *The Sun*, *Daily Mirror*, *Daily Mail* and *Daily Express*, stating that they are cutting all dealings with them, refusing to "offer themselves up as currency for an economy of clickbait and distortion".

Four days later, the first hearing of the Duchess of Sussex's legal action against Associated Newspapers starts with the judge, Mr Justice Warby, hearing an application by the newspaper group to strike out parts of her claim against them. These include allegations that the publisher acted dishonestly by editing out parts of the letter, and that they stirred up matters between the duchess and her father, as well as having an agenda to publish intrusive, offensive content about her. Associated Newspapers were successful in this application.

In July, Mr Justice Warby hears an application from the Duchess of Sussex to stop Associated Newspapers from naming her five friends who spoke anonymously to *People* magazine apparently to defend her, raising suggestions that she was subject to tabloid "bullying".

2021: On 11 February, the duchess wins her privacy claim at the High Court against Associated Newspapers, the publisher of the *Mail on Sunday*. Mr Justice Warby granted her summary judgement in her claim for misuse of private information against the publisher, which means that part of the case is resolved without the need for a trial. He states that Meghan had a "reasonable expectation that the contents of the letter would remain private".

The following month, the judge allows the *Mail on Sunday* to reduce the size of the front-page statement they were ordered to publish that declared they had infringed her copyright.

In March, millions of viewers in the UK and USA tune in to a controversial interview given by the Duke and Duchess of Sussex with the American media VIP, Oprah Winfrey. The couple claim they did the interview in order to explain their reasons for their self-imposed exile from the royal family. However, it results in a media frenzy over their claims about the monarchy's attitudes to mental health issues, race, privacy and the press, amongst other matters. While the American press coverage and social media responses are generally positive, the UK media and some citizens on social media condemn them as selfish, causing harm to the Queen and denigrating the monarchy as an institution. Others support their actions as their revelations, particularly on racism, resonate with many.

Piers Morgan leaves ITV's *Good Morning Britain* after a row over comments he made about the duchess. Remarking on the Oprah Winfrey interview, he said he "didn't believe a word" Meghan had said in the interview about her mental health. Later in a tweet, he says "freedom of speech is a hill I'm happy to die on". Ofcom receives a record 41,000 complaints about his comments and starts an investigation.

During her controversial interview with Oprah Winfrey, Meghan made the case that public figures as well as ordinary people deserve a basic right to privacy where there are recognised boundaries and where individuals are treated with respect. She said: "I think *everyone* has a basic right to privacy. Basic. We're not talking about anything that anybody else wouldn't expect" (Nicolaou, 2021). She explained she and Prince Harry understood that as public figures they could not expect complete privacy but asked to be able to share the "parts of their lives" they were "comfortable" with revealing (ibid).

Given that privacy is deemed to be a justified claim and a right based on people's desire to remove themselves from public view on certain occasions, and that obliges others to respect it by refraining from interfering, then the duke and duchess's assertion would appear to be valid despite the fact that they are such high-profile public figures. Their decision to withdraw from royal duties, to withhold information about themselves gives scope to reduce the opportunity of others to interfere with that right. If the press must refrain from interfering with the couple's privacy, then it can be argued that the duke and duchess must withhold information about their private lives. However, as we have seen, deciding the boundaries of what constitutes public and private can be complex for celebrities, especially when they are former royals. Edwards and Fieschi (2008) explain that in guarding our privacy we fear the loss of a personal space to reflect and be autonomous, where we are "free from scrutiny, pressure or risk". They add: "We fear that dignity and power have been wrested from us to the extent that we are no longer in control of the access others have to us" (p. 13). Thus, their desire to limit the access others have to them and to be free to choose what information to release about themselves and their loved ones opens Harry and Meghan up to accusations by some elements of the media, as well as the public on social media, of hypocrisy, of wanting to turn press attention on and off when they desire, and in so doing use the media for their own ends.

But privacy is not an absolute right and can be compromised by a person's conduct or consent, and therefore, what they disclose in the public domain can adversely affect their privacy regardless. Individuals need to take responsibility for protecting their own privacy as it is not a commodity that can be used on one person's terms, for example, courting attention when they want it and shunning intrusion when they don't. They must weigh up the consequences of revealing private information or allowing access to their private lives. The press, in turn, should balance any intrusion with the public's right to be informed and to freedom of expression, and should avoid commoditizing a public figure to the point that they are no longer respected as a person. Therefore, the media should have a moral justification for any intrusion and persistent publication. Steven Barnett, professor of communications at the University of Westminster, said: "Too often, however, the norm of journalistic scrutiny is exploited as a fig-leaf to justify monumental invasions of privacy and downright lies that cannot be justified by any arguments around accountability" (2021).

Some media commentators fear that the Duchess of Sussex's privacy case will be detrimental to freedom of expression. In the future, news outlets may be curtailed in how they report the lives of those in the public eye as a result.

There are also concerns as to whether the judgement will limit the manner in which journalists can use and publish leaked documents. Hence, some critics fear that the consequences of this case could have a chilling effect on media freedom and legitimate investigative journalism. However, Barnett (2021) adds: "A healthy journalistic culture knows the difference between exposing incompetence, corruption or dishonesty in high places and the vindictive hounding of individuals designed simply to maximise corporate profit."

There are ethical lessons that news outlets can learn from the case too. Dominic Ponsford, a journalist with *Press Gazette*, a news site for those in the journalism industry, outlined these as:

- Be aware that family members owe a duty of confidence to each other. Their right to freedom of expression does not eclipse the right to privacy of spouses, parents, siblings and so on. He says: "So be careful disclosing private details about relationships where one of those involved has a reasonable expectation of privacy and they have not sanctioned disclosure."
- Public figures may be more likely to sue, and therefore, to avoid such probabilities, news outlets should be more wary about assessing a reasonable expectation of privacy and the nature of private information. Ponsford comments: "Harry and Meghan have succeeded in ensuring that an alarm will go off in the brain of every Fleet Street night lawyer when their names appear in copy as they have shown themselves to be highly litigious."
- News outlets should keep disclosures proportionate to what is needed to tell the story. Be moderate and avoid excessive inclusions. "Judges take a dim view when publishers include gratuitous detail when it comes to privacy," Ponsford warns.
- Ask whether the public figure has a reasonable expectation of privacy and if there is a public interest in overriding their right to privacy. If the justification is not watertight, then editors should seriously question whether to publish.
- Be cautious when reporting stories based on leaked documents. Think through the consequences of publication and preferably report the contents of the document rather than reproduce all of it (Ponsford, 2021a).

What about the privacy of ordinary people?

Most journalists would apply different criteria when covering the private lives of ordinary people because they do not normally find themselves in the media spotlight, unlike celebrities. But the distinction between public figures and private citizens is more complex than this binary prioritization. As Frost (2020) notes, most ordinary people will have some exposure to public life and will therefore have some potential to be accountable to the public for their actions, whether that is through their job or status in a community, a newsworthy event or involvement in criminal proceedings.

He explains that a person's job might carry serious responsibilities that makes them accountable to the public, such as police officers, health professionals, senior civil servants, those who work with children or deal with public money. Equally, volunteers, parish or community councillors or those who undertake charity work may find themselves appearing in news stories as a result of their benevolence. But these same citizens are entitled to keep private those parts of their lives that do not impinge on their civic work. Once again, the test for a reasonable expectation of privacy must be used. That expectation of privacy, however, does not always apply *at* work. IPSO rejected a complaint by a pilot who claimed that a newspaper intruded on his privacy when he was pictured at work watching police escort several passengers off his plane. The regulator said the pilot was carrying out his duties in the main cabin of the aircraft, witnessed by passengers and crew, and as he was not doing anything private, he could not have a reasonable expectation of privacy at that time (see Howell v Metro.co.uk, Editors' Codebook (2021), p. 42).

Ordinary citizens might also attract the attention of the media if they inadvertently become involved in a newsworthy event. Most often, this happens during breaking news, such as road crashes, disasters or terrorist attacks, but can also occur where an individual unintentionally appears in a street shot or other public place. In fast-paced news situations—or crowded streets—it is not always possible for journalists to seek consent from members of the public but where possible they should try to judge what level of intrusion is warranted. Journalists also have a responsibility to help people who are not used to interacting with the media to assess the consequences of telling their story, according to Palmer (2017). She claims it is important for journalists to help ordinary interviewees or contributors to be aware of the potential negative effects of speaking out on a topic and the likely intrusion that can occur, particularly now that news outlets promote stories on social media where they can go viral and users can comment or speculate on a news source's personal life. Additionally, ordinary citizens with little experience of dealing with news outlets might reveal more than they intended to a journalist, even in the most benign stories, and as reporters make decisions about what aspects of an interview to include in a story, an ethical journalist should attempt to manage their interviewee's expectations about what parts of their private information will or will not be published. Palmer says: "In most situations, journalists need to very seriously consider whether damage to a private citizen's privacy and integrity is really worth the public good" (quoted in Verdecchia, 2020). She warns, due to the internet and search engine optimization (SEO), that news stories can reappear over and over and that news outlets need to ask themselves: "What is the public benefit? You have to weigh that against the, in some cases very long-term negative repercussions on a private citizen's life" (ibid).

Those who find themselves involved in criminal proceedings have less opportunity to influence media reporting. Evidence presented in a court room, including private details of people's lives, can be reported by news outlets unless restrictions have been placed on coverage by the judge. Therefore, information that might seem private can be made public by a news outlet if those details are said in court. Once again, the news outlet must assess the public benefit of publication, how much private information they should report and who could be harmed by that coverage.

Should news outlets take special care with children's privacy?

Much of the discussion of covering celebrities' children applies to those who are not in the public eye. The child's welfare and well-being should be paramount unless there is an overriding public interest in reporting stories about them or that affect them directly because of a family connection. Journalists must balance the importance of reporting stories about children that inform the public and are in the interests of the public good with the need to protect children's privacy and welfare. The same heightened expectation of privacy applies, although children's autonomy and agency to have their voices heard must also be considered. Prioritization of children's rights has been embedded into the IMPRESS code through the need to seek consent for publication for children under the age of 16. In doing so, they establish that at 16 years of age a child has sufficient maturity to make their own decisions about consent and in such cases journalists should seek consent from the child to photograph, reveal their identity or publish content about them and need not gain parental consent. The code also recognises the responsibility placed on journalists to assess the age and capacity of the child to consent (Clause 3.1). However, one complication, particularly when accessing information on social media, is how can a journalist be sure the child is of the age they claim to be. Contacting a parent or responsible adult might be wise, but it could undermine trust between the young person and the reporter. Applying news values, gathering context and considering the balance between the right to inform the public and the right to protect the child's welfare will assist journalists in fulfilling this responsibility. However, some journalists may be less scrupulous and might prioritise news values over the child's welfare rather than risk losing the story.

Since young people now live a great deal of their lives in public via social media, news outlets must adopt rigorous press standards when considering using children's digital content, particularly given its accessibility and lasting nature. According to Oswald et al (2016), "harm may be caused in years to come, and that harm may alter in nature". Deciding how to balance the right to report content involving children (freedom of expression), especially when it is in the public domain via social media platforms, and their right to be protected (privacy), including the use of social media posts for purposes they were not intended, for example, publication by news outlets, is arduous. Morris and Messenger Davies (2018) add:

> Courts and press regulators are increasingly grappling with this balance, a challenge compounded by the instantaneous spread of images and information on social media that can be quickly adopted and appropriated by newspapers–often without seeking prior consent or verifying the authenticity of content.
>
> p. 93

Ethics in action: Joshua King, head of digital engagement and development at the *Scotsman*: "Social media is a minefield for reporters from a privacy ethics point of view."

Joshua King is the digital editor at the *Scotsman*, *Scotland on Sunday* and *Edinburgh Evening News*. In more than a decade of work in print and digital media, his byline has also appeared in *The Times*, *The Big Issue*, the *Press and Journal*, *The i* and *The Face*. Joshua has written advice for trainee journalists for JournoResources, served on the NCTJ Student Council and developed a team of young breaking news reporters. He studied at the University of Edinburgh and trained to be a journalist at Robert Gordon University in Aberdeen. He has worked both as a staff reporter and as a freelance writer. Joshua has written extensively about his experiences with epilepsy, has interviewed politicians including Alex Salmond, Nick Clegg and Ruth Davidson, trailed The Queen on royal events and spent a year behind the scenes with Peterhead FC on their historic 2013–2014 title-winning campaign.

Ten years on from the Leveson Inquiry and its revelations of phone hacking, do you think the media are less intrusive, much the same as 2011 or more intrusive?

The *News of the World* phone hacking revelations—particularly the targeting of Milly Dowler's voicemail—probably mark the nadir of British journalism in my lifetime. I don't think there is anyone in the industry today who doesn't consider what happened disgraceful. I certainly hope there isn't. The collapse of the *News of the World* came just as I was first working in newsrooms in Scotland. In that sense, I didn't see the 'before', only what newsrooms were like in the aftermath.

In the wake of the phone hacking scandal, News International took out full page adverts in British newspapers to run a letter signed by Rupert Murdoch. "The *News of the World* was in the business of holding others to account. It failed when it came to itself", he wrote. I believe the media are now held to account in a way it wasn't before 2011. It is scrutinised like never before and quite frankly cannot act with the impunity that allowed phone hacking to take place.

What the Leveson Inquiry and the public fallout from the collapse of the *News of the World* did establish beyond any doubt is that clandestine methods to investigate people's private lives will not be tolerated. Not by newsrooms, not by regulators, not by the police and certainly not by the public. I cannot think of many more intrusive breaches of privacy than illicitly monitoring a person's messages. The fact that is over means our industry is less intrusive than it was before. We mustn't ever go back.

What effect do you think high-profile legal cases like those involving Sir Cliff Richard and the Duchess of Sussex have on media reporting of the private lives of public figures?

The financial penalties faced by publications found to have breached privacy laws are fierce and should give editors pause for thought. In both those cases, the media outlets in question were broadly investigating topics in the public interest but crossed an ethical line in how they obtained the specifics and it cost them. It cost them financially, and it cost them from a public perception point of view. It cost the wider industry, too—particularly in the case of the BBC and Sir Cliff Richard. When outlets cross legal lines and face legal penalties, often those lines get tightened. Of course, testing privacy laws in court goes both ways—media victories can strengthen free speech and public interest precedent. But these high-profile cases, so big that they themselves were splashed on the front pages of papers, have hampered the media's reporting of public figures. Yes, ethically, the approaches adopted went too far. But does that mean that other more responsible reporting should be in any way curtailed in a backlash?

What decisions do journalists need to make about intruding on the private lives of ordinary people?

The IPSO is pretty unequivocal about the issue of privacy. Everyone, the code makes clear, has a right to privacy, covering family life and their mental health to a person's home and correspondence. That final stipulation, 'correspondence', covers digital communication and has never been more important. And the recognition of privacy goes way beyond IPSO. Our right to a private life is codified in the European Convention on Human Rights, and in law under our own Human Rights Act 1998. In short, an individual's private life is protected not just by guideline and regulation but by principle and statute.

So is it ever acceptable for a journalist to consider intruding on a person's private life? Simply put, yes. 'Privacy' is one of nine IPSO clauses caveated with a public interest justification. Uncovering injustice, criminal behaviour and hypocrisy as well as protecting public health and public safety are the fundamental tenets of journalism. It's what we're supposed to be doing. And it's not uncommon that those objectives collide with a person's right to privacy.

What we have to ask ourselves—and our colleagues in our newsroom, because these ethical decisions should be made as part of a team—is *why* we are considering intruding on someone's privacy. Is this the only approach we can take? Is information available in a different way? Is what we are uncovering, or what we're aiming to uncover, justifiably in the public interest? Not only should we be asking these questions, we should be asking them quite formally in the newsroom so that if IPSO came knocking with a complaint in hand, an editor can show that serious consideration was given to the ethics of our actions.

Another factor well worth considering is how much detail of their private life—specifically material relevant to the story—has a person already shared publicly. A person has a right to privacy, but the ever expanding nature of social media means that the pool of what can truly be considered private to a person is shrinking.

It's worth saying something specific about images. In a case I'm sure picture desks are all very familiar with, the *Dorking Advertiser* fell foul of a complaint from a Mr Hugh Tunbridge. The complainer had been snapped in the background of a photo of a restaurant used to accompany a food review. A pretty innocent story all round. Not so to Mr Tunbridge who argued, in a complaint upheld by the then Press Complaints Commission, that he and his dining companion had a reasonable expectation of privacy in a restaurant, even if it was a public place. It goes to show how careful we must be, and that what we as reporters might consider to be in the public domain is not the same standard held by regulators or the public at large.

Are social media platforms encouraging a culture of intrusion with many people— ordinary citizens and celebrities—sharing large parts of their private lives? What are the ethical implications for journalists using this content in their stories?

The collision of social media and privacy is one of the big questions not just of contemporary journalism, but of contemporary society. Privacy, identity and personal data have all been thrown into sharp relief by the emergence of giants like Facebook and Tik Tok, and the trend shows no signs of slowing. Social media has been a big boon for the media, both as a way of sourcing stories, pictures and video—a bomb could go off in a city halfway around the world and the footage would be on our screens in minutes—and as a way of presenting the news to our audiences.

But as much of a boon as it is, social media is also a minefield for reporters from a privacy ethics point of view. Just because someone has opened a very large, very digital window to their private life does not necessarily give us the right to look through and report on it. The lines are blurred, particularly in the world of celebrities. Much of their social media output is deliberately public-facing or even curated: public figures, sportspeople, movie stars and musicians know that the statements they make or the pictures they share could be featured in the media. But the fact that these figures know this material could be picked up and don't challenge that is not the same as the journalists having free rein to use material from social media.

That false assumption on the part of reporters becomes problematic when dealing with members of the general public and what they post online. Are we to consider that content as readily available to report on as an A-list star's tweets? The lines continue to blur. For instance, where a person posts a fundraising campaign on their profile, it does not seem unethical to promotethat in the local media. But what if that same person posts an emotional tribute to a loved one who has just been killed in a terrible accident? Lifting that without approaching them for comment can be considered an intrusion into that person's privacy and grief. They intended for it to be seen by friends and family, not splashed on the front pages of newspapers. It would be hard to argue that such reporting without consent had such a strong public interest justification as to override the grieving person's right to privacy.

Material posted on social media can often be the starting point for a story, but rarely will using a social media post without permission, context or follow-up amount to good, ethical reporting.

Have you ever worked on a story that involved you in making decisions about intruding on a person's privacy? Can you tell us about it and what you learned from it?

I worked as a district reporter for the *Press & Journal* (P&J) earlier in my career. 'Death knocks' were a common part of the job. Chapping the door of a grieving family to ask if they would consider a story about their lost loved one. Perhaps after a terrible car crash or a long illness. It could be a controversial practice for some, and it was hard as a young reporter. I was working for the P&J right after the phone hacking, and Milly Dowler revelations emerged, a time when all the press were lumped in with those illicit practices. I think some saw little difference between illegally hacking a phone and a death knock. In my experience, the two are not equivalent. The first is a shortcut, an underhanded cheat for finding stories you have no right or responsibility to be reporting. The second is an opportunity to pay tribute to loved ones.

Several decisions were made before we went out to knock on the door. And there were rules we stuck to—our news desk (rightly) insisted we always approach a family in person rather than on the phone or on social media. And we would only go if we knew the family were aware of the death. There was a case after the Manchester Arena bombing when one family was approached by a reporter from one publication before the person had been officially confirmed dead. When it came to who and when to knock, we considered how the person had died and their place in the community. Did they die in an accident or a crime, the reporting of which could raise awareness or bring justice? Were they a prominent local figure whose life was worthy of paying tribute beyond the usual death notices and memorials?

We would also have to consider when it would be appropriate and sensitive to approach. Sometimes, the decision making was easier if, for instance, the family launched a fundraiser to bring a loved one's body home from abroad, or were raising awareness about a rare disease. In cases like that, the family had taken a decision to speak publicly. In other cases, families pre-emptively asked the press not to approach, or would say 'no' immediately on the doorstep. That's when knowing your IPSO code was vital. Whether you consider knocking the door of a grieving family to be unethical or not, harassing a person after you have already been turned away unquestionably is. IPSO requires us to approach people in these situations with discretion and sympathy. It sometimes goes badly wrong—I was sent to knock the door of the family of a trawlerman who had just been lost at sea. All the relatives had gathered at the house and I was threatened and asked to leave. But on another occasion, I worked with the family of a missing local man, who had disappeared in bizarre circumstances, on a series of stories to shed light on the case. The stories ran over several weeks and months, they kept his name in the public eye and they called on the police to do all they could. That, I believe, showed the news and ethical value in approaching a grieving family to tell their story.

What advice do you give to young journalists at your news outlet regarding privacy and intrusion?

My number one piece of advice would be: know your IPSO Editors Code of Practice. It is the gold standard statement of ethics we should and must hold ourselves to. Beyond that, communication is crucial in a newsroom. Young journalists shouldn't have to make these decisions alone. If you are in doubt, do not act alone. A more senior person on the news desk or above should be involved in the decision to advise and approve. If you're a young, inexperienced or trainee journalist who is unsure of where you stand on matters of privacy, always, always ask for support. Guidance should come before, during and after any possible intrusion into a person's privacy. Before, all staff should be trained and know their ethical code backwards and forwards. During, there should be communication and oversight on how a story is being approached. After, there should be discussion about how the decisions were made in an ethically sensitive story: were they the right calls, what lessons could be learned?

Ethical workout

- Do celebrities have more, less or the same rights to their privacy as politicians?
- When is a photograph that invades the news subject's privacy necessary to the story?
- If you have given a source anonymity to protect their privacy and dignity, what happens when rumours of their identity circulate on social media? Should the journalist step in?
- In what situations is it legitimate to invade a child's privacy? Do children have greater rights to privacy than others?

Five takeaways from this chapter

- Everyone has a right to privacy but this is not an absolute right and it must be weighed with the right to freedom of expression.
- Codes of conduct contain provisions to protect people's privacy and stipulate that any intrusion by journalists must be in the public interest.
- Journalists should ask themselves if a person has a reasonable expectation of privacy before they intrude.
- Privacy is not a commodity that public figures can barter on one person's terms. Equally, the media should not commoditise a public figure merely because the public are interested in them and the coverage helps to sell newspapers, increase audience figures or generate clicks.
- The media should take greater care regarding intrusion when reporting on ordinary citizens, particularly during breaking news such as disasters and terrorist attacks.

Ethics toolbox

- Council of Europe (2018) Guidelines on Safeguarding Privacy in the Media. Available at: https://rm.coe.int/prems-guidelines-on-safeguarding-privacy-in-the-media-2018-/168090289b
- Frost, Chris (2020) *Privacy and the News Media*. Abingdon: Routledge.
- McStay, Andrew (2017) *Privacy and the Media*. London: Sage
- Whittle, Stephen and Cooper, Glenda (2009) Privacy, probity and public interest. Available at: https://reutersinstitute.politics.ox.ac.uk/sites/default/files/2017-12/Privacy%2C%20Probity%20and%20Public%20Interest.pdf

References

Barnett, S. (2021) 'Meghan and Harry's Oprah interview: Why British media coverage could backfire', *The Conversation*, 8 March 2021. Available at: https://theconversation.com/meghan-and-harrys-oprah-interview-why-british-media-coverage-could-backfire-156424 (Accessed: 26 May 2021).

Barrett-Maitland, N. and Lynch, J. (2020) 'Social media, ethics and the privacy paradox', in Kalloniatis, C. and Travieso-Gonzales, C. (eds.), *Security and privacy from a legal, ethical, and technical perspective*. IntechOpen. doi:10.5772/intechopen.90906. Available at: www.intechopen.com/online-first/social-media-ethics-and-the-privacy-paradox (Accessed: 31 July 2020).

BBC (2016) 'Celebrity injunction: PJS cannot be named, says Supreme Court'. Available at .www.bbc.co.uk/news/uk-36329818 (Accessed: 5 August 20).

BBC. (2018) 'Cliff Richard: Singer wins BBC privacy case at High Court', *BBC*, 18 July. Available at: www.bbc.co.uk/news/uk-44871799 (Accessed: 5 August 2020).

BBC. (2019) 'The BBC's editorial standards'. Available at: http://downloads.bbc.co.uk/guidelines/editorialguidelines/pdfs/bbc-editorial-guidelines-whole-document.pdf (Accessed: 5 August 2020).

Bowcott, O. and O'Carroll, L. (2016) 'Supreme court upholds "celebrity threesome" injunction', *The Guardian*, 19 May. Available at: www.theguardian.com/law/2016/may/19/supreme-court-upholds-celebrity-threesome-injunction (Accessed: 5 August 2020).

Brandwood, J. (n.d.) 'Launch Government inquiry into the British tabloids following the death of Caroline Flack', Petition at *change.org*. Available at: www.change.org/p/secretary-of-state-for-digital-culture-media-and-sport-launch-government-inquiry-into-the-british-tabloids-following-death-of-caroline-flack (Accessed: 5 August 2020).

Brewer, D. (2007) 'Respecting privacy as a journalist'. Available at: https://mediah elpingmedia.org/2007/07/14/respecting-privacy-as-a-journalist/ (Accessed: 11 August 2020).

Davis, S. (2020) 'Exploiting people in the public eye', Petition at *change.org*, 15 February. Available at: www.change.org/p/exploiting-people-in-the-public-eye?recruiter= 1043078149&recruited_by_id=f9302730-505b-11ea-b922-2181c12388a3&use_re act=false (Accessed: 5 August 2020).

Debatin, B. (2011) 'Ethics, privacy, and self-restraint in social networking', in Trepte, S. and Reinecke, L. (eds.), *Privacy online: Perspectives on privacy and self-disclosure in the social web*. Berlin, Heidelberg: Springer, pp. 47–60.

Editors' Codebook. (2021) *The handbook of the Editors' Code of Practice'*, IPSO. Available at: www.editorscode.org.uk/downloads/codebook/Codebook-2021.pdf (Accessed: 26 May 2021).

Edwards, C. and Fieschi, C. (2008) *UK confidential*. London: Demos. Available at: www.demos.co.uk/files/UKConfidential.pdf (Accessed: 2 March 2021).

Frost, Chris. (2020) *Privacy and the news media*. Abingdon: Routledge.

Gibson, O. (2004) 'Campbell wins privacy case against mirror', *The Guardian*, 6 May. Available at: www.theguardian.com/media/2004/may/06/mirror.pressandpublishi ng1 (Accessed: 5 August 2020).

Greenslade, R. (2018) 'The Cliff Richard ruling is a chilling blow to press freedom', *The Guardian*, 18 July. Available at: www.theguardian.com/commentisfree/2018/jul/18/cliff-richard-bbc-press-freedom-privacy (Accessed: 5 August 2020).

Hacked Off. (2019) 'Hacked Off says The Sun's Ben Stokes front page is "appalling invasion of privacy with no public interest justification"', 17 September. Available at: https://hackinginquiry.org/ben-stokes-front-page/ (Accessed: 5 August 2020).

Hammarberg, T. (2011) 'Ethical journalism and human rights', *Commissioner for Human Rights*. Available at: www.coe.int/t/dg4/cultureheritage/mars/source/resources/ref erences/04%20-%20CM%20ComDH%20Ethical%20Journalism%20and%20Hu man%20Rights%202011.pdf (Accessed: 31 July 2020).

Heawood, J. (2018) 'The Impress Podcast – Episode #2 – Privacy in the News: The case of Sir Cliff Richard vs. the BBC [Podcast]', 3 September. Available at: www.impress.press/multimedia/podcast/the-impress-podcast-episode-2-privacy-in-the-news-the-case-of-sir-cliff-richard-vs-the-bbc-by-impress-podcast.html (Accessed: 5 August 2020).

Hong, S.C. (2016) 'Kids sell: Celebrity kids' right to privacy', *Laws*, 5(2). https://doi.org/10.3390/laws5020018. Available at www.mdpi.com/2075-471X/5/2/18/htm (Accessed: 1 August 2020).

IMPRESS. (2017) 'The Impress standards code'. Available at: www.impress.press/downloads/file/code/the-impress-standards-code.pdf (Accessed: 1 August 2020).

Ingram, D. and Henshall, P. (2019) 'Chapter 62: Privacy and the public interest', *News Manual*. Available at: www.thenewsmanual.net/Manuals%20Volume%203/volume3_62.htm (Accessed: 5 August 2020).

IPSO. (2021) 'The editors' code of practice'. Available at: www.ipso.co.uk/editors-code-of-practice/ (Accessed on 1 August 2020).

Marshall, A. (2020) 'A TV Star's suicide prompts a blame game in Britain', *The New York Times*, 19 February. Available at: www.nytimes.com/2020/02/17/arts/television/caroline-flack-suicide.html (Accessed: 5 August 2020).

Moosavian, R. (2019) 'Ben Stokes v The Sun: Gross intrusion or simple reportage? How media privacy law works', *The Conversation*, 19 September. Available at: https://theconversation.com/ben-stokes-v-the-sun-gross-intrusion-or-simple-reportage-how-media-privacy-law-works-123827 (Accessed: 11 August 2020).

Morris, B. and Messenger Davies, M. (2018) 'Can children's privacy rights be adequately protected through press regulation? What press regulation can learn from the courts', *Journal of Media Law*, 10(1), pp. 92–113. doi: 10.1080/17577632.2018.1467597

National Union of Journalists. (2011) 'NUJ code of conduct'. Available at: www.nuj.org.uk/about/nuj-code/ (Accessed: 27 October 2020).

Nicolaou, E. (2021). 'Meghan Markle tells Oprah everyone should have a right to privacy in an exclusive clip', *Oprah Daily*, 9 March. Available at: www.oprahdaily.com/entertainment/a35773234/meghan-markle-oprah-privacy-tabloids-exclusive-clip/ (Accessed 26 May 2021).

Ofcom. (2019) 'The Ofcom broadcasting code, section eight: Privacy'. Available at: www.ofcom.org.uk/tv-radio-and-on-demand/broadcast-codes/broadcast-code/section-eight-privacy (Accessed: 5 August 2020).

Olsson, J. (2018) 'Cliff Richard v the BBC: A landmark case on privacy rights'. Available at: www.lexology.com/library/detail.aspx?g=2d4ac203-3823-4834-8a74-deb2b7e44f37 (Accessed: 5 August 2020).

Oswald, M., James, H. and Nottingham, E. (2016) 'The not-so-secret life of five-year-olds: Legal and ethical issues relating to disclosure of information and the depiction of children on broadcast and social media', *Journal of Media Law*, 8(2), pp.198–228. https://doi.org/10.1080/17577632.2016.1239942

Palmer, R. (2017) *Becoming the news: How ordinary people respond to the media spotlight*. New York: Columbia University Press.

PA Media Lawyer and Press Gazette. (2019). 'Meghan Markle v Mail on Sunday will be "privacy case of the century", says media law expert', *Press Gazette*, 3 October. Available at: www.pressgazette.co.uk/meghan-markle-vs-mail-on-sunday-will-be-privacy-case-of-the-century-says-media-law-expert/ (Accessed 26 May 2021).

Ponsford, D. (2021a) 'Five lessons for the media over Meghan's Mail on Sunday privacy victory'. *Press Gazette*, 12 February. Available at: https://pressgazette.co.uk/meghan-mail-on-sunday-privacy-victory-five-lessons-for-media/ (Accessed: 26 May 2021).

Ponsford, D. (2021b) 'The Sun says it never should have published Ben Stokes story and pays substantial privacy damages', *Press Gazette*, 31 August. Available at: www.pressgazette.co.uk/the-sun-ben-stokes-privacy-apology/ (Accessed: 8 October 2021).

Prince Harry, Duke of Sussex, (2019) 'Statement by his royal highness Prince Harry, Duke of Sussex'. Available at: https://sussexofficial.uk/ (Accessed: 26 May 2021).

Privacy International. (2017) 'What is privacy?', *PI Explainer*. Available at: https://privacyinternational.org/explainer/56/what-privacy (Accessed: 31 July 2020).

Quinn, F. (2018) *Law for journalists: A guide to media law*, 6th ed. Harlow: Pearson.

Society of Professional Journalists. (2014) 'SPJ code of ethics'. Available at: www.spj.org/pdf/spj-code-of-ethics.pdf (Accessed: 5 August 2020).

Steel, J. (2012) *Journalism and free speech*. Abingdon: Routledge.

UK Government. (1998) 'Human Rights Act 1998, Article 8'. Available at: www.legislation.gov.uk/ukpga/1998/42/schedule/1/part/I/chapter/7 (Accessed: 31 July 2020).

Verdecchia, L. (2020) 'When ordinary people become part of the news: A Q&A with Ruth Palmer', *Center for Journalism Ethics, School of Journalism and Mass Communication, University of Wisconsin-Madison*, 17 February. Available at: https://ethics.journalism.wisc.edu/2020/02/17/when-ordinary-people-become-a-part-of-the-news-a-qa-with-ruth-palmer/ (Accessed: 9 July 2021).

Warren, S.D. and Brandeis, L.D. (1890) 'The right to privacy', *Harvard Law Review*, 4(5), pp. 193–220.

Waterson, J. (2019) 'Ben Stokes takes legal action against Sun over story of family tragedy', *The Guardian*, 10 October. Available at: www.theguardian.com/media/2019/oct/10/ben-stokes-takes-legal-action-against-sun-over-story-about-his-mother (Accessed: 5 August 2020).

6
Covering death and trauma
Focus on compassion and respect

Sallyanne Duncan

Interviewing grieving or traumatized people is a task that most journalists dread. They fear adding to people's pain and suffering by asking what might seem like inappropriate or impertinent questions at probably the worst time in a family's life. However, deaths that happen in public places and some that occur in private, such as celebrity deaths, are newsworthy so journalists have a duty to report them. Citizens have a right to be informed about events that happen in their communities, and death and trauma are no exceptions, but equally those who are experiencing death and trauma have a right to privacy. With the coronavirus pandemic it is likely that journalists will increasingly report on death, as well as trauma associated with long COVID. Therefore, getting the balance right is a major concern for journalists who wish to report responsibly. This chapter looks at some of the ethical issues when covering death and trauma including approaching traumatized people, using social media and covering funerals. It then examines specific types of trauma, such as responsibly reporting road crashes, murder, domestic violence and abuse. In the *Ethics in Action* section, journalist, author and trauma training specialist, Jo Healey gives her insights into ethically reporting people's personal tragedies.

What are the main ethical issues journalists need to consider when covering death and trauma?

Most journalists who report stories about traumatized people are caring and empathetic and far from the public's general perception of reporters as exploitative vultures. However, even when journalists behave responsibly the act of reporting is intrusive. Stories of death and trauma deal with human emotions like pain and suffering, grief, remembrance and loss. Road crashes, murder investigations, traumatic court cases, terrorist attacks, natural disasters, extreme weather, suicide, and the pandemic are all news events. Additionally, topics like historic child abuse, terminal illness and stillbirth regularly appear on the

DOI: 10.4324/9780429505386-7

features pages. However, unlike general news where the journalist's instinct is to concentrate on the story, death and trauma journalism needs to also prioritize those at the *heart* of the story—traumatized people—if news outlets are to avoid further distress. Consequently, an essential ethical concern for journalists is to try to minimize harm to those in their stories by considering how they approach grieving people, their behaviour when reporting, and the content they publish or broadcast. They should treat the traumatized and bereaved as ends in themselves, i.e. it is the interviewee's story told in their way, not the journalist's, and not as means to an end, i.e. a way to get a tear-jerking exclusive that increases clicks or ratings.

Minimizing harm appears in most codes of ethics. In the UK, IPSO and IMPRESS warn news outlets to avoid exacerbating grief and distress by acting with sympathy, discretion and sensitivity, whilst Ofcom asks broadcast news teams to assess whether interviewing traumatized individuals is intrusive or infringes their privacy. The American Society of Professional Journalists code goes further with a whole section on minimizing harm and while its advice only applies to some US news organizations it provides useful guidance for journalists elsewhere. It starts from the position of treating people as "human beings deserving of respect" and suggests journalists do this by assessing the public's need for information against any potential harm. It then asks journalists to show compassion for those affected by news coverage, particularly those who have experienced trauma, and to consider cultural differences when reporting. Journalists are also warned to avoid pandering to lurid curiosity, even if others do, an issue that has been prevalent in some UK tabloids over the years. We have seen this in the reporting of Madeleine McCann, a three-year-old child who disappeared while on holiday with her family in Portugal in 2007, where numerous rumours, speculation and inventions regarding her and her family were regular fodder for the tabloids, and continue to be so to this day. In 2008 Madeleine's parents, Kate and Gerry McCann, won a libel case against Express Newspapers and secured unprecedented front page apologies after the publisher ran stories suggesting the couple were responsible for their daughter's death and that they had sold her to pay off debts. Giving evidence at the Leveson Inquiry into press standards in 2011, the McCanns stated that the UK press had declared "open season" on them after Madeleine's disappearance, describing the reporting as "disgusting" and "offensive". Some journalists at the time told them that their daughter's disappearance had caught the British public's imagination and was driving sales in the UK. Accordingly, journalists were being put under intense pressure to file more copy. Kate McCann told the inquiry she felt "totally violated" when her private diary, where she revealed her feelings about her daughter's disappearance, was leaked to the now defunct, *News of the World*. She said that the tabloid had "absolutely no respect for me as a grieving mother" (BBC, 2008; Robinson, 2011).

Minimizing harm does not appear to have been on the radar for these news outlets when reporting on the McCanns and their daughter. But some journalists, including those on tabloid publications, strive to treat those in their stories with greater thoughtfulness. A journalist from the *Scottish Sun* explained:

> It helps if people understand that we're not there to give them a hard time. If they say "no" they are not going to get harassed but we give them the opportunity [to talk], give them the courtesy of letting them know it's going to be in the paper. Once the police put something out [a press statement] it's going to be in the paper.

They added:

> The legacy of red top tabloid journalists is that maybe in the past they have been like that [insensitive and intrusive]. Things have changed so much. We have to be so careful. … If someone says "no" we won't go back. That's part of the Editors Code (IPSO). But if it comes from another party the problem is that your desk will continue to send you back until we get that "no" (from the bereaved person).
> *Scottish Sun journalist, personal communication with the author, 2017*

Minimizing harm also has to be balanced with the need for the journalist to seek the truth and report it. And even this action can appear intrusive, with personal matters necessary to the story becoming public knowledge. These two ethical issues can sometimes be in conflict with the result that one has to take precedence over the other. Journalists should strive to report the truth and as a result some information may be included in a story that distresses bereaved relatives. Uncomfortable truths have to be reported, but as fact not speculation or sensationalism, and there needs to be a legitimate justification for their inclusion. Whilst a *Mail Online* story about the death in London in 2019 of Sheikh Khalid bin Sultan Al Qasimi, the son of the ruler of Sharjah in the United Arab Emirates, did contain speculation from another publication about a "drug-fuelled party at which some guests were having sex", they also reported the fact that his brother died from a heroin overdose. Complaining to IPSO about this, amongst other issues, his family said it had compounded and deepened their hurt and distress. However, IPSO remarked that this was factual information that was already in the public domain, and as it was relevant to Prince Khalid's death, reporting it was in the public interest. The committee stated in their findings: "Journalists have a right to report the fact of a person's death, even if surviving family members would prefer for there to be no reporting" (see Sultan bin Muhammad Al Qasimi and the Al Qasimi family v Mail Online, IPSO, 2019).

Minimizing harm does not mean that journalists should sanitize their content or self-censor but it does mean them respecting the traumatized people they report on and treating them with dignity. Partly, that entails journalists making judgements about how relevant some content is to the story they are currently reporting. Whilst a criminal conviction might have been reported publicly previously, is it appropriate to dig through the archives and include that information in the story of a person's death merely because it is available? The New Zealand Media Council did not believe so. They found that a news outlet, *Stuff*, acted unfairly towards a man's grieving family when their report of his death included his conviction ten years previously for a sexual offence against a child. They acknowledged that the media should report all available facts about the deceased but cautioned against including "irrelevant information" that is likely to distress the family. *Stuff* claimed that an article that failed to acknowledge his victim's experience would be "a breach of basic journalism ethics" as it would amount to misleading by omission, which could be insulting to her. The media council dismissed this as speculation, citing the potential harm that could be caused to the victim by reawakening unwelcome memories of the traumatic experience and by her reading it online without advanced warning. They recognized this was a marginal case based on individual facts and their decision was not a general disapproval of publishing objectionable information about a dead person. Indeed, some media council members disagreed with the decision stating that while they sympathized with bereaved relatives the media has a duty to the public at large and not only to the grieving family. "Sound, honest and factual reporting can often cause discomfort", the dissenting members said. They added that the news outlet did not sensationalize the story but reported the facts accurately and proportionately, and gave the family an opportunity to comment (New Zealand Media Council, 2021).

These difficult judgements need careful thought in order to determine which ethical principle prevails over the other. These are decisions for editors and their teams, not for individual journalist working on a traumatic story. They apply whether journalists report stories about the bereaved without their involvement or knowledge, or whether traumatized people participate in the story by agreeing to be interviewed. Weighing up the public interest in reporting uncomfortable facts about a deceased—what public good is served by doing so—and balancing that against the potential harm to those involved in the story, such as grieving family and friends and any victims of crime, is a challenging task at any time, let alone on deadline.

How should journalists treat someone who is in grief or shock?

At a time of death and trauma those in the midst of it have little control over what is happening to them. They may be unable to absorb information or to understand what is occurring. The sudden barrage of contact from reporters, news desks or TV crews, whether at their front doors, by phone or via social media, can be intense and gruelling. They may not have been informed that stories about their loss are to be published. The shock from seeing the death or serious injury of their loved one printed in a news story or announced as part of a news bulletin may be overwhelming. And yet, many bereaved and traumatized families agree to speak to journalists about their loss. Some regret it because of the treatment they receive from news outlets but others find it cathartic. Their experience of this encounter is very dependent on the treatment they receive from news organizations and their individual journalists.

As a means of achieving a more constructive experience for both grieving relatives and news outlets, Duncan and Newton (2017) devised a model of ethical participation, designed to enable traumatized and bereaved relatives to have greater involvement in how their stories of loss are told. Most death and trauma reporting is *journalist-driven* where stories are shaped according to preconceived news frames and agendas, a formulaic approach that can result in stereotypical reporting with little emphasis on the deceased's individuality, character or even the specific circumstances of their death, resulting in a story that is no longer recognizable as the grieving relative's own experience. Journalists can address these issues by applying the principles of ethical participation: context, clarity and control.

By providing greater context about the deceased, their life and their death, journalists can overcome a concern that is often raised by grieving families: journalists' reporting gives an incomplete or biased impression of their loved one. The hurt from this action can be immense when the person depicted in the news outlet's article bears little resemblance to their dead child, sibling or parent, or the news outlet chooses to pursue a particular angle or suggests that the deceased may in some way be responsible for their own death. These incomplete or biased views can cause lasting damage to their memory of their loved one.

Additionally, bereaved and traumatized people need greater clarity about what will happen to their story within the news process. They need reassurance that the information they provide and their precious memories will be handled with care and respect. At a time of chaos through grief and shock bereaved and traumatized families need to feel involved in the process of producing their story, not managed or manipulated, so explaining what will happen, what is and is not within the control of the reporter, will help build trust between them and the journalist. Melody, who survived childhood rape, says it is important for journalists to involve interviewees in the reporting process. Speaking about being filmed for TV she said: "I definitely needed to know why they were doing it ... Someone who's been a victim of abuse, they've already had too many people making them do things without explanation and it wasn't pleasant" (Healey, 2020, p. 121).

Also, taking time to connect with grieving relatives as a human being, not only as a journalist, by talking to them and genuinely showing that you are sorry for their loss, will enhance that trust. Being more open when discussing consent to use the information they provide will also restore some control to them over what is happening to them at that moment. Journalists should not assume that because a traumatized person agrees to be interviewed that they are approving the use of everything they say in the interview. Remember they are in shock. Explaining what it means to consent to publication is a way to treat an interviewee fairly and with respect. It is also important to ask clear, simple questions and avoid confusing interviewees with technical or complex questions that require them to speculate. The potential anxiety from having given misleading or wrong information can add further harm to them and reinforce feelings of remorse.

By following the principles of context and clarity journalists give bereaved and traumatized people an element of control over the telling of their stories and if news outlets adopt a more *bereaved-focussed* approach in their reporting it could have a profound effect on grieving families' encounters with the media.

> An element of control is important to families at this time and having a journalist deal honestly and respectfully with them is preferable to being excluded from the report, either by failing to interview them or by revising their story such that it is no longer recognisable to them.
> Duncan and Newton, 2017, p. 86; for a greater explanation of this ethical process see Reporting Bad News by Duncan and Newton, 2017

But all that work of treating bereaved and traumatized people fairly, honestly and with compassion can be undone if journalists are inaccurate. Families feel angry and hurt when news outlets and their reporters misspell their loved one's name, or give them the wrong job title, or worse, invent some minor details to liven up the story. To the journalist these are errors; to the families these are insults that can rankle for decades. These "small errors" can be perceived by grieving relatives as a lack of respect for their loved one. Worse still, is when journalists fail to check even basic details before speaking to a traumatized person. Pam Dix, of the charity Disaster Action, lost her brother when a bomb blew up flight Pan Am 103 over Lockerbie in 1988. She said:

> Some of you won't know the questions you're going to ask. Some of the most obvious things like: "How do you and your husband feel about this?" Where the answer turns out to be: "Well, actually it was my husband who was killed!" Can't you just look something up? Get a little bit of the groundwork

done. Because of the nature of open access resources you won't always get the right answer, but try and do well-founded research if you have time.

Dix et al., 2016

Taking care over personal details, checking with grieving relatives before the interview ends or contacting them afterwards when writing the story will all ensure that journalists minimize harm to those experiencing bereavement and trauma. Inaccuracies equate to a lack of care and to families that exacerbates their pain and suffering. Showing compassion, connection and empathy towards interviewees, on the other hand, can alleviate their pain and suffering to a small extent.

These sensitive stories cannot be told in a rush. They need time, and sometimes for the journalist time is scarce. However, this dilemma can be eased to a certain extent by journalists being honest with their interviewees. They can explain they are on a deadline, have limited time and therefore can reduce their questions to a few key points. They can also suggest doing another story later where they can speak at length, when the family are ready to do so. Rushing to tell the story in order to be part of the news cycle or to be first seldom works for ethical reporting of death and trauma, especially where there are complex issues associated with it, such as historic child abuse. It is important to balance the urgency to report with the potential harm to those who are grieving or are part of a traumatized community from reading or viewing such stories without warning and without any support.

[For practical advice on how to approach bereaved or traumatized people see Jo Healey's book, *Trauma Reporting: A journalist's guide to covering sensitive stories* (Routledge, 2020).]

Using social media content to write a story will spare a grieving family from dealing with the press, won't it? Is that an ethical way to report?

Using content from social media in stories of death and trauma is fairly standard practice these days. Whole articles can be written about an incident where people have been seriously injured or died without a reporter ever approaching a family member. Indeed, the family might not even know that a story about their loved one has been published or broadcast. Some news outlets do this to expedite the story, to get it up online or in the news bulletin as quickly and as efficiently as possible. Reduced staff in the newsroom, tighter deadlines, more platforms requiring content, all curtail reporters' opportunities to leave the office or even make a phone or Zoom call. Tender reminiscences from grieving relatives, which would normally be gathered by reporters sensitively exploring the life and death of a loved one, are replaced by Facebook, Twitter and Instagram RIP messages, which were written as expressions of grief, not as statements for wider dissemination by the media. The user's content is repurposed without their knowledge and without consultation with the deceased's relatives. But, news outlets might argue that if something is posted on social media and put into the public domain without any privacy settings such that it can be seen by anyone then they are entitled to publish or broadcast it. However, that should not be a license for irresponsible reporting. IPSO cautions news outlets to consider to what extent social media content was in the public domain and who placed it there, how many people were able to view the material, their relationship to the deceased and the person who posted it, and whether they had a reasonable expectation that it would not be circulated further (IPSO, 2020).

IPSO recognizes that news outlets will use social media content to illustrate stories involving personal grief and shock, but they warn editors and journalists to take care and avoid insensitive publication that would ridicule the deceased or is particularly gory. They also urge caution when selecting photos of the deceased by asking news outlets to consider the length of time that has elapsed since the newsworthy incident as well as the content of the picture in relation to the context of the death (see IPSO ruling Farrow v Lancashire Evening Post, Editors' Codebook, 2021, p. 67). But even using apparently straightforward pictures raises ethical issues. Rose Dixon, whose daughter Avril was murdered when she was 22, told journalist and trauma trainer, Jo Healey, about the harm caused to her family when news outlets used their daughter's social media content without their knowledge.

> We felt invaded by the press when pictures of our daughter had been taken from her social media sites without our approval. We would have liked the opportunity to choose. Many were out of date and we found it very upsetting to see pictures of our daughter together with her murderer.
> *Healey, 2020, p. 31*

Yes, taking pictures and posts from social media will spare a family the anguish of being interviewed by a journalist at probably the most horrendous time in their lives, but doing so also excludes them from participating in how that story is told. No context, no clarity or consent, resulting in them being denied control over another aspect of their lives. So, there are certainly ethical tensions here.

Messages, pictures and videos might be publicly available on social media but they might have been posted and shared at speed by people the family barely know or have little communication with. Unless a journalist contacts grieving relatives they will not know their feelings on the matter so news outlets by publishing these messages run the risk of causing unnecessary distress. When news organizations use these without checking the poster's relationship with the deceased they are adding to the family's anguish and are giving those messages, which were intended for a more intimate community of family and friends, greater weight by circulating them to a broader audience who have no relationship with the deceased other than as news subjects in a story. Grieving relatives may find these condolence messages helpful and healing but they might also be upset that they have been posted before they have had a chance to break the news to friends and family themselves. Taya Dunn Johnson, whose 36-year-old husband died in 2012, urges people to pause for a few hours before posting in order to give the family time to deal with the enormity of their tragedy. "The 'RIP' posts started hitting my timeline about an hour after my husband's death, and I certainly didn't start them. This created a sense of confusion, fear, anxiety, panic, dread, and shock for the people who knew me, too" (Dunn Johnson, 2019). Journalists may be able to mitigate this distress if they pause a little then select posts from those who are at the centre of the loss, such as parents, spouses, siblings or adult children. Even then, without seeking approval from them to use their social media content the potential for harm is high. Recognizing social media's role in displacing traditional protocols about how and who should inform people about a death, Gibson observes:

> Randomness, the decentralization of media sources and 24-hour information flow have enabled strangers, acquaintances and friends to announce a death, offer condolence and set up memorial pages before official sources or more centrally bereaved persons are able to act or make decisions about their response mechanisms.
>
> Gibson, 2015, p. 339

Should the media cover funerals?

Before the COVID-19 pandemic media reporting of funerals was mostly restricted to the deaths of celebrities and public figures or ordinary citizens who were the victims of terrorist attacks or major disasters. The funerals of murder victims, especially where the killing has severely impacted a community, may also be covered particularly by the local media, but news outlets don't report the funerals of every death that appears in their publications.

Deciding which funerals to report—from an ethics perspective—has to be weighed up in terms of the family's wishes, mitigation of potential intrusion and the ability of individual journalists to behave respectfully and sensitively towards mourners. There also has to be a public interest in intruding at this most sensitive time. What public good is served by doing so? Editors and reporters should discuss the benefits to their communities of attending such events, making judgements on a case-by-case basis.

Some families may welcome media coverage because they see the funeral as means of bringing people together to grieve and to remember their loved one. For others a funeral is a wholly private matter and consider any media attention intrusive and insensitive. Those who wish to avoid media interest can ask IPSO, the body that regulates most mainstream national and regional print media in the UK, to issue a private advisory notice to inform journalists that they should not attend. Ascertaining the family's wishes is imperative so although there is the potential to cause further distress by contacting them to ask to attend, this is preferable to turning up unannounced. Contacting relatives in advance to ask permission and to emotionally prepare them for a forthcoming publication seems like a responsible approach. Going through a funeral director or an officiant to ascertain the family's wishes and to inform them of who the news outlet is and how they plan to approach their coverage might also be appropriate. However, not all family members might agree on the best action and if there is dissent it might be better for a news outlet to sensitively consider the specific circumstances. Contacting IPSO for advice using their pre-publication 24-hour phone line would be prudent.

Even those parts of a funeral that are in public view, where a reporter or photographer would have a legitimate right to observe, such as a funeral procession, need to be undertaken with care, particularly regarding images of people in states of extreme distress. Two notable cases offer guidance here, emphasizing that the responsibility for sensitive coverage lies firmly with the media. Relatives of Olympic cycling champion Sir Chris Hoy complained to the Press Complaints Commission (PCC), the forerunner of IPSO, about intrusion into their grief and shock when attending the funeral of his uncle. The photograph that accompanied the article in the *Scottish Sun* on 18 November 2012 showed the deceased's wife being comforted. In defence, the newspaper said the pictures were taken on the street after the photographer had been asked to leave the churchyard. This, said the PCC, was a clear indication that the family did not want pictures taken at the funeral. The regulator upheld the complaint, stating that the photographs were intrusive (Turvill, 2013). The second case, also adjudicated by the PCC, involved a photographer who took pictures at the cremation of a teenager who had taken his own life, despite being warned off. The newspaper, the *Bristol Evening Post*, argued that cremations were public events and therefore the press could cover them. They also claimed that they did not know that the family objected to photographs being published in a picture spread in the newspaper on 26 February 2009. However, in upholding the complaint the regulator stressed that "grieving parents should not have to be concerned with journalistic behaviour" and that the newspaper should have established the family's wishes in advance (see Mrs Hazel Cattermole v Bristol Evening Post in Editors' Codebook, 2021, p. 70).

However, news outlets need to take care of the copy they produce as well as images. Matthew Pearson of the *Ottawa Citizen*, who has covered several funerals, advises reporters to take care to produce responsible articles.

> Covering funerals is not easy. They are often profoundly sad, but that doesn't mean many aren't also filled with joy, celebration and humour. The writing requires a gentle hand—one that is able to capture in words the pulse of the room.

He added:

> When writing think about how certain anecdotes or stories told at the funeral could be misinterpreted by readers. The last thing you want is to cause a grieving family more harm by including details that cast aspersions on the deceased's character.
>
> Pearson, 2013

How can we report road crashes more responsibly?

In their careers some journalists may never report a war, disaster, terrorist attack or a murder but they will probably cover a road crash, especially if they work in the regional media. For journalists, exposure to road crashes and to survivors or grieving families is a recognized, customary part of their job (Backholm and Bjorkqvist, 2012; Dworznik and Garvey, 2018). Their articles are usually of a single incident so the scale of death and injury on our roads is minimized by the reporting of individual events in particular places. We don't see the bigger picture. Yet, more than 1.35 million people die each year in road crashes globally and between 20 and 50 million more suffer non-fatal injuries (WHO, 2018, 2021). It is no surprise then that road traffic incidents are the eighth leading cause of death in the world. Children and young adults are most at risk: more 5–29 year olds die than any other group, and 73% of them are males under the age of 25 (WHO, 2021). In the UK, 1,752 people were killed on the roads in 2019 but a staggering 30,144 people were seriously injured and a further 121,262 were slightly injured that year, according to incidents reported to the police (Department of Transport, 2020). The effects from road crashes can ripple out beyond the incident itself to change the lives of individual families and friends in terms of grief and loss, coping with serious injuries, psychological effects, loss of income, time off work to recover or to care for the injured, or adapting to disability. Given the amount of coverage road crashes receive, the media are ideally placed to influence public policy and preventative measures through accurate, responsible reporting. Including vital context in road crash stories can help the public understand wider trends in road usage, street design and traffic management. For example, referring to regional, national and international statistics means news outlets are treating road deaths and injuries as more than isolated incidents. In doing so journalists provide greater accuracy, accountability and independence of thought. RoadPeace, the charity for victims of road crashes, advises journalists to avoid using of the word "accident" as it embodies society's tolerance of road danger, implies that a driver's action is a matter of chance, and suggests that these deaths and injuries are inevitable and unavoidable. Media Guidelines for Reporting Road Collisions advocate that using crash or collision "leaves the question of who or what is to blame open, pending further details" (Laker, 2021). They also recommend journalists refer to a driver rather than their vehicle, particularly when describing actions like speeding or leaving the scene of a crash, as research indicates that naming only one human actor implicitly attaches blame to them. Where little is known about the incident they suggest describing both people, using neutral language, for example a driver and cyclist were in collision. Journalists are also asked to refer to deaths and injuries before any information on traffic delays, as well as to add context on perceived risk on the roads by providing local and national collision trends and statistics, which can emphasize the scale of the issue and avoid portraying road crashes as isolated (ibid). Editors are also urged to adopt a consistent approach regarding the stories they run. Professor Sally Kyd of Leicester Law School told *Press Gazette*: "I have seen newspapers complaining about speed cameras and the 'war on motorists' on one page, whilst on another page in the same edition there is a report on sentencing of a road death case where the defendant is portrayed as a monster whose sentence is wholly inadequate, despite the fact that the main reason they were convicted was that they were speeding at the time they collided with the deceased" (Tobitt, 2021). Care should be taken over photographs including user-generated images. News outlets should check images for anything that could identify those involved in the crash, such as personal items left at the scene, vehicle number plates or make and model of the vehicle, especially if it is distinctive or an unusual colour. The aim is to avoid distressing family and friends who may stumble across coverage on social media before they are informed by the police. (For further advice on reporting road crashes see www.rc-rg.com/guidelines.)

What are some of the ethical complications of reporting violent crimes?

Sensitivity and balance are also important when reporting violent crimes. The public, it seems, have "an insatiable appetite for crime" (Chermak, 1994, p. 567) but for every incident reported in the news there is a grieving family and friends who remember the person, not the dramatic story of violence. News stories of crimes like murder, rape and serious assault invariably frame the perpetrator as an evil stranger attacking a vulnerable victim, but incidents of crime can be more complex than that, and might involve wider societal issues. According to Keeble, news outlets need to pay special attention to the reporting of murders and serial killers, who often target women as their victims. He said: "Too often tabloids emphasise the abnormality of the killer (with words such as 'evil', 'monster', 'beast', 'sick', vicious', 'brute', 'fiend' and 'bizarre') and the randomness of the attack" (2009, p. 211). In actual fact, killers are often known to their victims, particularly where the victim is female. Of the 2,075 women killed from 2010 to 2020 in England and Wales around 57% of them were killed by someone they knew, usually a partner or ex-partner, and 70% of them were killed in their own homes. Of the 4,493 men who were killed during this period, 39% of them were killed by someone they knew, 35% of them in their own homes (BBC, 2021). Additionally, most violent assaults are committed by people who are known to the victim: 92% for women and 79% for men (ibid). So the framing of an evil stranger is not altogether accurate and may be the result of sensationalizing the crime in order to increase clicks, views or circulation, making the story dramatic, entertaining and of interest to the public. However, whilst crime reporting serves a public interest (rather than an interest to the public), sensationalist reporting can result in inaccuracy, exacerbate public fear, emphasize unusual incidents over more routine crimes that can severely impact individual citizens' lives, and can lead to a skewed impression of crime in a community. Sensationalist language here can be subtle as well as blatant. Even where journalists strive to be impartial they might influence the audience's perception of the perpetrator and the victim by inadvertently employing strategies that increase sensationalism. For example, listing the facts of the incident, especially if the audience can easily associate their lives with them, could raise alarm amongst some people. Mencher (2003) believes that because "writing is as much an act of the unconscious as it is the conscious use of controlled and disciplined intelligence" (p. 53) then journalists' subjectivity will occasionally creep in. This "unbalanced representation" may be caused by journalists' twin obligations of the need to inform the public, and to generate income for their news outlet through engaging content (Duwe, 2000; Grundlingh, 2017, p. 121). Works and Wong (2020) identify four crime-related themes that journalists tend to use in their reporting. These are (1) sympathetic victims, where elements of the journalists' storytelling results in a sense of loss and injustice in the audience; (2) fear of personal victimization, where revealing the circumstances of the murder can cause the public to fear for their own safety; (3) sensational murders, where the unusualness, unexpectedness or shocking nature of the murder stand out from other incidents, and (4) media construction of social issues, where the coverage of the murder suggests that a greater social issue contributed to the incident (ibid, p. 428). The coverage of 33-year-old Sarah Everard, who was abducted, raped and murdered by a serving Metropolitan Police officer in March 2021, fits all four themes. As a young women who believed and trusted a police officer when he stopped her in the street, falsely arrested her, handcuffed her and required her to get into his car, citing an apparent breach of COVID-19 regulations, news outlets emphasized the sense of loss and injustice and framed her as a sympathetic victim. Their reporting of the facts about her killer: that he was a serving police officer, that there were allegations of inappropriate sexual behaviour prior to Ms Everard's murder, and that his nickname amongst some of his colleagues was "the rapist" because he made women feel uncomfortable and had a reputation for alleged drug abuse and extreme pornography use (McCann, 2021), reinforced women's fears about their personal safety in the UK. Not all this reporting was sensational but the presentation of the facts of how he abducted her and how she died has the potential to become a strategy that inadvertently results in sensationalism. The weight the media gave to the unusualness, unexpectedness and shocking nature of the killing—that a person in authority whose remit is to protect the public and keep them safe could use his position of trust to kidnap, plus the brutality of her rape and murder—made this a sensational murder. There is also some evidence of the final theme, media construction of social issues where the coverage suggested wider concerns contributed to the murder. When Sarah Everard's body was found a week after her disappearance on 3 March, fear amongst women grew into outrage. This brought into sharp focus the ongoing issue of violence against women and girls, which has been a societal crisis for many decades. Thus, the contributory factor, it seems, is a culture of tolerance and malaise regarding inappropriate sexual behaviour and violence towards women and girls.

Complex killings like murder-suicide resulting from coercive control require journalists to look beyond formulaic, stereotypical reporting to understand the context that has resulted in the deaths. Coercive control is a form of controlling behaviour that is "designed to make a person dependent by isolating them from support, exploiting them, depriving them of independence and regulating their everyday behaviour" (Women's Aid, 2021). Making assumptions that the incident was the result of some family tragedy that pushed the murderer over the brink should be avoided. In the early stages of the incident it is not possible for journalists to determine from talking to neighbours and acquaintances of the deceased how the family lived their lives. Luke and Ryan Hart, whose father killed their mother and sister then took his own life in 2016, were appalled at the press coverage that characterized their father as a "nice guy" and used victim-blaming and murderer-sympathizing headlines. They said:

> In the aftermath of the murders, we witnessed a commentary that described our father as a "nice guy" who was "always caring" and "good at DIY". One report even stated that the murder of our sister and mother was

"understandable". The sympathising male angle of the reporting revealed our default societal perspective: we were forced to read of our father's "suicide note" rather than the "murder note" that it was to our mother and sister. The murders were treated as an isolated, random and unpreventable news story for which nothing needed to change

Hart and Hart, 2019

They added:

> The emotional language used in the media betrays the true motivations of men who kill women and children. They are not "provoked", they do not "snap", they do not "lose it". They are calculated and cold-blooded.
>
> ibid

Some individuals and groups impacted by mass shootings have called for change in the media's approach to reporting perpetrators in particular. Although this is specifically in relation to mass random shootings (normally defined as a crime in which three or more people who are selected indiscriminately are killed), the principles could be applied to individual murders. The Don't Name Them campaign aims to shift media focus on to the victim, survivors and those who try to help and away from the perpetrator. They state:

> … let's not glorify the attacker by giving them valuable airtime. Don't share their manifestos, their letters, their Facebook posts. Be above sensationalism. Tell the real stories—the stories of the victims, heroes and the communities who come together to help the families heal
>
> Don't Name Them, n.d.

Change appears to be taking place. Greensmith (2019) states: "Increasingly, news outlets, law enforcement officers and public officials, have refused to name the shooter and this suggests a new appetite for understanding the ramifications of the dominant narrative of coverage of these crimes" (p. 112).

Ethics in action: Jo Healey, journalist, author and founder of Trauma Reporting training : "Do your job, do it well, do no harm"

Jo Healey worked as a reporter for newspapers and radio before moving to BBC TV, becoming a senior news journalist. There she devised and introduced Trauma Reporting training for journalists and crews. She is the author of *Trauma Reporting, A journalist's guide to covering sensitive stories*. The founder of Trauma Reporting training, Jo now trains journalists and media teams all over the world on how best to work with victims, survivors and vulnerable interviewees. Here, she shares her insights into reporting people's personal tragedies.

Tell us about the first time you contacted a bereaved family

Reporters invariably remember their first death knock. It was viewed as a rite of passage, an initiation into intrusion of the toughest kind: forced to face people's big emotions, forced to face their own fear.

I was dispatched to knock on the door of a father whose young daughter had taken her own life. I was working for the local paper in a mining community. Not much older than the teenaged daughter who had died, I was terrified. Approaching the family felt hard to square.

The editor's words of "encouragement" to a cub reporter as he sent me out were: "You look sympathetic and the dad's less likely to hit a woman…"

The dad didn't hit me, he was weary and washed out when I turned up. He chose to talk to me. The hairstyle in his daughter's "pick up pic" was the same as mine.

I have no idea how I went about the interview. But maybe it stirred the first inklings that this should be done differently. Or, more likely, I was just relieved to have got through it and delivered. I was ambitious and it was a long time ago.

What are your thoughts about covering people's trauma?

As with many thousands of journalists in newsrooms worldwide, I've gone on to work with hundreds of people whose lives were upended, whose emotions were shredded, but who wanted to share. Stuff so bad it's newsworthy. People telling me intimate experiences of grief, violation, loss.

I tend to recall the tiny details they shared off camera: a mum at her newly buried young son's grave leaning into me and whispering how she yearned to push her hands through the soil, grab his body and just hold him. The granny, deep in the mining community where I worked, ironing her lace hankies. She was going to need them, she told me. It would be her grandson's funeral the following morning, he was being buried with full military honours. She wanted to do him proud.

It is endlessly a privilege to be at the heart of people's stories of trauma, loss and anguish. Whether covering lost livelihoods and fractured communities as the pits and coalfields folded like dominoes, to covering lost lives.

Whose trauma has had an intense effect on you as a reporter?

The people who touch me are the ordinary people who have extraordinarily bad or difficult things happen to them. People who chose to share those experiences with me and, through my telling of them, went on to share them with thousands of others.

One of them was Emma Humphreys. Her story had a profound effect personally and professionally.

Emma had a brutal home life, spent time in care and by the time she was 16 she was homeless and selling sex. She moved in with one of her punters. He was twice her age and subjected her to extreme physical, sexual and emotional abuse.

One day, panicked with fear that he would rape her yet again, Emma stabbed him once with the knife she had earlier used to cut her own wrists. He died shortly afterwards.

Deeply traumatized, Emma was unable to speak of the violence she'd endured. Without a decent defence, she was given an indefinite sentence for murder. Years later, she made contact with Justice for Women. They started a campaign, and that's how Emma's story reached me.

After working for newspapers and then radio, I had moved to work for TV regional news. I was researching a series of features around domestic violence. Emma's story caught my eye because the killing had happened in our patch.

I remember vividly meeting Emma. She agreed to an interview with me on a day release from prison. We met in a park and a campaigner with Justice for Women was with us. Emma was tiny and terrified and not much younger than me. We sat in the park on a bench and only when she felt ready we attempted to film her. She was shaking like a leaf but determined finally to have her say, and she did.

For the first time, in public and on film, Emma's story of abuse, violence, terror and injustice were captured and would be told.

As a young reporter, I felt a huge responsibility. Emma and I had got on really well. Instinctively I had taken the interview slowly and given her space and control to share what she chose to share. But she had attempted suicide many times in prison, she was monumentally vulnerable. When we were getting shots of her walking through the park, she could barely walk in front of the camera. We filmed her feeding the ducks and those shots would go on to be used endlessly by network TV in the future as her story unfolded. Because it did unfold.

Emma's story caused a stir even in the days before social media. The campaign hotted up but the legal process was slow. I headed off on maternity leave and returned to work just as Emma's case was up at the Court of Appeal. Two and half years after the campaign started, ten years after she had been jailed.

It was a baking hot day, campaigners were out in force, chanting, singing and brandishing placards. And then came the news they were longing to hear. Emma was free, her murder conviction overturned.

I stood on the appeal steps, amid the commotion and watched as Emma, tiny and frail but with a megawatt smile, walked tentatively out into the sunshine. Her life was so unlike mine, a childhood filled with fear and abuse, an adulthood in jail. Yet here she was not only walking free and making international headlines but having achieved a change in the law around provocation.

It is people like Emma who inspire me.

What responsibilities did you think are on you when you tell the story of a person's tragedy?

Tragic stories can run and run with inquests, court cases, appeals, inquiries, anniversaries and many other forms of follow ups to cover.

Extraordinary to me has been witnessing people's resilience as they navigate the early stages of a traumatic death; the strength they then find to keep going through the morass of after-shocks; the determination to find something good out of something dreadful; and the drive to stop anyone else having to go through something similar.

The families whose stories I have followed have consistently welcomed our cameras into their homes, sometimes shifting furniture, sifting through the attic for mementoes, taking us to gravesides and adapting to our strange broadcasting requests with incredible grace.

I worked closely with three police widows, each of their husbands had been killed on duty. They were a similar age to me with similar-aged children. I empathized so strongly with their loss and pain, it was a struggle at times to work with them.

Again, the sense of responsibility was enormous as I sat, faced with raw grief and the weighty trust that I would tell their story well. I was initially interviewing and filming with them for court backgrounders to run on the day of the verdicts.

I felt I owed it to them to involve them as much as I could and was permitted to bring them in to the edit suite to show them the pieces before they were transmitted. My relief that they loved the backgrounders was immense.

I went on to cover several follow up stories over the next ten years or so. We never filmed with their children, so it was a surprise one day to get a text from one of their daughters. Now 18, she was doing a skydive for a charity to help police families whose mums or dads had been killed on duty, could we cover it? Of course we could.

What led you to write your book?

Among the most harrowing deaths to cover are those of a child. The pain of a parent is ever palpable.

Faith's teenage son Joshua was cycling to school when he was hit by a car. He died 11 days later in intensive car, his mum at his bedside.

Faith is private and unassuming; her grief for Josh is towering; working with journalists was the last thing she would wish to do. But Josh loved BMX biking and Faith chose to build the skate park of his dreams. To raise funds, she needed publicity, to go public she had to speak to reporters about her loss.

It was around this time that I was beginning to think reporters should have training in how best to work with interviewees like Faith. She and I worked together on a couple of pieces and I asked her what sorts of things upset or helped her when working with journalists.

She shared her distress when they turned up having done no research, not knowing Josh's name or age or much about what had happened: the need for her to have some idea of the questions they'd ask; of what they needed from her and why.

She told me how important it was to give her time to process requests because her mind was in turmoil, to allow breaks, to recognize how exhausting it was for her to talk about Josh and to be filmed at the skate park.

She stressed the importance of acknowledgement "the simple sorry that makes it so much easier for me to move forward with the report you are doing," she told me.

Faith is now part of your trauma reporting training sessions, tell us about that

Together with other bereaved parents, survivors of sexual abuse and trauma, Faith agreed to be filmed for my trauma reporting training sessions, offering insight to journalists.

"Being part of your training," she told me, "I feel Josh's life wasn't totally wasted. It helps me to push through the grieving knowing others are benefitting from my loss and trauma."

The sessions teach good practice when working with victims, survivors and interviewees who are vulnerable. Their success led to me writing *Trauma Reporting, A journalist's guide to covering sensitive stories* filled with testimony from families and news correspondents.

It is the culmination of years of following people's tough emotional stories, something journalists do endlessly. As a broadcaster the temptation once your piece has aired is to let it go. It vanishes into the airwaves and often from your mind. But with these pieces and these people who have suffered death and trauma, they tend to live with you. I can remember all of mine.

Ethical workout

- What would be your initial thoughts if you were asked by an editor to contact a bereaved family?
- What do you think should be your priorities when interviewing bereaved relatives?
- How do you feel about taking content from a dead person's social media account?
- Analyse coverage of some recent murder cases and see how many of Works and Wong's themes apply to them. Do those cases that get intense coverage fit more of the themes or less?

Five takeaways from this chapter

- Journalists should weigh up the need for the public to have information against the potential harm to those involved in the story. They need to strike a balance.
- They should treat those involved in the stories with compassion and respect, avoiding sensationalism or pandering to lurid curiosity.
- Journalists need to do their groundwork before interviewing grieving relatives and friends. They need to research basic facts about the deceased, be accurate regarding personal information, and give interviewees time to tell their story. They should also ask permission to use social media images. Failure to do so can distress bereaved family and friends, causing them unnecessary harm.
- They should be aware of the ripple effect from road crashes and not consider them isolated incidents that only affect one family, but should place them in context of wider societal issues. They should not refer to them as road "accidents".
- Journalists should be careful about how they frame victims of violent crime and perpetrators, how they present the facts of killing and how their coverage could be perceived by those close to the deceased or injured.

Ethics toolbox

- Duncan, Sallyanne and Newton, Jackie (2017) *Reporting Bad News: Negotiating the boundaries between intrusion and fair representation in media coverage of death*. New York: Peter Lang.
- Healey, Jo (2020) *Trauma Reporting: A journalist's guide to covering sensitive stories*. Abingdon: Routledge. See also her website, Trauma Reporting, at https://traumareporting.com

- Various guidance from the Dart Center for Journalism and Trauma including *Resources for journalists coping with trauma*; *Tips for interviewing victims of tragedy, witnesses and survivors*; *Aftermath and anniversaries*; *Disasters*; *Homicide and mass shooting* and *Sexual violence*. More details at https://dartcenter.org
- Media guidelines for reporting road collisions. Active Travel Academy/ University of Westminster. Available at www.rc-rg.com/guidelines
- Good section on crime reporting in this report from the Council for Europe, *Guidelines for Safeguarding Privacy in the Media*. Available at www.coe.int/en/web/freedom-expression/-/guidelines-on-safeguarding-privacy-in-the-med-1
- The International Center for Journalists, a global network, has numerous resources to help journalists report on COVID-19 accurately and ethically. See *Covering COVID-19: Resources for journalists*, available at www.icfj.org/our-work/covering-covid-19-resources-journalists
- Journalists should also look after their own mental health and well-being as reporting death and trauma can have an adverse emotional effect on them. This website, https://headlines-network.com/, run by Hannah Storm and John Crowley, offers support and advice.

References

Backholm, K. and Bjorkqvist, K. (2012) "The mediating effect of depression between exposure to potentially traumatic events and PTSD in news journalists". *European Journal of Psychotraumatology*, 3(1). https://doi.org/10.3402/ejpt.v3i0.18388

BBC. (2008) "Papers paying damages to McCanns". *BBC News*, 19 March. Available at: http://news.bbc.co.uk/1/hi/uk/7303801.stm (Accessed: 3 May 2021).

BBC. (2021) "How many violent attacks and sexual assaults on women are there?" *BBC News*, 24 September. Available at: www.bbc.co.uk/news/explainers-56365412 (Accessed: 20 October 2021).

Chermak, S.M. (1994) "Body count news: How crime is presented in the news media". *Justice Quarterly*, 11(4), pp. 561–582. https://doi.org/10.1080/07418829400092431

Department of Transport. (2020) "Reported Road Casualties Great Britain: 2019 Annual Report". *Department of Transport*, 30 September. Available at: www.gov.uk/government/statistics/reported-road-casualties-great-britain-annual-report-2019 (Accessed: 26 June 2021).

Dix, P., Eyre, A. and Rees, G. (2016) "Looking back on disaster". 21 October. Available at: https://dartcenter.org/resources/looking=back-disaster (Accessed: 6 May 2021)

Don't Name Them. (n.d.) "The reasons". Available at: www.dontnamethem.org/ (Accessed: 27 October 2021).

Duncan, S. and Newton, J. (2017) *Reporting Bad News: Negotiating the boundaries between intrusion and fair representation in media coverage of death*. New York: Peter Lang.

Dunn Johnson, T. (2019) "Please read this before you post another RIP on social media". *Good*, 5 July. Available at: www.good.is/articles/social-media-rip (Accessed: 6 May 2021).

Duwe, G. (2000) "Body-count journalism: The presentation of mass murder in the news media". *Homicide Studies*, 4(4), pp. 364–399. https://doi.org/10.1177/1088767900004004004

Dworznik, G. and Garvey, A. (2018) "Are we teaching trauma? A survey of accredited journalism schools in the United States". *Journalism Practice*. doi: 10.1080/17512786.2018.1423630

Editors' Codebook. (2021) "Editors' Codebook, The handbook to the Editors' Code of Practice". Available at: www.editorscode.org.uk/downloads/codebook/Codebook-2021.pdf (Accessed: 5 May 2021).

Gibson, M. (2015) "Automatic and automated mourning: Messengers of death and messages from the dead". *Continuum*, 29(3), pp. 339–353. https://doi.org/10.1080/10304312.2015.1025369

Greensmith, G. (2019) "Reporting mass shootings", in Luce, A. (ed.) *Ethical reporting of sensitive issues*. Abingdon: Routledge, pp. 97–114.

Grundlingh, L. (2017) "Identifying markers of sensationalism in online news reports on crime", *Language Matters*, 48(2), pp.117–136, doi: 10.1080/10228195.2017.1341543

Hart, L. and Hart, R. (2019) "Our 'nice guy' father murdered our mother and sister yet the media focused on his suicide". *Independent.ie*., 29 April. Available at: www.independent.ie/irish-news/our-nice-guy-father-murdered-our-mother-and-sister-yet-the-media-focused-on-his-suicide-38058754.html (Accessed: 26 October 2021).

Healey, J. (2020) *Trauma reporting: A journalist's guide to covering sensitive stories*. Abingdon: Routledge.

IPSO. (2019) "05601–19 Sultan bin Muhammad Al Qasimi and the Al Qasimi family v Mail Online". Available at: www.ipso.co.uk/rulings-and-resolution-statements/ruling/?id=05601-19 (Accessed: 5 May 2021).

IPSO. (2020) "Social media guidance". Available at: www.ipso.co.uk/member-publishers/guidance-for-journalists-and-editors/social-media-guidance/ (Accessed: 5 May 2021).

Keeble, R.L. (2009) *Ethics for journalists*. 2nd ed. Abingdon: Routledge.

Laker, L. (2021) "Media guidelines for reporting road collisions". *Active Travel Academy/University of Westminster*. Available at: www.rc-rg.com/guidelines (Accessed: 26 June 2021).

McCann, J. (2021) "Why was Wayne Couzins known as 'the rapist'? Origins of the nickname of Sarah Everard's killer explained". *Inews*, 3 October. Available at: https://inews.co.uk/news/uk/wayne-couzens-the-rapist-nickname-why-known-as-sarah-everard-killer-explained-1227129 (Accessed: 27 October 2021).

Mencher, M. (2003) *News reporting and writing*. 9th ed. New York: McGraw-Hill.

New Zealand Media Council. (2021) "Three complaints against stuff". April 2021. Available at: www.mediacouncil.org.nz/rulings/three-complaints-against-stuff (Accessed: 5 May 2021).

Pearson, M. (2013) "10 tips for covering funerals". *J-Source, The Canadian Journalism Project*. Available at: https://j-source.ca/10-tips-for-covering-funerals/ (Accessed: 7 May 2021).

Robinson, J. (2011) "Leveson Inquiry: McCanns deliver damning two-hour testimony". *The Guardian*, 23 November. Available at www.theguardian.com/media/2011/nov/23/leveson-inquiry-mccann-testimony-tabloids (Accessed: 3 May 2021).

Scottish Sun journalist. (2017) Face-to-face interview with the author. 4 May.

Tobbit, C. (2021) "New crash guidelines urge journalists to avoid 'accident' and refer to drivers rather than vehicles". *Press Gazette*, 19 May. Available at: www.pressgazette.co.uk/road-collision-reporting-guidelines-finalised/ (Accessed: 26 June 2021).

Turvill, W. (2013) "PCC: Scottish Sun photographs from funeral of Sir Chris Hoy's uncle 'intrusive'". *Press Gazette*, 23 April. Available at: www.pressgazette.co.uk/pcc-scottish-sun-photographs-funeral-sir-chris-hoys-uncle-intrusive/ (Accessed: 7 May 2021).

Women's Aid. (2021) "What is coercive control?". Available at: www.womensaid.org.uk/information-support/what-is-domestic-abuse/coercive-control/ (Accessed: 27 October 2021).

Works, W. and Wong, J.S. (2020) "Using crime news reporting themes to predict image inclusion in newspaper homicide articles", *Journalism Studies*, 21:4, 425–442, doi: 10.1080/1461670X.2019.1670719

World Health Organization. (2018). "Global status report on road safety 2018". Available at: www.who.int/violence_injury_prevention/road_safety_status/2018/en/ (Accessed: 26 June 2021).

World Health Organization. (2021). "Road traffic injuries". Available at: www.who.int/news-room/fact-sheets/detail/road-traffic-injuries (Accessed: 26 June 2021).

7
Reporting suicide responsibly
A force for good

Sallyanne Duncan

The question of suicide lies at the heart of the human predicament—drawing in a vast range of philosophical, ethical, social and cultural issues. The media bear an enormous responsibility to cover the fundamental issues surrounding suicide with appropriate sensitivity as coverage could cause deep distress to close family and friends (Keeble, 2009). A significant amount of suicide coverage globally contains shocking, graphic depictions about deaths involving celebrities, unusual methods or ordinary citizens who become newsworthy because of the circumstances of their death. Yet, media reporting of suicide can be a force for good, if it is reported responsibly. This chapter examines the ethical concerns raised by media coverage of suicide and explains the Responsible Suicide Reporting (RSR) model, a tool that hard-pressed journalists can use to ethically report suicide whilst under pressure of deadline. Using this model as a foundation, the chapter explores balancing accurate, truthful reporting with minimizing harm to vulnerable people; concerns about descriptions of method and location; copycat suicides and contagion; avoiding stigma; speculation, blame and simplistic reasons for suicide and the necessity of using helplines. The chapter ends with a poignant, personal story from Gordon Allan, who was suddenly thrust into the media spotlight when his wife Sally went missing and later died by suicide.

What are the important factors to consider when reporting suicide responsibly?

There are many ethical pitfalls for journalists when they report on suicide. Get it wrong and there are potentially damaging consequences. Principally, journalists need to think about minimizing harm in order to protect those who may be vulnerable to suicidal thoughts (see the section on *Have I minimized harm?* below). A total of 6,773 people killed themselves in the UK in 2019, with around 75% being men. (ONS, 2020; NRS, 2020; NIRSA, 2020). Every

DOI: 10.4324/9780429505386-8

40 seconds somewhere in the world a person takes their own life and for every individual who dies, at least 20 more will attempt to kill themselves (WHO, 2017b). Also, researchers estimate that for every one person who dies by suicide around 135 people are significantly impacted by that death (Cerel et al., 2018). In the UK alone, using the 2019 figure, that is 914,355 people. Given the magnitude and effect that deaths by suicide have there is a definite public interest justification for covering them, but only if it is done responsibly. Englehardt and Barney observe (2002, p. 84):

> Reporters and editors, while fully aware of the anguish they will cause with the publication of such information, need to identify the greater goods that may result from such publication, that is, identify the benefits that may more than offset the harm. The basic good, of course, is that to gather and distribute information is good—the journalist's basic function.

Missing persons

Suicide stories can be messy and complex. Some start with the death itself and the discovery of a body, where the focus is on who died, what happened and how they died. Others, however, enter the news agenda as a plea to help find a missing person. For these stories the emphasis shifts to the search, the hope of finding the person safe and sound, and of solving a mystery. Most media, particularly local news outlets, enlist the help of the community in the search. Here, the media are fulfilling Englehardt and Barney's comment about the journalist's basic function to gather and distribute information, and the public interest in them doing so is extremely high. Pleas to find a missing mother, daughter, father, son, brother or sister can generate huge amounts of interest from the public, who invest emotionally in the story. The benefits are greater goods including the public reporting sightings or providing information; media coverage keeping the search at the forefront of people's minds; the family being comforted by taking action to find their loved one, and the potential for the missing person to see a news story and choosing to make contact. However, relatives need to consider the downside of involving the media in their search, although responsible journalists can do much to mitigate these. The family can quickly lose control of their interaction with the media and coverage can seem overwhelming, intrusive and frightening. Telling their story to numerous news outlets can be emotional with no guarantee that their story will be used or that it will be covered in a way that they wanted (Missing People, 2021). Here, a journalist should act responsibly by giving a family more control over their story and what happens to it, by explaining the news process, the news outlet's approach and by being honest and compassionate with them.

There are other complications for the missing person too. When reporting these stories journalists should also be aware that a missing person may not want to be found and news coverage might make it more difficult for them to return home (Missing People, 2021). It is challenging for journalists to address these issues whilst reporting a missing person story but if they wish to act responsibly in this regard they could take care over their use of language and the tone within the story, as well as including a helpline like Samaritans or Missing People in a prominent position.

In many respects news outlets are performing a proactive and positive act through their storytelling when covering the search for a missing person, if the reporting is done responsibly and ethically. But when a suicide or attempted suicide occurs the challenges facing journalists are heightened and complicated. Having supported a traumatised family through the search for their loved one through their storytelling, journalists now need to refocus to satisfy their audience's desire to know what happened to the missing person: how did they die. But they need to do this with care as they balance the public's right to be informed with respecting the family's wishes. At this point the family have lost hope, are experiencing the raw edges of bereavement and may wish to step back from contact with the very journalists whose reports had assisted with the search. Here, journalists should be conscious of avoiding potential harm to the newly bereaved family and friends or to other vulnerable people who may be influenced by the story. Responsible media reporting of the suicide can however help families to tell their story, particularly if there is speculation and misguided attempts to assign blame on social media. The greater the missing person story was in the media, the greater the need for responsible journalists to work with the family to complete the story to correct unhelpful and potentially damaging speculative posts on social media. It is important for news outlets to fulfill their public service role of informing their audiences about events in their communities but it is also vital that vulnerable people are protected from harm. And while missing persons and suicides make powerful human interest stories they should always be told responsibly, with humanity, dignity and empathy.

The media's positive role in working with the bereaved

News outlets that choose to report responsibly can make a constructive contribution to public understanding of suicide by telling the stories of those who have lived through it. They can help those bereaved by suicide to raise awareness, promote self-care and point to sources of help for vulnerable people. Through relating the personal stories of those with lived experience the media can play a positive role in helping to end the stigma around suicide. In doing so they perform their public service role of contributing to and framing discussions about issues of shared concern. Accountability through public service reporting means that news outlets can raise awareness of suicide as a serious public health issue, and in doing so can support people who have been bereaved by suicide to break through the silence often associated with these deaths. Families who have lost a loved one can be passionate about trying to prevent suicide, so other families don't have to suffer the pain and loss they have felt. Helping to prevent suicide can give individuals a positive focus to help them recover and process their grief. Reporting the stories of those with lived experience fulfills an important civic aim of informing people to encourage them to take action and make changes over issues of common concern, no matter how small. By enabling people who have been bereaved by suicide to tell their own stories of trauma and loss in their own way, the media assist in breaking down barriers to people seeking help or to understanding. They show through the storytelling of those with lived experience that suicide can touch us all. Gordon Allan, who lost his wife to suicide, says:

> Audiences engage with people and from my experience they connect, listen and learn more intensely when they know the story and lessons learned are based on your own lived experience. Telling my story to try and help and inform others has also been important in helping me to move forward and recover.

Therefore, reporters should consider contacting people who have been bereaved by suicide and are keen to use their experience to raise awareness and prevent further suicides. Reporters should take time to listen, empathise and build trust with those who want to use their lived experience to help others, rather than shy away from them because they fear they might upset them by asking questions. In doing so, a greater good is served.

Working under pressure

Making decisions about what to report and what to leave out is often done under pressure and whilst there are many useful guidelines to help news teams navigate this difficult terrain journalists seldom have the time to consult them when on deadline. Duncan and Luce (2020) devised the Responsible Suicide Reporting (RSR) model to combat this problem by creating a means for journalists to make sound ethical decisions based on the guidelines' advice as they reported their stories. In doing so journalists are testing their stories for key ethical principles, as well as balancing being truthful, independent and fair, alongside minimizing harm.

Journalists should recognise they are accountable to those affected by their coverage, including their sources and their audience. Avoiding stereotypes, harmful content and stigmatising narratives are urgent factors to consider in all stories. The people who could be hurt are a segment of their audience, which is far from homogenous.

Duncan and Luce, 2020

What is the Responsible Suicide Reporting (RSR) model? How does it work?

The RSR model is a practical tool that mirrors the news process and has storytelling at its heart. Journalists can habitually use it while reporting a suicide story without having to recollect or search online for external media reporting guidance when they are under pressure. They can do this safe in the knowledge that their coverage will be responsible, i.e. in line with suicide reporting guidelines, relevant sections of ethical codes and journalism regulators' advice.

There are three parts to the model that encourage journalists to act reflectively as they tell the story of a suicide. These are: determining the type of suicide story; following simple rules, and importantly, reflecting on whether their reporting is responsible using six guiding questions.

Part one is a familiar first step for reporters: settling on the type of story they are producing, and this is usually determined by where the incident occurs within the news cycle. Stories generally fall into five categories that journalists routinely use when covering death, each requiring slightly different considerations regarding suicide. These are:

- Events: what has happened, when and where. Here, journalists should be vigilant as to whether their description of the method and location is too graphic, whether the word suicide should go in the headline, subheading or the intro or lead. They should also think carefully about the effect that frequently using suicide in the text has on search ability and web analytics.
- Tributes: who has it happened to, what was the person it happened to like. These focus on a grieving family who pay tribute to their loved one and here reporters should be sensitive to the language they use regarding the method and circumstances of the death. They should aim to be compassionate, empathetic and honest in their approaches.
- Inquests, court cases, public inquiries: how has this happened, why has it happened, who is to blame. Care must be taken here regarding journalists' judgements about explicit details presented as evidence. Including too much

can result in gratuitous, sensational and stigmatising coverage so journalists need to balance accurate, full disclosure with potentially harmful content.
- Anniversaries: those that mark time passing from when the suicide happened. Like tribute stories, here journalists should be compassionate, empathetic and honest in their approaches but should also be conscious of the potential harm resulting from revisiting the circumstances of the death, alongside telling the story of how the bereaved are coping.
- Action as memorials: these look to the future, where loved ones are preserving the memory of the person who died through some constructive action. Although this is a more positive narrative where the circumstances of the death are less prominent, journalists should be aware that bereaved survivors may still be grieving.

Having taken that routine step of determining the type of story to be produced, journalists, during the reporting of the story, now consider four simple ethical rules to assess whether their article harms anyone. While creating content they can apply the rules of do not sensationalise; do not stigmatise; do not glorify and do not gratuitously report. If they do this then they will be acting responsibly.

In the final part of the model, reporters test their stories for ethical compliance by asking themselves six questions while they produce their content. These are:

- Have I minimized harm to those affected by suicide?
- Have I told the truth yet avoided explicit details of method and location?
- Have I taken care in producing the story, including tone and language?
- Have I used social media responsibly?
- Have I avoided stereotypes, harmful content and stigmatising stories?
- Have I provided support via helplines?

If they answer yes to each one then they have written an ethical suicide story and can be confident that it complies with guideline advice. If they answer no to any question then they need to rethink what they have written.

So let's look at each of the six questions in turn.

Have I minimized harm to those affected by suicide?

To answer this question journalists and editors should think about who could be harmed by what they report and how they report it. Here, the concern is the *effect* of their reporting. So identifying who is at risk is the first step. Two groups dominate: those who have been bereaved by suicide and those who may have suicidal thoughts. Sometimes these two groups are the same people so reporters should take great care when interviewing friends and family who have been bereaved by suicide. They should be compassionate, empathetic and honest in their approaches and be alert to the effect that their questions might have on their interviewees. They should also be truthful in what they report, stick to the facts and not speculate about reasons why a person took their own life. Not all teenagers who die by suicide were bullied at school.

Journalists who choose not to interview bereaved family and friends can remain detached or distant in their coverage by reporting a suicide as if it was any other news item, which it is not, and this apparent "impartiality" can seem callous to bereaved families and friends, especially if unverified information is published as fact. Instead, journalists could consider "walking in the shoes" of the vulnerable people at the centre of their stories and think about how those who are bereaved might feel when, without the forewarning gained from participating in an interview, they come across the content of their lived one's suicide, even years later.

As noted earlier, when the media cover suicide irresponsibly by sensationalising, stigmatising, glorifying or gratuitously reporting, they run the risk of harming vulnerable people who may be susceptible to suicidal ideation. The effect can be a single attempt or death or it can ripple out amongst specific communities, resulting in copycat suicides or contagion. A copycat suicide is when a person at risk imitates another suicide as a result of knowing about the original death by some means such as local knowledge, social media, fictional depictions or news coverage. (It is also known as the Werther effect after Goethe's 1774 novel, *The Sorrows of Young Werther*, which was believed to have triggered a series of suicides across Europe.) Suicide contagion, direct or indirect exposure to suicide or suicide behaviours, can precede an increase in suicidal behaviour in vulnerable people, particularly adolescents and young adults. Suicide prevention charities Papyrus and Samaritans caution news outlets to take extra care when reporting on young people. They warn against portraying the deceased as heroic or using emotive, romanticised language. Using large photographs of the deceased, especially pretty, young women, can also romanticise a suicide and lead to it going viral on social media. Repeated use of photographs, including galleries, can be triggering for vulnerable young people. Instead, Papyrus and Samaritans recommend straightforward reporting that provides context on the wider issues of suicide and that emphasises suicide as a public health issue that is preventable (Samaritans, 2020a; Papyrus, 2021). Those who identify with a person who has taken their own life, perhaps because they are the same gender or ethnicity, are more at risk of suicide (Fekete and Macsai, 1990; Stack, 1991). Celebrity suicides can also trigger imitative attempts, particularly if coverage is splashed across newspaper front pages and their online sites. This extensive, prolonged exposure can have an effect on non-celebrity stories too, if they receive enough publicity.

Numerous researchers identify a correlation between media reporting of suicide and vulnerable people's susceptibility to repeat the action by taking their own lives (Phillips, 1974; Wasserman, 1984; Gould and Davidson, 1988; Velting and Gould, 1997; Pirkis and Blood, 2001; Stack 2003, 2005; Pirkis et al., 2006, 2007). Others note an increase in the rate of suicide when news coverage is extensive, prominent, sensational, lengthy or explicitly describes the method, especially when it is unusual, or when there is intensive coverage across news publications and TV, and if they were completed suicides (Hawton et al., 1999; Gould, 2001; Pirkis et al., 2006). However, this research does not mean that media reporting of suicide *causes* vulnerable people to take their own lives, as some scholars have observed (Cross, 2007; Luce, 2019), but it does indicate a connection between the two and therefore journalists should take great care. Cross explains that the only person people who can confirm whether media depictions of suicide have influenced their decision to kill themselves is dead. He states:

> This simple but decisive point pulls the rug from under the common sense view that some suicides must be copycats because they have chosen to kill themselves in a manner akin to someone whose suicide has been reported. However, correlation does not equal causality i.e. because events occur in near time does not mean that one causes the other. To surmise that a depiction of suicide influenced someone to take their own life obfuscates the myriad psychological and social complexities engulfing individuals, and which contribute to their decision to end their life.
>
> *2007, p. 20*

The media, however, can have a positive influence. The US Department of Health and Human Services advises that the risk of suicide contagion stemming from media reporting can be minimized by "factual and concise media reports of suicide" rather than repetitive, prolonged exposure that "can increase the likelihood of suicide contagion" (US Dept of Health and Human Services, 2019).

Have I told the truth yet avoided explicit details of method and location?

Normally when journalists cover a story they are expected to include as much detail as possible, not only to inform their audience but as evidence that their reporting is truthful. Providing detailed factual information is one of the functions of ethical journalism but too much detail when reporting suicide can be immensely harmful or life-threatening, even if it is truthful and accurate. Media guidelines throughout the world, such as those from WHO (World Health Organisation, 2017a), National Union of Journalists (2014), Samaritans (2020b), Mindframe in Australia (2020) and the American Association of Suicidology (2020), warn that explicit descriptions of the suicide method should be avoided to prevent copycat suicides or contagion. When journalists include explicit depictions in their stories they provide a "roadmap" of how someone who may be susceptible to suicide can take their own life.

Where possible it is better for news outlets to decide not to refer to the method at all, but instead to record the death as a suicide. However, some editors may wish to give their audiences a more precise explanation of what has occurred in their communities in order to be accurate and to quell any rumours. Here, the method can be mentioned in general terms, such as a person died by hanging, rather than explicit information about the type of ligature and how the death was achieved. The death of actor Robin Williams is a classic example of how not to report the method. The circumstances of his death were revealed by the US police in a press conference and many news outlets globally chose to splash them across their front pages and at the top of their bulletins. A minority took a more responsible approach by refusing to publish or broadcast the specific details of the method. Similarly, when a person dies from an overdose the type of drugs and the number taken should not be included in the article. Or when someone dies by drowning the story should not contain the specific place that it occurred, the height of the bridge or cliff, the depth of the water or the currents at the time of the incident, amongst other information. Journalists should also be particularly cautious when reporting an unusual method, which goes against standard journalism practice as reporters are taught to seek out novelty or surprise, but research has shown that there can be an increase in suicides when the media report unusual methods. Additionally, care should be taken with the location. Ongoing coverage at a certain location can lead to the place becoming a shrine or a likely place for others to take their own lives. This is a tricky issue, however, because sometimes the location is fundamental to the story and here news outlets should take care to consider their earlier reporting within the context of the current story.

Most suicide stories in England and Wales are sourced by news outlets from Coroners' inquests, a formal inquiry into a death, and research by Duncan and Luce (2020) found that 41% of these stories contained explicit details of the method and circumstances of the death that had been disclosed during the inquest as part of the judicial process. Families are often dismayed by this coverage, seeing it as disrespectful and an intrusion into their grief and shock. However, some news outlets argue that it is important for them to include this level of detail in order to give an accurate summary of the inquest. Judgements need to be exercised here about how much and what type of content to include in a story, regardless of it having been stated in a public court room. If the media are to report suicide responsibly in the public interest then news organisations and journalists need to find a balance between these two positions.

Have I taken care in producing the story, including tone and language?

Tone and language are really important in media reporting of suicide. The use of words, whether oral or written, can cause significant damage to those affected by a suicide death and can result in wanton stigmatisation. Guidelines emphasise that journalists should avoid the phrase "committed suicide" as it reduces a person to a type of death and has criminal overtones. Suicide is not a crime in the UK, although it is illegal in 25 countries throughout the world with an additional 20 countries following Islamic or Sharia law where those who attempt suicide may be punished with jail sentences (Mishara and Weisstub, 2016). Instead, guidelines recommend using alternative phrases like "died by suicide" or "ended their own life". In addition to these two terms, suicide prevention organisations suggest news outlets use language like "took their own life", or the rarer "completed suicide" rather than describing a suicide as "successful" if someone dies or "unsuccessful", "failed" or a "suicide bid" if someone does not die. The aim is to use more neutral language that avoids judgements about criminality and accomplishment.

Samaritans (2020a, 2020b) also warns journalists to avoid implying that someone died instantly, that their death was quick, uncomplicated, painless or an escape route. Also, phrases like "suicide epidemic" when several suicides occur can be alarmist, particularly when included in a headline, and implies that suicide spreads like a disease. Equally, mental health charities recommend avoiding the language of diagnosis to describe political unrest, such as the unnecessary use of "suicide" in terms like "political suicide" (Chakalain, 2019).

Where words are placed in the story can also be damaging. Putting "suicide" in a headline or in the top line of a bulletin is believed to increase the probability of copycat suicides and contagion because of the prominence it has been given. Imagine seeing the news stand at a supermarket after a celebrity death by suicide like Avicii, Robin Williams or Caroline Flack, where each newspaper headline contains the word suicide or names the method. Research suggests that including "suicide" in the headline can increase the appeal of the story to vulnerable people by glamorising or normalising suicide (Duncan and Newton, 2017). Instead, those deaths that are likely to have a great impact on audiences and communities should be described in direct, impartial language with straightforward headlines, as research shows that sensationalist headlines can lead to an increase in suicides.

Tone is also important and journalists should be wary of adopting a superior tone that suggests the person who has taken their life is to blame for their actions, that their death was "self-inflicted", that they were weak or that their suicide provided a solution to their personal problems. Therefore, reporters should avoid stigmatising phrases such as "suicide victim", "a cry for help" or describing the deceased as a "suicide-prone person". Equally, sensationalist or sentimental language can result in a dramatic tone akin to fictional accounts of suicide that distances the actual death from reality.

Have I used social media responsibly?

Being active on social media is now a core part of a journalist's work. Some of the practices that are acceptable for other news stories might not work for suicide reporting, however. Again, if the media are to minimize harm to those who are affected by their reporting then they need to pay attention to certain advice on social media use when covering suicides. News alerts and push notifications, standard practice on general news, are not recommended for suicide stories because of their immediacy, unexpectedness and concise messaging of breaking events. Samaritans also suggest closing comment sections on suicide stories in order to avoid offensive, harmful remarks about the death (2020a, 2020b).

Guidance on the Suicide Reporting Toolkit (2020) recommends paying particular attention to using a deceased person's posts; including them in news articles can glamorise or glorify suicide. Posts from the deceased should not be used unless the journalist or news outlet has explicit permission from the family because the reporter does not know the context in which they were posted, or the deceased's state of mind when they did so. In particular, suicide notes left on social media accounts should not be published because of their potential influence on others. However, media coverage increasingly contains suicide notes, sometimes with the consent of the family, despite major guidelines stating that this is highly dangerous to vulnerable people. Samaritans state that including suicide notes or last messages can increase the possibility of people identifying with the deceased, and if a news outlet publishes these messages without informing relatives it can cause distress to family and friends.

Regarding online memorial sites, reporters should take care when using any material from these sites because those who post on them are grieving and vulnerable. Remember, for every person who dies by suicide, at least 20 more will attempt to kill themselves (WHO, 2017b). Again, journalists who use content from memorial sites should ensure that they have explicit consent from the person responsible for posting the information. Seeing this personal content included in a news story without their knowledge or consent when it was only intended as a mark of respect or expression of their loss can be extremely painful for those bereaved by suicide. Therefore, news outlets and journalists have a responsibility to ensure that they do not cause unnecessary anxiety or harm to those who have been bereaved by suicide.

Have I avoided stereotypes, harmful content and stigmatising stories?

It is important that journalists think about how they tell stories about suicide and the messages that they convey through their reporting. The way they describe a suicide—or frame it—can result in stigmatising stories that can negatively affect people who may identify with the deceased. Mental illness, despair, isolation and bullying are common frames within suicide stories but they tend to be dealt with superficially and stereotypically, which can lead to stigmatisation. Duncan and Luce (2020) found that in inquest stories journalists present stigmatising narratives around morality, mental illness and infantilising the act itself, by for example describing the deceased's youthfulness or nonconformity. Yet, people who take their own lives don't fit into a "type" for suicide, and not all those who attempt suicide or die by suicide have mental health issues at the time of their death. Some might be undiagnosed or rather than mental ill-health they might be experiencing circumstances in their lives that result in feelings of desperation or hopelessness, which are more accurate predictors of suicide (National Union of Journalists, 2014).

Answering the *why* question is important for journalists in order to provide context and explanation, and these are central to suicide coverage too, but unless the deceased has left a message stating clearly why they took their own life, journalists cannot provide undisputed facts of why someone died by suicide. Therefore, speculating on the reason why someone took their own life oversimplifies the factors leading up to the death. There is never one simple explanation as to why someone kills themselves and journalists should avoid distilling the information available to them down into a single cause, which may be speculation anyway. Looking for an answer to the why question defines the deceased by the circumstances of their death, and not as a complete person with a life before they died, which is stigmatising.

Stigmatised reporting can occur through labelling, stereotyping and separating. Labelling is where someone is defined by their mental health condition or vulnerability, rather than seeing the person. Stereotyping defines a person by recognised undesirable characteristics, either in the minds of other people or in their own minds. Separating is where journalists present an "us and them" frame where those who take their own lives, or attempt suicide, are seen as "them", outsiders or abnormal, leading to perceived differences and inferiorities. Olson (no date) states that those who have attempted suicide or know someone who has died by suicide suffer tangible psychological scars from the hurt and shame of the act. He adds: "Misunderstanding, ignorance, and fear are at the root of stigmatisation, and these factors have inflicted immense suffering on those who are in any way perceived as 'not normal'." These myths can be perpetuated in media reporting, particularly when reporting celebrity suicides, leading to sensationalist coverage and contributing to the persistence of stigma. Examples are framing those who take their own lives as "cowards" or "selfish", or portraying people who attempt suicide as "attention seekers". The actual words may not be used but the message of worthlessness can be perceived through a derogatory tone inferred from the choice of language, images, quotes and story angle. Additionally, suggesting that suicidal risk is hereditary can "sometimes serve to further torture families who experience a suicidal death" (Olson, no date). Hinting within a story that there was nothing anyone could do to prevent a person taking their own life is harmful and stigmatising for those who may identify with the deceased. In actual fact feeling suicidal is often a temporary state of mind. Most people contemplating suicide do not want to die; instead they want to end the pain they are experiencing in their lives (National Union of Journalists, 2014).

Offering narratives of hope, help and recovery instead of such harmful content could save lives. Journalists have a duty to ensure their reporting is accurate and adheres to the ethical principle of truth-telling and therefore they should thwart myths or false information with fact. They can counter stigma by emphasising suicide is preventable and where mental health issues are an acknowledged factor, that mental illness can be temporary, curable and does not define a person.

Have I provided support via helplines?

The media can play a vital role in suicide prevention by simply including a helpline with suicide stories. Yet, despite numerous guidelines recommending they do so their use by the media is inconsistent. Duncan and Luce (2020) found that 60% of news stories did not contain a helpline, and in some cases articles with helplines breached other guideline recommendations on avoiding explicit details of the method or stigmatising content. The result was that, ironically, some potentially harmful content that ignored guidance on responsible reporting included a helpline at the end. An earlier study by Pirkis et al. (2009) found that only 17.7% of suicide coverage in the Australian media during 2006–2007 contained a helpline, suggesting that 82.3% did not. Yet, the public tends to be prepared to use helplines because they are free or low cost with immediate access 24 hours a day, as well as being anonymous and confidential and therefore less stigmatising than other forms of help (Machlin et al., 2017).

How news outlets report stories can also have an effect on uptake of helplines. Machlin et al.'s study into media reports of depression and anxiety in males found use of helplines increased when stories were about hope and recovery that featured role models they could identify with. Conversely, stories that lacked hope or identifiable role models were not associated with positive change in helpline use. They concluded that news stories can have a positive impact on help-seeking amongst men but articles need to contain accurate representations of depression and anxiety (and by inference, suicide) whilst focussing on hope and recovery. This positive theme can be further developed by journalists including references to suicide being preventable and that specific organisations can aid recovery. Therefore, as well as including a helpline reporters can encourage people to seek help by emphasising the type of support available from each organisation. By doing so they could save lives. Helpline information helps prevent further suicides and signposts to an audience where they can access further support for themselves or their loved ones. There are hundreds of helplines throughout the world so a tailored approach is best. Providing a long list of support groups can be counter-productive, therefore it is best to choose one or two specific phone numbers or websites. Find a Helpline is an online resource that lists around 1,600 organisations globally that offer emotional support and is a useful tool for journalists looking for the most appropriate helplines to include in their stories (see the Ethics Toolkit at the end of this chapter for more information.)

Tell me more about the Suicide Reporting Toolkit

Duncan and Luce created the Suicide Reporting Toolkit as an online resource to advise journalists, journalism educators and students on ways to cover suicide stories while avoiding stigmatisation and putting others at risk. It has sections on method and location, language and tone, helplines, reporting bereaved people, use of statistics, using multimedia content, celebrity suicides, social media and self-care. It also provides lesson plans for educators to use in their journalism classes, as well as academic research and further resources. You can find out more here: www.suicidereportingtoolkit.com.

Ethics in action: Gordon Allan, who was bereaved by suicide

Gordon Allan lost his wife, Sally, to suicide on Boxing Day 2015. Sally took her own life due to mental health issues that she kept hidden from everyone who knew her. Since then Gordon has worked as a volunteer mental health champion. He and his family set up the Sally Allan Fund in her memory along with Tyneside and Northumberland Mind. It aims to raise awareness and understanding of mental health, self-care and stigma. Gordon also works with, or has worked with, the North East and North Cumbria Suicide

Prevention Network, the Northumberland Mental Health Promotion and Suicide Prevention Group and Talking Matters Northumberland and Active Northumberland on the Being Active Matters project.

Gordon's story below gives an insight into the impact of suicide on a family, a community and a region. The story began as a missing person story. In those situations, the family and police are keen to involve the local media in an effort to help find the person. However, having placed the story in the media brings an added responsibility for journalists to complete the story. How do they inform their audience who have become engaged with the story, whilst respecting the feeling and wishes of the bereaved family and not giving information that might harm others?

"My story starts just after 3 o'clock on Boxing Day morning 2015. That was around the time, Sally my wife of 37 years, left our family home. Myself and five other family members were fast asleep in our beds, we didn't know this was happening.

By the time we woke up, Sally was dead. Sally had taken her own life. The family knows that now, but we didn't know it then. When we woke up, Sally was missing and we didn't know why. It would take a week of searching for her before it was confirmed Sally was dead. Another five weeks before the police found her body, and another week, before Sally's body was released back to the family. Two weeks later her hearse reversed on to our drive. Finally, mum was back home. Sally's journey was over. The family and I could start to grieve.

At the inquest the Coroner gave an open verdict, 'He could not be certain "beyond reasonable doubt" that Sally intended to take her own life'.

The family disagreed; it was suicide.

Those are the facts. What is the story?

The family and I believe Sally died because she had a mental illness. A mental illness she kept hidden from myself, our three children, her friends and work colleagues. Sally never saw a doctor or a nurse about her mental health. I have spent hours and hours trying to understand why she stayed silent.

My search to understand why Sally stayed silent is one story I could tell.

I have lots of stories to tell:

> the story, when it became clear to me that Sally was dead, but I had no story and no body. I had nothing. That was the hardest time,
>
> or

the story of being a prime suspect in a police missing person investigation,

or

the story of organising the biggest search for someone missing, that Northumbria Police had ever seen,

or

the story of what it was like to be at the heart of the main regional news story, day after day after day,

or

the story of how my family received no suicide bereavement support?

So many stories.

The story I have chosen to tell is my story. A story of love and forgiveness.

My story begins with the note Sally left, it said: "I'm sorry, I just can't carry on. Please look after each other. You deserve happier times than I can give you."

The note was signed Sally, mum and ended with two kisses. There seemed to be a space left for the word love, but it wasn't written. Why had Sally not written the word love? It hurt. That missing word caused me many days of self-doubt, guilt and soul searching. I now believe Sally did love me to the very end, but I have to live with the fact I will never know the truth.

Let us explore love.

In my experience, love after death is complicated. Love before death is so much simpler. A kind thought. A loving kiss. A warm smile. It just happens and the wonderful thing is it doesn't need a lot of thought. Like magic love is just there. In your heart every minute of every day.

Loving my wife, of 37 years, after death isn't so simple. That love has to be worked at, thought about, memories kept alive, cherished and remembered. It can be hard work.

The loss of love after death, can drag you down, isolate you, hold you back, make you scared, steal your energy, drag you down with guilt and even make you doubt your own worth. Sometimes my love is like that. That love makes me hide in the shadows.

But, my love for Sally is still my greatest strength. Our love is our history; it made our family and I want to pass that love onto my children and their children. My love makes me smile, talks to me, gives me advice, holds my hand and makes me a better person. It gives me the hope and energy to build towards a better future. That love takes me forward into the light.

When people ask me, what is life like without Sally, I give this answer 'the sun doesn't sparkle for me as brightly as it once did, but I still enjoy sunny, blue-sky days'.

To keep loving Sally as I do. First, I had to forgive her, and then I had to forgive myself. Forgiveness is the way I have found peace.

These words written in a letter someone sent to me, explain how I came to forgive Sally. The person who wrote these words had attempted suicide but survived.

They explain better than I ever could.

> I knew in that very confused mental state that my family would be so much better off without me. Feelings of absolutely zero self-esteem and depression do that to a person. No matter what anyone said it wouldn't have changed my mind.
>
> So whatever else you may think, please remember two things.
>
> 1) No matter what you did or didn't say, or did or didn't do, it wouldn't have changed what was in Sally's head. That can only come from the person, when and if they are ready.
> 2) Sally didn't do what she did because she didn't love you and her family; she did it because she did love you all. Sadly, when mental illness takes hold it is easy to convince yourself that those you love will be better off without the burden of you around.

It took me six to nine months to forgive Sally and to forgive myself. Forgiveness that gave me peace and a future.

To finish my story, I will explore the power of community love.

The community love of the North East, who threw a comfort blanket of love over my family.

A community, who at the very worst moment in our lives, felt our pain, reached out and gave us their love. These are their stories:

> the story of how hundreds, gave up their Christmas holiday to go out searching for Sally,

or

the story of the tens of thousands of messages of love and support on Facebook, or the millions of tweets and retweets on Twitter,

or

the story of the community of who organised a flower ceremony in Newcastle, in memory of Sally, attended by 300 people,

or

the story of all the people who donated £40,000 and told me to end the stigma that surrounds mental health and suicide,

or,

and this is the end of my story,

the story of Sally's memorial service and the 350 people who clapped, when the vicar said "I don't know how this family just did that".

When I think of those two minutes of clapping inside the church, it still sends a shiver down my spine. That moment was a miracle. Every single clap was full of love and forgiveness but together they had the power to heal.

When the clapping stopped, whatever happened, I knew I would be okay.

That is my story."

To learn more from Gordon about Sally's story and the need to talk about suicide go to https://beta.northumbria.police.uk/latest-news/2020/september/let-s-talk-about-suicide-and-save-lives-the-heartfelt-message-from-widower-gordon-allan-this-world-suicide-prevention-day/

Ethical workout

- Should the media report suicides? What arguments can you present for and against in answer to this question?
- Take a look at media coverage of the suicide of celebrities like Robin Williams, Kurt Cobain, Caroline Flack, Kate Spade, Gary Speed or Avicii. How could they have been reported more responsibly?

- The WHO, the Office of National Statistics, the National Records of Scotland and the Northern Ireland Statistics and Research Agency, all offer a wealth of data on suicide. How could you turn this data into an engaging, informative and ethical infographic?
- Find some recent suicide stories and identify any language, tone, descriptions or frames that are stigmatising.
- How would you write a solutions-based, constructive article about suicide? What would be your idea, angle and approach?

Five takeaways from this chapter

- Applying and affirming the six questions from the RSR model will ensure that journalists' reporting of suicide is ethical.
- Suicide is preventable. Most people contemplating suicide do not want to die; instead they want to end the pain they are experiencing in their lives. The media can assist in prevention by including appropriate helplines or support links with their coverage.
- There is a correlation between media reporting of suicide and incidents of copycat suicides or contagion but that does not mean that media coverage causes someone to take their own life.
- Journalists should take great care to ensure they do not include too much explicit detail about the method or location. Providing a roadmap could suggest a means by which a vulnerable person might take their own life.
- The reasons why a person chooses to die by suicide are complex and the media should not suggest there is a single, simple explanation or speculate on possible reasons as this can be inaccurate and harmful to grieving relatives and friends.

Ethics toolkit

- Suicide Reporting Toolkit, an online resource for journalists and journalism educators that assists them in making ethical decisions about telling stories about suicide while under newsroom pressure. See www.suicidereportingtoolkit.com
- Mindframe, an Australian national programme that works collaboratively to support media and communications professionals to safely and accurately report on suicide, mental ill-health, alcohol and other drugs. For guidance on reporting suicide see: https://mindframe.org.au/suicide/communicating-about-suicide/mindframe-guidelines

- Dart Center for Journalism and Trauma, a resource and global network of journalists, journalism educators and health professionals dedicated to improving media coverage of trauma, conflict and tragedy. For guidance/resources on reporting suicide see: https://dartcenter.org/topic/suicide. For advice on self-care see: https://dartcenter.org/topic/self-care-peer-support
- National Union of Journalists (NUJ) (2014) *Responsible reporting on mental health, mental illness and death by suicide: A practical guide for journalists.* Available at: www.nuj.org.uk/resource/nuj-guidelines-for-reporting-mental-health-and-death-by-suicide.html
- Samaritans *Media guidelines and resources.* For advice on covering specific aspects of suicide such as those involving celebrities, young people, railways, murder suicide, inquests in England and Wales, and more see: www.samaritans.org/about-samaritans/media-guidelines/
- World Health Organisation (WHO) & International Association of Suicide Prevention (IASP) (2017) *Preventing suicide: A resource for media professionals.* Available at: www.who.int/mental_health/suicide-
- American Association of Suicidology (AAS) (2020) *Reporting recommendations.* Available at: https://suicidology.org/reporting-recommendations/
- Find a helpline, an online resource of more than 1,600 helplines worldwide that offer emotional support that can also be used as an accurate database for journalists. Available at: https://findahelpline.com/

References

Cerel J, Brown M.M., Maple M, et al. (2018) 'How many people are exposed to suicide? Not six'. *Suicide and Life-Threatening Behaviour*, 49(2), pp. 529–534. https://doi.org/10.1111/sltb.12450

Chakalain, A. (2019). '"Political suicide!" Our peculiar urge to describe Brexit as a mental illness'. *New Statesman*, 7 March. Available at: www.newstatesman.com/politics/uk/2019/03/political-suicide-our-peculiar-urge-describe-brexit-mental-illness (Accessed: 27 July 2021).

Cross, S. (2007) 'Why the copycat theory on suicide coverage is a conceptual red herring', *Ethical Space: The International Journal of Communication Ethics*, 4(4), pp. 19–21.

Duncan, S. and Luce, A. (2020) 'Using the Responsible Suicide Reporting Model to increase adherence to global media reporting guidelines'. *Journalism: Theory, Practice and Criticism*, pp. 1–17. https://doi.org/10.1177/1464884920952685 (Accessed: 27 July 2021).

Duncan, S. and Newton, J. (2017) *Reporting bad news: Negotiating the boundaries between intrusion and fair representation in media coverage of death*. New York: Peter Lang.

Englehardt, E. and Barney, R. (2002). *Media and ethics: Principles for moral decisions*. Belmont, CA: Wadsworth Cengage Learning.

Fekete, S. & Macsai, E. (1990) 'Hungarian suicide models, past and present'. in Ferrari, G. (ed.) *Suicidal behaviour and risk factors*. Bologna: Monduzzi Editore, pp. 149–156.

Gould, M. (2001) 'Suicide and the media', in Hendin, H. and Mann, J.J. (eds.) *Suicide prevention: Clinical and scientific aspects*. (Annals of the New York Academy of Sciences). New York: New York Academy of Sciences, pp. 200–224.

Gould, M. and Davidson, L. (1988) 'Suicide contagion among adolescents', in Stiffman, A.R. and Felman, R.A. (eds.) *Advances in adolescent mental health*. Greenwich, CT: JAI, vol. 3, pp. 29–59.

Hawton, K., Simkin, S., Deeks, J.J., O'Connor, S., Keen, A., Altman, D.G. et al. (1999) 'Effects of a drug overdose in a television drama on presentation to hospital for self-poisoning: Time series and questionnaire study'. *British Medical Journal*, 318, pp. 972–977.

Luce, A. (2019) *Ethical reporting of sensitive topics*. Abingdon: Routledge.

Machlin, A., King, K., Spittal, M. and Pirkis, J. (2017) 'Preliminary evidence for the role of newsprint media in encouraging males to make contact with helplines'. *International Journal of Mental Health Promotion*, 19(2), pp. 85–103, doi: 10.1080/14623730.2017.1307774

Mindframe (2020) Reporting suicide and mental illness: A Mindframe resource for media professionals. Available at: https://mindframe.org.au/suicide/communicating-aboutsuicide/mindframe-guidelines (Accessed: 27 July 2021).

Mishara, B.L. and Weisstub, D.N. (2016) 'The legal status of suicide: A global review'. *International Journal of Law and Psychiatry*, 44, pp. 54–74. https://doi.org/10.1016/j.ijlp.2015.08.032

Missing People. (2021) 'Deciding whether to use the media in your search'. Available at: www.missingpeople.org.uk/get-help/help-services/publicity/working-with-the-media (Accessed: 8 September 2021).

National Records of Scotland (NRS). (2020) 'Probable suicides: Deaths which are the result of intentional self-harm or events of undetermined intent'. Available at: www.nrscotland.gov.uk/statistics-and-data/statistics/statistics-by-theme/vital-events/deaths/suicides (Accessed: 27 July 2021).

National Union of Journalists (Scotland) (NUJ). (2014) 'Responsible reporting on mental health, mental illness and death by suicide'. Available at: www.nuj.org.uk/documents/nuj-guidelines-for-responsible-reporting-on-mental-health/ (Accessed: 27 July 2021).

Northern Ireland Statistics and Research Agency (NISRA). (2020) 'Suicide statistics 2019'. Available at: www.nisra.gov.uk/publications/suicide-statistics-2019 (Accessed: 27 July 2021).

Office of National Statistics (ONS). (2020) 'Suicides in England and Wales, 2019'. Available at: www.ons.gov.uk/peoplepopulationandcommunity/birthsdeathsandmarriages/deaths/bulletins/suicidesintheunitedkingdom/2019registrations (Accessed: 27 July 2021).

Olson, R. (no date) 'Suicide stigma, centre for suicide prevention'. Available at: www.suicideinfo.ca/resource/suicideandstigma/ (Accessed: 27 July 2021).

Papyrus, Prevention of Young Suicide. (2021) 'Guidelines for journalists reporting suicide'. Available at: www.papyrus-uk.org/guidelines-for-journalists-reporting-suicide/ (Accessed: 29 July 2021).

Phillips, D.P. (1974) 'The influence of suggestion on suicide: Substantive and theoretical implications of the Werther effect'. *American Sociological Review*, 39, pp. 340–354.

Pirkis, J. and Blood, R.W. (2001) 'Suicide and the media: Part I: Reportage in non-fictional media'. *Crisis*, 22(4), pp. 146–154. doi: 10.1027//0227-5910.22.4.146

Pirkis, J., Blood, R.W., Beautrais, A., Burgess, P. and Skehan, J. (2006) 'Media guidelines on the reporting of suicide'. *Crisis*, 27(2), pp. 82–87. doi: 10.1027/0227-5910.27.2.82

Pirkis, J., Burgess, P., Blood, R.W. and Francis, C. (2007) 'The newsworthiness of suicide'. *Suicide & Life-Threatening Behavior*, 37(3), pp. 278–283. doi: 10.1521/suli.2007.37.3.278.

Pirkis, J., Dare, A., Blood, R., Rankin, B., Williamson, M., Burgess, P., et al. (2009). 'Changes in media reporting of suicide in Australia between 2000/01 and 2006/07'. *Crisis*, 30(1), 25–33. doi: 10.1027/0227-5910.30.1.25

Samaritans. (2020a) '10 top tips for reporting suicide'. Available at: www.samaritans.org/scotland/about-samaritans/media-guidelines/10-top-tips-reporting-suicide/ (Accessed: 27 July 2021).

Samaritans. (2020b) 'Media guidelines for reporting suicide'. September. Samaritans. Available at: https://media.samaritans.org/documents/Media_Guidelines_FINAL.pdf (Accessed: 27 July 2021).

Stack, S. (1991). 'Social correlates of suicide by age: Media impacts', in Leenaars, A. (ed.) *Life span perspectives on suicide: Timeliness in the suicide process*. New York: Plenum, pp. 187–213.

Stack, S. (2003). 'Media coverage as a risk factor in suicide'. *Journal of Epidemiology and Community Health*, 57(4), pp. 238–240. doi: 10.1136/jech.57.4.238

Stack, S. (2005). 'Suicide in the media: A quantitative review of studies based on non-fictional stories'. *Suicide & Life-Threatening Behavior*, 35(2), pp. 121–133. doi: 10.1521/suli.35.2.121.62877

Suicide Reporting Toolkit. (2020) 'Suicide reporting toolkit for journalists'. Available at: www.suicidereportingtoolkit.com/journalists (Accessed: 25 July 2021).

US Department of Health and Human Services. (2019) 'What does "suicide contagion" mean, and what can be done to prevent it?' Available at: www.hhs.gov/answers/mental-health-and-substance-abuse/what-does-suicide-contagion-mean/index.html (Accessed: 1 August 2021).

Velting, D.M. and Gould, M. (1997) 'Suicide contagion', in Maris, R., Canetto, S. and Silverman, M.M. (eds.) *Annual review of suicidology*. New York: Guilford, pp. 96–137.

Wasserman, I.M. (1984) 'Imitation and suicide: A re-examination of the Werther effect'. *American Sociological Review*. 49(3), pp. 427–435.

World Health Organisation and International Association of Suicide Prevention. (2017a) 'Preventing suicide: A resource for media professionals'. Available at: www.who.int/mental_health/suicide-prevention/resource_booklet_2017/en/ (Accessed: 1 August 2021).

World Health Organisation. (2017b) 'Suicide data'. Available at: www.who.int/mental_health/prevention/suicide/suicideprevent/en/ (Accessed: 25 July 2021).

8
Diversity in the news
Seeking fair representation and inclusivity

Sallyanne Duncan

Diversity is a significant ethical issue for news outlets. It has a bearing on accuracy and truth-telling, minimizing harm, fairness, being accountable, respecting human dignity and inevitably, trust. Numerous minorities are under-represented in the news in the UK and worldwide, and this is reflected in some newsrooms where the number of people of colour or who are LGBTQ+ is small. This chapter explores the effects of this lack of diversity, some of the attitudes that prevail and some ways that news organisations can overcome a lack of diversity. It examines the current position regarding discrimination and perspectives on unconscious bias. Specifically, it also looks at media treatment of women, people with disabilities, LGBTQ+ communities and ethnic minorities. The chapter ends with a comprehensive discussion of the media's relationship with diversity by award-winning journalist, academic and editor-at-large of *Eastern Eye*, Barnie Choudhury. As well as offering insightful observations on mainstream media's reporting of race and on the approach of publications that have diversity at their heart, like *Eastern Eye*, Barnie provides his own diversity framework tool that enables him to produce stories of human interest based on irrefutable data that give him the chance to amplify untold experiences from diverse communities.

To what extent can the mainstream media's coverage be described as discriminatory?

In 2009 Keeble wrote:

> Many journalists are concerned to remove discrimination on grounds of gender, sexual orientation, race, disability, age, mental health and so on. At the same time there is a dominant culture which tends to regard

DOI: 10.4324/9780429505386-9

sceptically lobby groups interfering with journalistic professionalism and seeking to bend coverage to match their own biases. Such groups are often condemned as PC (political correctness) fanatics. Inevitably, in such emotionally charged contexts, argument, protest and defensiveness result—as well as lots of ideas for creative responses.

p. 174

More than a decade on from Keeble's comment, has much changed? Some would argue, not a great deal. Some news outlets may not discriminate as explicitly as previously but racism, sexism, bias and ignorance still occur in the UK media across sectors. A survey by *Press Gazette* (2021), the journalism profession's trade publication, found that 41% of UK journalists who responded said they had personally experienced or witnessed racism and bigotry in the newsroom. Amongst black journalists the figure rose to 74%, whilst 37% of white journalists experienced discrimination. And if this is occurring in newsrooms it is likely to filter into the journalism produced by news outlets too. One survey respondent said that while racism is less overt, they believed bias operated more subtly "in terms of what gets prioritised on the news agenda" and that racism towards how individual people in the news are treated can be hidden, "unacknowledged even by the people who perpetrate it" (Mayhew, 2021). A white tabloid reporter/sub-editor who worked at a news agency until 2017 said they were told and witnessed for themselves that "real-life stories about black people would not be so readily commissioned by newspapers and magazines". When they were, publications paid less and featured the stories less prominently. They added: "Outside of BLM [Black Lives Matter] coverage, there's a general lack of stories published about issues that affect black and ethnic minority communities" (ibid). Racism or racial bias in the media was a reflection of British society according to many respondents. One said: "Racial bias is in play across all UK media. It is endemic, systemic and deeply engrained as it is in society as a whole" (Majid, 2021).

Yet, in March 2021 the Society of Editors, which represents almost 400 members from the national and regional press and broadcasting, claimed the UK media is not bigoted. Their executive director, Ian Murray, made the statement in response to Prince Harry's assertion that the UK press were bigoted, specifically the tabloids, as a result of their coverage of his wife, Mehgan Markle, whose father is Caucasian and whose mother is African American. Rather than being racist Murray claimed that the UK press were fulfilling their function to hold the rich and powerful to account following an attack on the media by the couple, adding that it was not acceptable for them to claim the UK press were racist "without supporting evidence" (Society of Editors, 2021). *The Sun* had taken a similar line in the previous year when they said in a leader column: "We are sick, though, of woke morons crying racism over press criticism of Meghan and Harry. It is ludicrous to conflate racist abuse on social media with legitimate newspaper scrutiny" (*The Sun*, 2020). Following Murray's statement, several journalists, news outlets and Society of Editors board members distanced themselves from his comments: ITN news presenter, Charlene White, withdrew from hosting the Society's National Press Awards and some shortlisted publications and journalists pulled their entries.

Whether this is an example of bigotry in the UK media or a case of holding power elites to account it is evident that diversity is a major issue for British news organisations. Numerous respondents in the *Press Gazette* survey emphasised how a lack of diversity in newsrooms leads to racial bias and other discrimination in media coverage. One said: "Most newsrooms lack the diversity and checks and balances when it comes to stories that concern minorities". Another added:

> I think there is a lack of diversity in journalism across the board, be that gender identity, race, ethnicity, or socio-economic status. Therefore, however hard we try, there are always going to be unconscious biases that are at play
>
> Majid, 2021

Regulatory bodies like the Independent Press Standards Organisation (IPSO) and the Office of Communications (Ofcom) have clauses to protect individuals and audiences from discrimination by the media. Both aim to minimize harm and Ofcom also stress the need to avoid offence. IPSO emphasises the need to avoid pejorative or prejudicial reference to a person's race, colour, religion, sex, gender identity, sexual orientation, or to any physical or mental illness or disability and details must be avoided unless genuinely relevant to the story (Clause 12, Editors' Code of Practice, 2021). Ofcom state that broadcasters must ensure that any material that could cause offence is justified by the context in which it is used. Such material goes beyond the discriminatory content outlined by IPSO to include amongst others, offensive language, violence, sex, violation of human dignity and the treatment of vulnerable people who may be at risk of harm as a result of taking part in a programme (Section 2.3, Broadcasting Code, 2021). However, neither regulator refers to inclusivity or the need to include under-represented voices in news content in their codes, although Ofcom do have a diversity and equality hub (see www.ofcom.org.uk/tv-radio-and-on-demand/information-for-industry/guidance/diversity). Diversity—or the lack of it—in newsrooms and in news content is an ethical issue as well as a business and a social issue. When journalists fail to reflect the actual diverse make up of a community in their reporting, they compromise accuracy and truth-telling. When only a handful of journalists in a newsroom are from minorities then audiences from diverse groups can lose trust in a news outlet's ability to report stories about them accurately, knowledgeably and responsibly.

As well as addressing inclusivity future code writers may have to tackle issues of technology and diversity. Debates around how artificial intelligence (AI) addresses diversity and discrimination are beginning to emerge and could involve a form of unconscious bias. Algorithms lack the ability to discern and apply lived experience or to interpret professional standards to the extent that human journalists can. Therefore, news outlets that wish to have a more diverse workforce but also to use bots to write stories as part of the everyday workflow may have to develop policies to "reconcile those potentially conflicting approaches" (Smith, 2021). According to journalist Naomi Smith:

> Journalists have a moral responsibility to provide accurate accounts and be aware that their reporting has the power to shape perceptions. If algorithms and AI are to be used within newsrooms, it is crucial that diversity initiatives focus not only on the identities of those who work in newsrooms but also those who program and work with these algorithms.

What is unconscious or implicit bias?

Unconscious bias is our automatic or unintentional tendency to associate certain characteristics with certain groups. It is where we subliminally categorise people—positively or negatively—based on our background, upbringing, personal or social experiences, cultural context, and consumption of media portrayals. We all have inner biases—this is normal and not necessarily malicious—but how we deal with these, particularly as journalists, can cause potential harm to some people (Bailey, 2018; Goldsmith, 2021; Whelan, 2019). Thus, journalists should be aware of their responsibility to ensure that these implicit biases do not result in damaging assumptions and stereotyping. For example, former US President Donald Trump's description of the Coronavirus as the Chinese virus was reported extensively in the media and whilst most people may not have agreed with that explicit statement, subliminally it established a negative association between Chinese people and illness from the Coronavirus. Benz (2019) sums this up: "Our job as journalists is not to pretend we have no bias—of course we do—our job as journalists is to acknowledge the biases we hold and work to mitigate them as best as we can." He adds: "Bias, when allowed to remain unconscious, damages our ability to report fairly and accurately", on groups as well as individuals.

But mistakes can also be made as a result of pressures from the need to generate ideas, reporting on unfamiliar subjects, impending deadlines and workplace stresses, or because of blind spots. During the 2017 Wimbledon tennis championship the *Wall Street Journal* found themselves in difficulty over a tweet about the tournament's all-white garment policy. They tweeted: "Something's not white! At Wimbledon, a player failed his pre-match undergarment check." To illustrate the tweet, they chose a picture of black tennis star, Venus Williams, who was doing particularly well in the tournament that year. This seemed like a sound journalistic decision that provided context, according to journalist, author and academic, Isaac Bailey, given her success and that earlier she had also fallen foul of the undergarment policy. However, it failed to take account of unconscious bias. He said:

> While the journalists who pulled together the tweet, story, and photo had reason to believe they had checked all the appropriate journalistic boxes, they neither accounted for implicit bias—their blind spots, or their audience's—nor appreciated the still potent issue of race
>
> *2018*

Our cognitive capacity to process information quickly means that our brains rely on data stored in our long-term memory rather than starting from first principles every time we encounter a situation or a person. We use heuristics—or shortcuts—to assess at speed whether they are a threat or not (Goldsmith, 2021), drawing on, as Whelan (2019) notes, "past experiences, stereotypes and the availability and frequency of information over time". However, in doing so the brain makes connections that lead to an assumption that enables us to quickly understand a situation and to move on. But in journalism relying on assumptions is a dangerous practice that can stereotype and stigmatise people, for example, by their race, gender, ethnicity, disability, mental health, age, physical appearance, or class. It can lead to othering where we think in terms of "us" and "them"—us, the normal people, and them, the abnormal people—but also to stereotyping where we define people by recognised, undesirable characteristics. This is particularly prevalent in media reporting of crime. Heitzig (2015) found double standards in how criminality was defined and controlled, with the media playing a central role in the way they framed depictions of criminals and crimes. White criminality was constructed as an individual aberration or mental illness, whereas blackness was synonymous with criminality. Duxbury et al.'s (2018) study on race in mass shootings found that white men were framed as sympathetic characters while black and Latino men were treated as violent threats to the public. They concluded that there is "racial variability in how the media assign blame to mass shooters". This also appears to be the case with media reporting of Muslims. The Centre for Media Monitoring found that within the UK media words identifying Muslims or Islam were more frequently placed beside words like terror, terrorism, terrorist(s) than those associated with far-right or white supremacist terrorism (Hanif, 2020).

Some critics claim that the emphasis on unconscious bias exonerates governments, organisations and indeed, the media, from taking responsibility and being accountable for their discrimination. The assertion that bias is unconscious and inevitable changes it from being a systemic problem resulting from social inequality to be addressed structurally by governments and corporations to one that is psychological and the responsibility of the individual (Bourne, 2019; Morris, 2021).

That said, individual journalists can counter unconscious bias through empathy, critically reflecting on their reporting and thinking through their own personal and professional beliefs and values. They can extend their usual source lists to be more diverse, get to know people from different backgrounds within their own communities, treating people as individuals and debunking stereotypes, and ensuring that language and images do not contain assumptions (on the part of the journalist, news outlet or audience), harmful stereotypes and inaccuracies (Goldsmith, 2021).

Has representation of women in the media improved in the last decade?

Not really. Throughout the world women are under-represented in the news, an on-going trend for the last 20 years or so. Additionally, women are marginalised in leadership roles in news organisations. They comprise 39% of journalists but only 26% of them are leaders in news organisations globally. Research commissioned by the Bill and Melinda Gates Foundation on women's under-representation in news media across six English-speaking countries (India, Kenya, Nigeria, South Africa, the UK and the USA) found that use of women as a primary source or quoted as experts was between 14% in India and 29% in the UK in 2019 (Kassova, 2020). When they do appear as a primary source it is usually in crime/violence and celebrity stories rather than high profile genres like politics, where men's share is between three and seven times higher than women. As sources on the economy, men dominate by up to 31 times more than women (Kassova, 2020). From a specifically British perspective, Women in Journalism, a network organisation for female journalists in the UK, found in a snapshot study of the news output of 11 UK newspapers in one week in July 2020, that only one black woman and just 16% of women overall were quoted on the front pages of UK newspapers out of a total of 111 experts (WIJ, 2020).

The argument is sometimes proffered that increasing the number of women in newsrooms will lead to women being more visible in the news. The Gates Foundation report, *The Missing Perspectives of Women in News*, found that close gender parity in newsrooms in South Africa, the UK and the USA has not led to gender-balanced coverage. Only 1% of all news coverage in the six countries had a gender angle to it (Kassova, 2020). Women in Journalism also found that of the 174 front page bylines they counted in UK newspapers as few as one in four went to women, despite more than one-third of the country's newspapers being edited by women (ibid).

The *Missing Perspectives* report added that even where there are relatively equal numbers of women and men, male-based cultural and professional standards prevail and are adhered to by both genders, meaning that a journalist's professional identity takes precedence over gender identity. Its author, Lubo Kassova said: "Unless news cultures change, the increased representation of women in the newsroom will not be enough to achieve gender-based coverage" (2020, p. 24). However, the problem extends beyond the journalism profession to wider society where, she says, pro-male bias among both women and men is significant. She explains that 90% of men and women worldwide hold at least one bias against women, according to the United Nations Development Programme (Byrnes, 2020)

> It's more pronounced in the Global South, but also very much latent and lingering in the Global North. Particularly in the US and UK people think, "Oh, we've dealt with that. Patriarchal norms are no longer an issue in our countries and we've reached gender equality." Actually we haven't, and these values are one of the key barriers to balanced representation of women in news coverage
>
> *ibid*

Gender-based coverage is not totally absent from news agendas but it tends to be sporadic and pegged on specific incidents, movements or campaigns. One example is media reporting of the #MeToo movement that raises awareness of sexual harassment and sexual assault of women and promotes solidarity amongst survivors. It went from a few mentions to a social media phenomenon through the hashtag MeToo that was picked up by mainstream media and reported extensively worldwide. The movement was founded by activist and survivor Tarana Burke in 2006 to bring support and healing to survivors of sexual assault. The hashtag went viral in 2017 when actor Alyssa Milano used it following allegations of sexual harassment against Hollywood producer Harvey Weinstein. It was tweeted more than 12 million times (Lambley, 2019).

Ennis and Wolfe, who wrote a report on #MeToo for the Women's Media Center in 2018, analysed more than 15,000 news stories from 14 of the USA's biggest newspapers for five months before and 10 months after the Weinstein revelations. They found that 53% of bylines on sexual assault stories during that time were by men, although they did see an increase in women's bylines during the research period from May 2017 to August 2018. They also found that media interest was at its highest when high-profile individuals were involved rather than ordinary people and that women of colour seldom appeared in coverage, even though they experience higher rates of sexual violence (Kwateng-Clark, 2018). There is no doubt that the MeToo movement has raised awareness and increased media reporting of sexual harassment and assault against women. The coverage continues to this day, with both the BBC and *The Guardian* having a dedicated #MeToo pages, although they may be the exception rather than the rule. Ennis and Wolfe believe that the media has a duty and obligation to act ethically and sensitively when reporting intimate, traumatising accounts of sexual violence (2018). In order to achieve ethical reporting, they recommend news outlets think carefully about the language they use for example use survivor rather than victim, and being clear about clinical and legal definitions of harassment and assault. They suggest actively considering which cases to cover and seeking out those whose stories have not been told, as well as being aware of how significantly news output can shape people's perceptions. They also recommend providing training for journalists on reporting sexual harassment/assault stories sensitively, as well as creating inclusive newsrooms (ibid).

Some organisations are striving to be more inclusive in their news coverage. The BBC are trying to address the gender imbalance in sources used in its news and current affairs output. One of their journalists and presenter on news programme, *Outside Source*, Ros Atkins, set up the 50:50 project to track the number of men and women who appeared on the programme. The aim was to have 50% female sources and 50% male. With this conscious effort to think about gender balance the percentage of women appearing on the programme as sources rose from 39% to 50% (Byrnes, 2020). The project now involves 670 BBC teams and more than 100 partner organisations in 26 countries. In 2021, 70% of the datasets contributed by BBC teams and partners showed that women made up 50% of sources. The BBC have extended the project to include representation of ethnicity and disability, with more than 220 BBC teams signed up to monitor their use of sources from these groups. The BBC has set itself ambitious targets for inclusion, aiming to reach 50% women, 20% black, Asian and minority ethnic, and 12% disabled representation on-screen, on-air or in lead roles across all genres (Joannides et al., 2021).

The BBC may be tackling inclusivity but they found themselves in the midst of equal pay claims from two prominent female journalists in 2018 and 2020. Former BBC China editor, Carrie Gracie, was awarded substantial back pay in 2018 after speaking publicly about how her equivalent male colleagues were paid substantially more. The corporation apologised for underpaying her and reached an agreement on her back pay, which she donated to the gender-equality campaign group, the Fawcett Society, to help pay for legal advice for women in similar situations (PA Media, 2020). After numerous informal and formal attempts over several years to resolve an equal pay grievance, journalist Samira Ahmed took her case to the London Central Employment Tribunal, claiming that she was underpaid by £700,000. On 24 February 2020, they ruled that the work she did was equal to her male colleague, Jeremy Vine. They said the BBC had failed to prove the pay discrepancy was not because of gender discrimination and therefore she was entitled to equal pay. As a result of her historic case around 700 women at the BBC have received pay rises. The broadcast organisation started to revise its pay structures prior to Ahmed's tribunal but she is not convinced they have resolved the matter. She said: "There is a lot of concern still that the new structures continue to disguise inequality and discrimination. They certainly aren't transparent." (IFJ, 2021). However, the Equality and Human Rights Commission carried out an 18-month, independent investigation of 10 pay claims, although there had been more than 1,000 complaints. The outcome, announced in 2020, found that the BBC had not broken the law on equal pay for doing the same work, but recognised that pay discrimination could potentially occur because individual managers had too much discretion to set salaries. At the time Gracie described the investigation as "a whitewash" (Waterson, 2020).

What about media reporting of ethnic minorities?

Despite the many sets of media guidelines on reporting minority groups (e.g. Muslims, Roma, Jews, migrants and asylum seekers, among others), British news outlets continue to produce negative, harmful portrayals of ethnic groups in their content. Muslims, in particular, seem to be the subject of this detrimental coverage. After analysing 48,000 online articles and 5,500 broadcast clips between 2018 and 2020, the Centre for Media Monitoring found that around 60% of online stories and 47% of television clips linked Muslims and/or Islam with negative behaviour. The greatest percentage of negative articles that were biased against or misrepresented Muslim belief or behaviour were right-leaning or religious. In broadcasting, guests who expressed right-wing views were seldom challenged when they generalised about or misrepresented Muslims (Hanif, 2021). Worryingly, hate speech and anti-Muslim attacks in particular have increased in recent years. Attacks spiked in August 2018 when former UK foreign secretary and ex-Prime Minister, Boris Johnson referred to veiled Muslim women as "letter boxes" and "bank robbers" in a column for *The Telegraph*. They rose by 375%—from eight to 38—in the week following the publication of his column, 22 of them directed at women wearing a face veil (niqab) or other veiling practices. During the rest of August 42% of street incidents referenced Boris Johnson or his words (Tell MAMA, 2018).

Columns where outspoken views are expressed by the writer seem to be particularly controversial and several have resulted in complaints to press regulator,

IPSO. Media personality and far-right political commentator, Katie Hopkins, was the subject of a complaint for the comment piece she wrote for *The Sun* in 2015, entitled, "Rescue boats? I'd use gunships to stop migrants". In the article she compared migrants to "cockroaches" and the "norovirus", amongst other descriptions. However, IPSO did not consider this complaint under Clause 12, Discrimination, but instead viewed it as a matter of accuracy. Their reasoning was that despite the outrage caused by the column the clause refers to prejudicial or pejorative language towards *individuals*, and thus did not restrict news outlets' commentary on groups. Indeed, the regulator often refuses to consider third-party complaints from groups. Since Hopkins' article did not refer to an individual the clause did not apply (see Greer v The Sun; Editors' Codebook, 2021).

And yet, a significant amount of offensive and harmful content is aimed at groups rather than individuals. On leaving his role as IPSO chair in 2019, Sir Alan Moses said that group discrimination was the "biggest criticism" made towards IPSO since it was set up in 2014, but he added that extending the clause to include groups could affect freedom of expression, stressing that it was important for news outlets to have the right to offend in order for them to challenge. He said: "In my view you have to strike a balance between allowing the press to write critically and pejoratively about a religious group rather than banning it" (Tobitt, 2019).

Recognising the difficulty and seriousness of drafting a clause on discrimination, Sir Alan (ibid.) said:

> We all know that if you write something offensive it can be dangerous because those who wish to stir up racial hatred will use that material as the baseline on which to build and I am very conscious of that danger.

However, in that same year the regulator faced criticism from 26 MPs, including senior politicians David Lammy and Baroness Warsi, when they published an open letter accusing IPSO of failing to act against racism and Islamophobia in the press. The letter, organised by campaign groups Hacked Off and the Media Diversity Institute, claimed: "Racist and faith-based attacks against communities are so common in parts of the press that they have become a dangerous normality." However, Sir Alan Moses refuted accusations that IPSO condoned religious or race-based hate or offensive attacks. He said: "The real issue, with which the letter fails to grapple, is how to strike a balance between the freedom of a journalist or newspaper to offend a group while protecting individuals" (Walker, 2019).

The National Union of Journalists is one organisation who is striving towards more responsible reporting of Muslims and Islam. They have produced guidelines for programme makers and journalists to improve coverage. They have structured the guidelines using the acronym, PART, which stands for portrayal, accuracy, representation and terminology—the elements journalists should consider in order to report responsibly. For example, under portrayal they emphasise the need for balance in reporting, suggest picture desks and programme makers consider whether the images they use are stereotyping, and ask journalists to assess their content through the viewpoint of the Muslim community in order to determine whether it is fair. Under Accuracy, they recommend avoiding sensationalising content, particularly relating to identity and belonging. They also advise on checking the accuracy of statements by public figures and ensuring that headlines accurately reflect the substance of a story. Regarding Representation, they suggest that when interviewing those with extreme views that journalists should research the points thoroughly in order to offer a knowledgeable challenger. They also recommend seeking the views of Muslims themselves but recognise that there are differing perspectives within the groups and between individuals. Finally, under Terminology they recommend discussing terminology with Muslim colleagues in the newsroom, and if there are none then contacting relevant Muslim organisations for help (NUJ, 2019).

For further discussion of diversity and ethnic minorities see the *Ethics in Action* section with Barnie Choudhury in this chapter.

How can coverage of people with a disability be improved?

Approximately one billion people experience disability globally. That's around 15% of the world's population. In the UK around 14.1 million people are disabled: 8% of them are children, just under 20% are working adults and around 46% are of pension age (Department of Work and Pensions, 2021; WHO, 2021).

Yet, people with disabilities seldom appear in the news. When they do it tends to be in stories about disability where journalists focus on medical angles or overcoming specific challenges rather than as sources in more general stories. The media sometimes present people with disabilities as homogenous, who all have similar needs. This entrenches stereotypes and fails to see them as individuals with different experiences and requirements (Tuneva, n.d.). The media are also missing out on unexplored stories relating to disability. According to the World Health Organisation, people with disabilities undergo numerous violations of their human rights, including violence, abuse, prejudice and disrespect that intersects with other forms of discrimination. They also experience stigmatisation and discrimination when trying to access health services (WHO, 2021).

Additionally, some news outlets have tended to define people with disabilities by their disability, which is only one part of who they are. People with disabilities can be portrayed as courageous, pathetic, helpless, victims, asexual, recipients of charity who are eternally cheerful and grateful and always looking for miracle cures (Keeble, 2009). Ironically, they can also be framed as superheroes, who achieve great feats, and in doing so become inspirational characters for non-disabled people (Sanchez, 2015). Stella Young, an Australian comedian, broadcaster for ABC and disability activist, took exception to this portrayal in her TED talk, "I'm not your inspiration, thank you very much" (2014). She described images of people adapting to their disability, such as the image of a girl with no hands drawing a picture with a pencil in her mouth or a child running on carbon fibre prosthetic legs as "inspirational porn" because they "objectify one group of people for the benefit of another group of people" (ibid, 3:03). Their purpose is to inspire or motivate non-disabled people to think their lives are not so bad, for them to put their worries into perspective, she said (ibid, 4:21).

As in other forms of discrimination language is important when describing people with disabilities. An outdated but common phrase is 'battling with', used to refer to several forms of incapacity including chronic or terminal illness, but it has connotations of struggle and frames disability as a fight, a battle or a war. This discourse can be damaging to people with disabilities and their loved ones. Scope, the disability equality charity in England and Wales, recommends referring to a disabled person or people rather than cripple, the disabled or sufferer; using non-disabled person rather than able-bodied or normal; referring to a deaf or blind person rather than the deaf or the blind; using a person with dwarfism rather than midget, and describing a person as a wheelchair user rather than wheelchair-bound or confined to a wheelchair (Scope, n.d.). 'A person with' is also a useful phrase, as for example, 'a person with celebral palsy', because it emphasises the person rather than their disability. Saad Bashir, a journalist who uses a wheelchair, says it is important to humanise the subject through language and to see people with disabilities in broader terms. "The man in the wheelchair is a father, accountant, brother, football fan who uses a wheelchair. The blind woman is a mother, wife, lawyer who happens to be blind." He adds that disabled people need to be listened to and included in non-disability stories through greater representation in vox pops, case studies and as commentators (Calver et al., 2017).

What should journalists consider when reporting the LGBT+ community?

Despite a growing acknowledgement of sexual diversity and increased coverage in the mainstream media, many journalists outside the LGBTQ+ community remain confused about how to report it. Their concerns about being ill-informed about LGBTQ+ rights or using the wrong pronouns can be exacerbated under the pressure of deadlines. But former news editor of the LGBTQ+ news site Pink News, Tufayel Ahmed, advised journalists not to shy away from reporting LGBTQ+ stories because they might unintentionally cause offence. However, he added that journalists need to ensure they are equipped to report these stories as "it is important that everybody is able to cover it" (Lamb, 2019). Journalists can take practical steps like:

- Speak to people in the LGBTQ+ community; talk to people with lived experience who are directly affected by an issue; for example, LGBTQ+ people often face higher rates of poverty and homelessness
- As well as speaking to people in the community do your own research into the issues to improve your understanding and to avoid unintentional distortion
- Bring in different voices from the community and expand the range of interviewees from the community; don't repeatedly use the same sources, especially if they are also used by other news outlets
- Recognise that a source is not a spokesperson for the whole LBGTQ+ community; they are individuals who may not be able to answer questions outside of their own experiences
- Who have you left out of the story; avoid erasing people by looking for who is missing and thoroughly researching the issue
- Seek guidance from LGBTQ+ charities and organisations, such as Stonewall, who have a glossary of terms on the terminology used by the LGBTQ+ community, or GLAAD, the US media monitoring organisation who publish their Media Reference Guide to assist journalists to report stories fairly and accurately, or NLGJA, the Association of LGBTQ Journalists in the USA who have compiled a Journalists Toolkit to provide thought-provoking resources for journalists who do not normally cover the LGBTQ+ community (Green, 2019; NLGJA, 2021)

Coverage of trans issues has increased by 400% in the last five years with an average of 224 stories being published per month during 2018–2019, according to research for press regulator, IPSO (Mediatique, 2020). Whilst news outlets may have become more respectful about the language they use, some in the transgender community believe that the reporting contains undercurrents suggesting trans people are dangerous, with some feeling demonised and misrepresented (Green, 2019; Tobitt, 2019). Consequently, they are reluctant to become involved with journalists. The result is that their voices and experiences are often missing from news reports. There are also concerns about the accuracy of pronouns when referring to trans people in published articles.

Jasmine Andersson, equalities reporter at the *i* and *inews.co.uk*, advises: "Simply asking at the start of an interview what a person's pronouns are can easily avoid unintentional hurt feelings later on" (Green, 2019). She also warns that 'deadnaming' a trans person—using their former name—is disrespectful and can be traumatic for them. Despite the ethical need to minimize harm to those affected by their reporting, this is something that news outlets repeatedly do, according to Andersson (ibid).

Ethics in action: Barnie Choudhury, editor-at-large of *Eastern Eye*: "Walk in their shoes"

Barnie Choudhury is an award-winning journalist. He is editor-at-large for the UK's number one Asian newspaper, *Eastern Eye*. During 2020–2021, parliamentarians mentioned Barnie's work six times, and his investigations into racism, sexism and bullying in the judiciary led to a select committee hearing. Ministers and civil servants praised his and *Eastern Eye's* coverage during the pandemic for reaching communities they could not. In November 2020, the House of Lords' inquiry into the future of journalism featured Barnie's submission (see https://publications.parliament.uk/pa/ld5801/ldselect/ldcomuni/176/176.pdf).

He worked for the BBC for 24 years, and his brand of journalism helped change UK laws and expose organised crime, health and racial inequalities in Britain. Barnie was the director of media and PR for the Commonwealth secretary general, Baroness Patricia Scotland. In 2017, he was appointed the inaugural professor of professional practice at the University of Buckingham, a private institution, where he lectures on journalism, communications, marketing and leadership. Barnie achieved one of his biggest ambitions in 2021 when completed his Masters degree in data journalism at Birmingham City University.

How would you describe the current state of media reporting of diversity?

When it comes to racial diversity, the media has improved, but it has some way to go. If we look at the coverage of Brexit, south Asian businesses in the UK have been all but ignored (Choudhury, 2021a). When it came to the pandemic, it was not until two weeks after *Eastern Eye* highlighted the disproportionate nature of cases and deaths affecting non-white communities that mainstream media latched on. Finally, when it comes to violence against women or children going missing, if you are white, blonde and blue-eyed, you are more likely to get greater and more extended coverage than if you are south Asian or black (Firmstone et al., 2019). Just compare the coverage of the murder of Sarah Everard and Sabina Nessa.

Broadcast media does try to reflect diversity, while print media appears not to understand that engagement of diversity would lead to more business. The question we need to ask ourselves is this: take away the race, social class, gender, religion, sexual orientation and disability, why is this a story worth doing? If the answer is that it matters, it is significant, and it tells us something we do not know or did not expect, then we should give it the same coverage, the same prominence, and the same respect we have when it comes to "white" stories.

What ethical issues do you think journalists need to be conscious of when reporting stories about people from diverse backgrounds and experiences?

The most important things for me are my ethical and moral values which lead to my conscience. Trust is at the heart of my ethical values. My primary concern is how I can win the trust of those about whom I am reporting and giving a voice. Of course, I want the story, but not at any cost. If I am described as trustworthy by the protagonists, then I think I have passed the ethical test. I want to be able to sleep at night. I want to be able to go back to that source, that interviewee, that leader and know I wrote or edited a piece which was honest and authentic. Was I impartial, accurate, fair and balanced? Did I approach the story without assumptions? Whatever my politics or beliefs, did I put these aside?

Remember too that we owe it to our sources to protect them (Keeble, 2009). The chances are that non-white sources are the minority in a company or institution you are trying to expose, so how will you protect them? My stories about judges who accuse the judiciary of racism, sexism and creating a culture of fear are a case in point (Choudhury, 2021b). The ethics behind protecting them while checking out their claims was immensely challenging, creating huge dilemmas.

So, my starting point with any story I cover is to try to walk in their shoes. What must it be like to be of a different ethnicity, physically disabled, young, gay and non-Christian? What is going to be the reaction of their parents, brothers, sisters or children when they read or hear the story? Would you approach, treat or write the story differently if they were part of your community or background? If the answer to that last question is yes, I would do it differently, then you need to ask yourself why?

I am always reminded that I do not know everything, and my job is to ask often uncomfortable questions, but I do so with respect, humility and tenacity. Your role is to find the story with impact, and not let yourself find people who fit into your thesis and ignore the rest of the evidence. I imagine myself as a prosecutor and try to prove my case beyond reasonable doubt rather than on the balance of probabilities. I do that by trying to prove what I think is wrong. Your ethics comes from knowing that no matter how much you have invested in that story, if your assumptions, thesis or what your boss wants, is not accurate, you should walk away.

How do you see your role as an editor-at-large and columnist in covering stories of diversity?

My role as an editor-at-large and columnist is a privilege. The fact my editor allows me huge freedom on what I wish to report, and the freedom of being able to say what I want, within legal boundaries, are things I value and appreciate.

I am fortunate to have grown up with feet in two camps—mainstream white UK and minority non-white communities. It affords me insights and an ability to look through a lens which, dare I say, many white journalists have not experienced, cannot imagine, or comprehend. I automatically think about the diversity angle, and how a story can be different from the mainstream. Over the past 40 years, I have become more interested and more committed to reporting from communities from which we do not hear or are not covered adequately or properly.

My role is to question assumptions and lazy stereotypes. Quite often, journalists do not understand the cultural factors which determine the way certain sections of our society react. If we take older south Asians, for example, they still have the concept of community and honour. The next generation less so. They have either been born or brought up in the UK, and they are more likely to think and act differently from their parents. But that does not mean they think solely as a white Briton.

I bring my entire being and experiences to my journalism as an editor-at-large and as a columnist. It gives me the confidence to be authentic. For example, I am of a generation when what you did, how you behaved and performed affected an entire community. If I made a mistake, then it was because I was Asian. When a white reporter made an error, it was because he had a bad day. Similarly, I can write unpalatable truths about south Asian communities without being branded a racist. I can say that an Asian faith leader is a paedophile, or I can condemn someone who terrorises us in the name of religion without being described as a bigot.

But the downside is that when someone does carry out a terror attack, I pray he or she is not a Muslim, even though I am a Hindu. When someone is murdered, I pray that the killer is not non-white. When a football match where England is playing goes to penalties, I pray the player who misses is not black. Why? Because all people see is the colour of my skin.

I see my role as giving a voice to those who would otherwise not have one. It is to create impact, influence change and right perceived wrongs.

What are your thoughts on the media coverage of Black Lives Matter?

Like Stephen Lawrence, the assumption about the death of George Floyd was that it was yet another black criminal who had defied the police and deserved what happened next. What changed this was the disturbing and compelling footage of a public lynching by a police officer who knew he could be judge, jury and executioner. That nine-minute film of someone being murdered with apparent impunity changed minds and recreated and re-energised a social movement.

I think the media was too slow to realise that we were witnessing an existing movement rising up and reminding us that institutional, systemic and structural racism have never gone away. I felt the reporting was through the lens of those who had never reported on past movements. Overall, it was lazy, shallow and lacked political and historic context. People in the UK forget that 2021 is 50 years since the trial of the Mangrove Nine, when racist Metropolitan police officers fitted up black people in Notting Hill; 20 years since the northern riots based on the fault lines of race; and 10 years since the shooting of Mark Duggan which sparked disturbances in London. BLM was not a new cry. It was simply ignored by the media because it has never gone away.

As ever with much of mainstream reporting of race, the coverage of BLM, focused too much on the wrong thing. We concentrated on the pulling down of statues rather than asking why was it significant. We spoke about it being hijacked by political activists, conveniently forgetting that historically all social change is through politics and, sadly, sometimes violence.

My biggest concern is that we have been here before, and it will become a footnote in history. Unfortunately, once the media circus leaves town, we will forget about Black Lives Matter, until it happens again. And then we will ask the same questions, expecting different answers.

It was lazy because the media reported in the same way. What I wanted to read, hear and see were articulate black men and women explaining why this was happening, how it would change their lives and what they were trying to achieve without the interference of reporters. Instead, more often than not, I saw and read accounts through the lens of white journalists and commentators.

How does Eastern Eye report stories of diversity? Do you feel a responsibility to the different communities?

Diversity is embedded into everything we do. We do not have to think about being diverse. In fact, we have been at the forefront of exploring, examining and exposing good and bad practice through our conferences and campaigns since our founder began them 20 years ago.

The entire Asian Media Group stable of publications automatically thinks of its different audiences. Our responsibility is to tell their stories, test what they are telling us, and provide them with news they would not get elsewhere. Our journalists live in the same communities as their readers. Unlike big media organisations, we meet our readers, who are not shy in letting us know what they think. We are their advocates, we provide them with a voice, and we do this by holding power to account unafraid of the consequences. That is why over the past 12 months, MPs have mentioned our work in parliament six times, a Downing Street press conference held up our work during the pandemic as an exemplar of public service, and why mainstream media are following our stories.

Everyone knows that diversity makes business sense.

Why is it important that people in diverse communities tell their own stories?

When anyone tells his or her own story, the authenticity and human interest shine through. It creates greater impact, greater engagement and greater connections. It also allows for creative diversity. It is an axiom that stories from different communities allow us to learn about one another. That breaks down barriers and hopefully leads us to understand one another better. And life would be dull if we reported on just the white majority.

Do you think that improving diversity in newsrooms will result in greater diversity of news?

I would love to agree with the premise of the question, and say, yes. But my experience is that the reporter, of any hue, must viscerally want to engage with diversity. Sadly, academic studies and anecdotal evidence suggest that non-white journalists do not want to cover the "ethnic beat" (Pritchard & Stonbely, 2007). They get annoyed with the thought they are being stereotyped into covering an inferior beat. What they do not realise is that it is an exciting and worthwhile beat which can lead to policy and political change. It is often an effective way to make your name. Similarly, newsrooms need to embed diversity in everything it does because, in the right hand, it can create high-impact-data-driven-human-interest-influential-interesting-must-read journalism.

I have created a diversity framework which I use (see Figure 1.1). Where many might see a box-ticking exercise, I see stories sprinkled with human interest, and wherever possible irrefutable data. Where many might see people of colour, I see the opportunity to create real impact and hold power to account. And where many might see "minority reporting", I see a chance to amplify untold experiences.

DIVERSITY/SUBJECT	Race/ethnicity	Religion	Gender	Sexual orientation	Disability	Age	Social class
Health & social care/Covid [social affairs]							
Criminal Justice System [home affairs; justice; crime]							
Business/economics/Industry/finance/Brexit							
Education							
Foreign/international affairs/development							
Defence							
Environment/climate change/rural affairs							
Transport							
Housing							
Digital, culture/media, entertainment, arts, fashion							
Sport							
Politics							
Community affairs							

Figure 1.1 Barnie Choudary's diversity framework.

What can we do to improve diversity in newsrooms and diverse coverage?

Ofcom's five-year study confirms what I have been writing for the past three decades (Ofcom, 2021a). Broadcasters continually hire junior non-white staff while their more experienced diverse employees leave because they feel unappreciated and hit a Berlin Wall when they wish to progress. For generations, media organisations have failed to understand that recruiting non-whites to junior positions while blocking the path to promotion into senior leadership stops the progress of diversity.

The starting point must be in journalism school, where diversity and inclusion [D&I] becomes a compulsory taught module, just as law, regulations and public admin. The next stage is to champion and reward those who create diverse newsrooms and a culture of recruitment, retention and promotion. Bosses need to analyse why someone, or a department, is succeeding when it comes to diversity and the benefits of doing so when compared to non-diverse departments using agreed metrics such as impact journalism. Organisations need to make D&I a part of everyone's annual appraisal with key performance indicators. For example, the senior leader runs a mentoring, development and championing programme where success is promoting people of colour to the next grade within 18 months.

But the biggest hurdles are two-fold. First, not enough people of colour have their hands on the levers of power. By this I mean a substantial budget and the power to hire first without deferring to anyone else who happens to be white. Second, once men found it difficult to take direction, instruction or orders from women. Now, a man refusing to do tasks when asked by a woman are, thankfully, a rare occurrence. Unfortunately, that is not the case for people of colour. We are not at a stage when a junior journalist of colour can speak up, the theory of microinequities if you will, and a non-white senior leader is often more likely to be questioned and challenged than a white manager.

Until we get to a position where the skin colour is secondary to talent and results, we will not have real progress. Finally, people of colour need to understand that the "old boys' network" succeeds for a reason. They work together and put pals in positions of power so they can benefit. Being the only "gay in the village", pulling the ladder up behind you, may help your career at that moment. But having a true support network with whom you can thrash out creative ideas and allow colleagues to challenge you, the diversity of creative thought, is often more successful for your business.

Ethical workout

- What are the ethical issues that journalists need to consider when reporting diversity issues?
- Do a snapshot survey of one day's coverage in six UK newspapers and/or news channels. Identify stories and images that represent diversity. How many did you find? How prominent were they? Were they positive or negative?
- What should journalists think about in terms of language, stereotypes and access if their reporting is to be inclusive?
- Is media coverage of crime discriminatory? How?
- What should the journalism profession do to change the news agenda on diversity?

Five takeaways from this chapter

- Many groups are under-represented in the news and newsrooms but diversity deficiencies can be tackled by news outlets being more inclusive and seeking out communities they don't normally report.
- Journalists should be aware of their responsibility to ensure that unconscious biases do not result in damaging assumptions and stereotyping.
- Increasing the number of women in a newsroom does not necessarily expand the number of stories with a gender angle. News cultures that are predominantly male-focussed need to change too.
- To avoid stereotyping, journalists should treat people with disabilities as individuals with specific conditions and needs, and not as a homogenous group.

- Journalists who are confused about what pronouns to use when interviewing someone from LGBTQ+ communities should ask their interviewee what their preferred pronouns are. They should seek guidance from LGBTQ+ organisations like Stonewall and GLAAD.

Ethics toolbox

- Media Diversity Institute—resources for journalists. Available at: www.media-diversity.org/for-journalists/
- Sir Lenny Henry Centre for Media Diversity, Birmingham University. Available at: www.bcu.ac.uk/media/research/sir-lenny-henry-centre-for-media-diversity
- GLAAD Media Reference Guide. Available at: www.glaad.org/reference
- Centre for Media Monitoring—promoting fair and responsible reporting of Muslims and Islam. Available at: https://cfmm.org.uk/
- The Fawcett Society—the UK's leading charity campaigning for gender equality and women's rights. Available at: www.fawcettsociety.org.uk/

References

Bailey, I. (2018) 'Avoiding the pitfalls of hidden biases can lead to better story selection and more inclusive reporting', *Nieman Reports*, 13 November. Available at: https://niemanreports.org/articles/how-implicit-bias-works-in-journalism/ (Accessed: 12 December 2021).

Benz, K. (2019) 'The value of bias in a quest for inclusive journalism', *RTDNA*, 10 June. Available at: www.rtdna.org/article/the_value_of_bias_in_a_quest_for_inclusive_journalism (Accessed: 12 December 2021).

Bourne, J. (2019) 'Unravelling the concept of unconscious bias', *Race and Class*, 60(4), pp. 70–75. https://doi.org/10.1177/0306396819828608

Byrnes, S. (2020) 'Missing perspectives: How women are left out of the news', *Bill and Melinda Gates Foundation*, 2 December. Available at: www.gatesfoundation.org/ideas/articles/women-in-media-report (Accessed: 14 December).

Calver, B., Kemp, D. and Ryder, M. (2017) 'Everybody in: A journalist's guide to inclusive reporting for journalism students'. Available at: https://bjtc.org.uk/wp-content/uploads/2019/07/everybodyinbook-copy.pdf (Accessed: 27 October 2021).

Choudhury, B. (2021a) 'A tale of two challenges: How did the media report Brexit and Covid in South Asian communities?' in Mair, J. Clark, T and Fowler, N. (eds.)

Populism, the Pandemic and the Media: Journalism in the Age of Covid, Trump, Brexit and Johnson. Bury St Edmunds: Abramis, pp. 217–222.

Choudhury, B. (2021b) '"Racist judiciary": Culture of denial'. *Eastern Eye*, 7 April. Available at: www.easterneye.biz/exclusive-racist-judiciary-culture-of-denial/ (Accessed: 1 October 2021).

Department of Work and Pensions. (2021) 'Family resource survey: Financial year 2019–2020'. *UK Government*, 25 March. Available at: www.gov.uk/government/statistics/family-resources-survey-financial-year-2019-to-2020/family-resources-survey-financial-year-2019-to-2020 (Accessed: 20 December 2021).

Duxbury, S.W., Frizell, L.C. and Lindsay, S.L. (2018) 'Mental illness, the media, and the moral politics of mass violence: The role of race in mass shootings coverage', *Journal of Research in Crime and Delinquency*, 55(6), pp. 766–797. https://doi.org/10.1177/0022427818787225

Editors' Codebook. (2021) 'The handbook of the editors' code of practice'. *IPSO*. Available at: www.editorscode.org.uk/downloads/codebook/Codebook-2021.pdf (Accessed: 23 December 2021).

Editors' Code of Practice. (2021) 'Clause 12: Discrimination'. Available at: www.ipso.co.uk/media/2032/ecop-2021-ipso-version-pdf.pdf (Accessed: 21 December 2021).

Ennis, E. and Wolfe, L. (2018) '#MeToo: Women's Media Center report', *Women's Media Center*. Available at: https://womensmediacenter.com/reports/media-and-metoo-how-a-movement-affected-press-coverage-of-sexual-assault (Accessed: 14 December 2021).

Firmstone, J., Georgiou, M., Husband, C., Marinkova and M., Steibel, F. (2019) 'Representation of minorities in the media (UK)'. Available at: https://eprints.whiterose.ac.uk/143385/1/FinalAnalysisReportRevisedUK%20-%20with%20pictures.pdf (Accessed: 1 October 2021).

Green, D. (2019) 'A guide to reporting on LGBTQ+ community', *journalism.co.uk*. 28 June. Available at: www.journalism.co.uk/news/a-guide-to-reporting-on-lgbtq-stories/s2/a740869/ (Accessed: 27 October 2021).

Goldsmith, N. (2021) 'Unconscious bias and its impact on journalism', *Media Helping Hand*. Available at: https://mediahelpingmedia.org/2019/08/22/unconscious-bias-and-its-impact-on-journalism/ (Accessed: 12 December 2021).

Hanif, F. (2020) 'How the British media report on terrorism'. Available at: https://cfmm.org.uk/wp-content/uploads/2020/08/CfMM-How-British-Media-Reports-Terrorism-ONLINE.pdf (Accessed: 12 December 2021).

Hanif, F. (2021) 'British media's coverage of Muslims and Islam (2018–2020)'. Available at: https://cfmm.org.uk/wp-content/uploads/2021/11/CfMM-Annual-Report-2018-2020-digital.pdf (Accessed: 23 December 2021).

Heitzig, N.A. (2015) '"Whiteness", criminality, and the double standards of deviance/social control', *Contemporary Justice Review: Issues in Criminal, Social and, and Restorative Justice*, 18(2), pp. 197–214. https://doi.org/10.1080/10282580.2015.1025630

IFJ (International Federation of Journalists). (2021) 'Equal pay: "700 BBC women have had pay rises since my case", Samira Ahmed', 5 March. *IFJ News*. Available at: www.ifj.org/media-centre/news/detail/category/women-workers/article/equal-pay-700-bbc-women-have-had-pay-rises-since-my-case-samira-ahmed.html (Accessed: 19 December 2021).

Joannides, L., Goswami, N. and Henshall, A. (2021) '50:50 The equality project, impact report 2021', *BBC*. Available at: www.bbc.com/5050/documents/50-50-impact-report-2021.pdf (Accessed: 14 December 2021).

Kassova, L. (2020) 'The missing perspectives of women in news', *Bill and Melinda Gates Foundation*, November 2020. Available at: www.iwmf.org/wp-content/uploads/2020/11/2020.11.19-The-Missing-Perspectives-of-Women-in-News-FINAL-REPORT.pdf (Accessed: 14 December 2021).

Keeble, R.L. (2009) *Ethics for Journalists*. 2nd ed. Abingdon: Routledge.

Kwateng-Clark, D. (2018) 'The Women's Media Center found that during a 15-month period, 53 percent of sexual assault story bylines came from men', *Vice*, 9 October. Available at: www.vice.com/en/article/vbkqmx/womens-media-center-metoo-coverage (Accessed: 19 December 2021).

Lamb, J. (2019) 'Why the media often gets LGBTQ+ stories so wrong', journalism.co.uk, 26 June. Available at https://www.journalism.co.uk/news/media-often-gets-lgbtq-stories-wrong/s2/a740757 (Accessed: 27 October 2021).

Lambley, E. (2019) '#MeToo movement and its impact on the media: #embracing diversity', *Indigo*, 5 March. Available at: www.indigopr.com/blog/metoo-movement-and-its-impact-on-the-media-embracingdiversity/ (Accessed: 17 December 2021).

Majid, A. (2021) 'Two thirds of journalists responding to our survey say UK media is racist or bigoted in some way'. Press Gazette Race and Media Survey 2021. *Press Gazette*, 1 April. Available at: www.pressgazette.co.uk/two-third-journalists-uk-media-bigoted-or-racist/?_gl=1*127ntap*_ga*MTQ4NDUyMzYyNi4xNjMzMjY3MTg5*_ga_4GW6S7C2VR*MTYzNDQ3MzgzNy43LjAuMTYzNDQ3MzgzNy42MA (Accessed: 17 October 2021).

Mayhew, F. (2021) 'Two in five journalists responding to survey say they have seen or experienced racism in UK media'. Press Gazette Race and Media Survey 2021. *Press Gazette*, 1 April. Available at: www.pressgazette.co.uk/two-third-journalists-uk-media-bigoted-or-racist/?_gl=1*127ntap*_ga*MTQ4NDUyMzYyNi4xNjMzMjY3MTg5*_ga_4GW6S7C2VR*MTYzNDQ3MzgzNy43LjAuMTYzNDQ3MzgzNy42MA (Accessed: 17 October 2021).

Mediatique (2020) 'Examining trends in editorial standards in coverage of transgender issues'. Available at: www.ipso.co.uk/media/1986/mediatique-report-on-coverage-of-transgender-issues.pdf (Accessed: 27 October 2021).

Morris, N. (2021) 'Is "unconscious bias" just a convenient' way to avoid acknowledging racism?' *Metro*, 21 January. Available at: www.metro.co.uk (Accessed: 12 December 2021).

NLGJA: The Association of LGBTQ Journalists. (2021) 'Stylebook on LGBTQ Terminology'. Available at: www.nlgja.org/stylebook/ (Accessed: 27 October 2021).

NUJ. (2019) 'Media guidelines: Reporting on Muslims and Islam'. Available at: www.nuj.org.uk/resource/media-guidelines-reporting-on-muslims-and-islam-summary.html (Accessed: 23 December 2021).

Ofcom. (2021a) 'Broadcasters facing diverse talent drain'. Available at: www.ofcom.org.uk/news-centre/2021/broadcasters-facing-diverse-talent-drain (Accessed: 1 October 2021).

Ofcom. (2021b) 'The Ofcom broadcasting code (with the cross-promotion code and on-demand programme service rules)'. Available at: www.ofcom.org.uk/tv-radio-and-on-demand/broadcast-codes/broadcast-code (Accessed: 21 December 2021)

PA Media. (2020) 'Carrie Grace leaves BBC after 33 years', *The Guardian*, 26 August. Available at: www.theguardian.com/media/2020/aug/26/carrie-gracie-leaves-bbc-after-33-years (Accessed: 19 December 2021).

Pritchard, D. and Stonbely, S. (2007) 'Racial profiling the newsroom'. Journalism and Mass *Communication Quarterly*, 84(2). Available at: https://journals.sagepub.com/doi/abs/10.1177/107769900708400203?journalCode=jmqc (Accessed: 29 September 2021).

Sanchez, J. (2015) Reporting on disability: Guidelines for the media. Geneva: International Labour Office Gender, Equality and Diversity Branch. Available at: www.ilo.org/wcmsp5/groups/public/---ed_emp/---ifp_skills/documents/publication/wcms_127002.pdf (Accessed: 23 December 2021).

Scope. (n.d.) 'End the awkward'. Available at: www.scope.org.uk/campaigns/end-the-awkward/#talking-about-disability (Accessed: 20 December 2021).

Smith, N. (2021) 'Diversifying news by bots', *The Journalist*, December–January. Available at: www.nuj.org.uk/resource/the-journalist-december-2021.html (Accessed: 20 December 2021).

Society of Editors. (2021) 'Society of Editors' executive director steps down', *Society of Editors News*, 10 March. Available at: www.societyofeditors.org/soe_news/society-of-editors-executive-director-steps-down/ (Accessed: 17 October).

Tell MAMA. (2018) 'Normalising hatred: Tell MAMA annual report 2018'. Available at: www.tellmamauk.org/wp-content/uploads/2019/09/Tell%20MAMA%20Annual%20Report%202018%20_%20Normalising%20Hate.pdf (Accessed: 23 December 2021).

The Sun. (2020) 'The Sun says Prince Harry and Meghan Markle's obnoxious behaviour betrays royalty and abuses the generosity and goodwill of taxpayers', *The*

Sun, 9 January. Available at: www.thesun.co.uk/news/10708941/prince-harry-meghan-markles-obnoxious-behaviour-betrays-royalty-taxpayers/ (Accessed: 17 October 2021).

Tobitt, C. (2019) 'Outgoing IPSO chairman Sir Alan Moses says group discrimination "greatest issue" regulator has grappled with'. *Press Gazette*, 5 December. Available at: https://pressgazette.co.uk/outgoing-ipso-chairman-sir-alan-moses-says-group-discrimination-greatest-issue-regulator-has-grappled-with/ (Accessed: 23 December 2021).

Tobitt, C. (2019) 'Society of Editors boss Ian Murray resigns amid row over Prince Harry "bigoted" press claims'. *Press Gazette*, 10 March. Available at: www.pressgazette.co.uk/society-of-editors-diversity-meghan-harry/ (Accessed: 17 October 2021).

Tuneva, M. (n.d.) 'Guidelines for inclusive media reporting on Covid-19'. Available at: https://en.unesco.org/sites/default/files/guide_inclusivemediareporting_covid19.pdf (Accessed: 27 October 2021).

Walker, J. (2019) 'Senior politicians accuse UK press regulator of "turning a blind eye" to racism in media', *Press Gazette*, 28 February. Available at: https://pressgazette.co.uk/senior-politicians-accuse-uk-press-regulator-of-turning-a-blind-eye-to-racism-in-the-media/ (Accessed: 23 December 2021).

Waterson, J. (2020) 'Carrie Gracie attacks BBC pay discrimination inquiry "whitewash"', *The Guardian*, 12 November. Available at: www.theguardian.com/media/2020/nov/12/equality-watchdog-clears-bbc-of-unlawful-pay-discrimination (Accessed: 19 December 2021).

Whelan, P. (2019) 'The state of unconscious bias in the UK', *HR Magazine*, 19 February. Available at: www.hrmagazine.co.uk (Accessed: 12 December 2021).

WHO (World Health Organisation). (2021) 'Disability and health factsheet'. Available at: www.who.int/en/news-room/fact-sheets/detail/disability-and-health (Accessed: 20 December 2021).

Women in Journalism. (2020) 'A week in British news: How diverse are the UK's newsrooms?', *Women in Journalism*, September 2020. Available at: https://womeninjournalism.co.uk/lack-diversity-british-newsrooms/ (Accessed: 14 December 2021).

Young, S. (2014) 'I'm not your inspiration, thank you very much', April 2014. Available at: www.ted.com/talks/stella_young_i_m_not_your_inspiration_thank_you_very_much (Accessed: 20 December 2021).

9
The ethics of health journalism
Reporting a pandemic

Petya Eckler and Ozan B. Mantar

Even before the COVID-19 pandemic hit the world in 2020, news about health was everywhere and attracted considerable attention. Many British broadsheets and tabloids had dedicated sections that ranged in topics from tips for better sleep to features on women's health to news about National Health Service (NHS) funding and hospital waiting times. What changed in early 2020, however, when a global pandemic started spreading quickly, was that health suddenly moved from its own section to the front pages of local and national newspapers and their respective websites, and to the news highlights of nightly TV and radio bulletins. As a crisis loomed on the horizon, health news became a daily, even hourly, fixture and everyone's new obsession.

However, while increasing numbers of people consume health news and more journalists create it, the peculiarities of health journalism as a specialism remain. Health journalism is a unique specialism, which follows the basic rules of journalism but also has its specific tenets. This uniqueness also relates to daily decisions on ethics, which all health journalists grapple with. Harcup states: "Arguably, everything a journalist does—or chooses not to do—has potential ethical implications" (2015, p. 26).

In making those decisions health journalists may be guided by the Society of Professional Journalists' four foundational principles for ethical journalism: "seek the truth and report it", "minimize harm", "act independently" and "be accountable and transparent" (2014). These principles also appear in UK codes of conduct including the Editors' Code of Practice, IMPRESS Standards Code, the National Union of Journalists' Code of Conduct and Ofcom's Broadcasting Code, some of which also address transparency and separating fact from opinion. In this chapter, we shall examine how some of these ethical principles relate to the practice of health journalism during the COVID-19 pandemic. In the *Ethics in Action* section, health correspondent at

DOI: 10.4324/9780429505386-10

The Herald, Helen McArdle, explains her approach to covering major health stories, including the need to rigorously check data to present accurate information to the public.

What is unique about health journalism? What are some of the ethical issues health journalists need to consider?

The expansive nature of health journalism

First, let us examine the very concept of health. The World Health Organisation (WHO) defines health as "a state of complete physical, mental, and social well-being and not merely the absence of disease or infirmity" (1946). It is evident from this definition that the issue of health is a very broad one, which stretches beyond hospitals, medical facilities and treatment, and incorporates psychological and social aspects. If we apply this framework to the coverage of the COVID-19 pandemic, all stories about social isolation due to lockdowns, economic inequalities and their consequences on people, physical and social surroundings and how they affect well-being would also fall under the domain of health. Thus, it quickly becomes apparent that health journalism does not focus strictly on health or the science behind it, but often involves politics, societal movements, policy, social norms and prejudices. This interconnectedness is important for health journalists, as they likely will have to expand their reporting into these related fields and build expertise in political or social topics, which may seem irrelevant to health reporting at first. However, this can contribute to more informed reporting and to better accountability from politicians and funders as their decisions shape access to healthcare and healthcare quality experienced by audiences.

The link between health and politics became apparent during the COVID-19 pandemic, when decisions about the timing of lockdowns, for example, were taken not only with public health and epidemiology in mind, but also with regards to the economic and social consequences of such drastic measures (Health and Social Care Committee and Science and Technology Committee, 2021). As became clear, the politics of these decisions ultimately delayed the lockdown in March 2020 and cost thousands of lives (ibid). A good health reporter should expose such connections, as they often have far-reaching consequences, which can quickly turn catastrophic, especially in times of crisis, as evidenced in the earlier report. By providing such content their reporting adheres to the ethical principles of accuracy, independence and holding those in authority to account.

The potential to do harm

This leads to another peculiarity of health journalism: the potential for real harm from the stories shared with the public. The aim to minimize harm is one of the foundational ethical principles for journalists (EJN, 2021; SPJ, 2014; Wilkins, 2005) and is especially relevant for health journalism. Health stories speak to people's personal experiences of health and carry the potential for changes in people's behaviour as a result of the coverage (e.g. Yanovitzky and Bennett, 1999). Therefore, what appears in the media about health, especially during a pandemic, matters immensely, as we discuss later in this chapter. Further, journalistic content spreads beyond the public during a pandemic and is also consumed by experts and decision-makers (Wilkins, 2005, p. 248). Thus, "journalists have a responsibility to make information sophisticated in the sense that it is both scientifically and, when appropriate, historically informed" (Wilkins, 2005, p. 252), because, as Wilkins notes, this mediated communication also affects medical practitioners and public officials, who may be monitoring the media and basing their decisions on that content. In this sense, the potential for harm goes beyond direct influence on the public and into potential impact on policy makers and medical practice.

For example, former US President Donald Trump announced in March 2020 that a prescription-only drug used to treat malaria (hydroxychloroquine, under trade name *Plaquenil®* in the USA) was beneficial for treating COVID-19. He did this eight days before the Federal Drug Administration approved it for COVID-19 treatment. However, around three months later on 15 June 2020 the FDA retracted and cancelled approval due to side effects, misuse and ineffectiveness against COVID-19 (Milman, 2020; Williams, 2020). As a result of the attention by social media and mainstream media, some people took the drug and were hospitalised due to drug poisoning and overdose, while others died (Spring, 2020).

Health journalists also need to be aware of the potential to do psychological or social harm when reporting on a pandemic. Since the virus broke out in China and spread globally, individuals of Asian descent were targeted worldwide and faced physical attacks in the UK (Mercer, 2020), Australia (Woolley, 2020), the USA (Human Rights Watch, 2020), Italy and France (Giuffrida and Willsher, 2020), Canada (Cecco, 2020), Japan, South Korea and Vietnam (Rich, 2020); and xenophobic comments and cyber-bullying over social media (Cummins, 2020). Despite WHO's advice to not use disease names associated with ethnic and racial references or geographic locations (WHO, 2015), some politicians and those following them were quick to label the COVID-19 virus as Chinese, which incited anti-Asian rhetoric and discrimination. Foremost amongst them was Donald Trump who referred to the Coronavirus as the "Chinese virus". Research on Twitter in March 2020 of the weeks before and after Trump tweeted the phrase, "Chinese virus", shows that anti-Asian sentiment was higher in the week after this label was used and was more often linked with the hashtag #ChineseVirus (Hswen et al., 2021). Noteworthy is the fact that these negative effects from health coverage were not localised to the United States, where the news originated, but were spread globally.

An example of positive health reporting

Parallel to these harmful consequences from the coverage of the pandemic some positive and uplifting effects developed. In the UK one major story was that of Captain Sir Thomas Moore, a retired army officer from Bedford who raised at least £38.9 million for the NHS by public donations (The Captain Tom Foundation, n.d.). In this example, the role of the news media is indisputable. It all started in April 2020, when Moore's daughter declared in a press release that "he would walk 100 laps around his garden before his 100th birthday to raise money for the NHS" (Pidd, 2020). The story was first reported in *The Bedford Times & Citizen* on 7 April 2020 (Pidd, 2020; Turner, 2020; MSN, 2021), followed the next day by a piece by regional broadcaster, *ITV News Anglia* (Bell, 2020). The story was picked up by social media users and went viral, resulting in the family's initial goal of £1,000 being quickly exceeded. Moore was described by the BBC as "a defining figure of England's first national lockdown" (Shearing, 2021). His story is a notable example of good journalism practices in a pandemic, as it was quickly published with an inspirational narrative while maintaining ethical principles, which may have contributed to its wide distribution on social media. It is evidence that the media can be very effective during times of crisis in boosting public morale and creating awareness about issues such as the financial hardship affecting the NHS.

Balancing the need to challenge with the risk of harm

The goal to minimize harm does not mean abstaining from investigations or from criticising and challenging those in power. Here develops one of the ethical dilemmas for health journalists: How much should they challenge medical and public health research and policies while balancing the risk for causing harm? Boeyink and Borden offer some insight: "Like the rest of us, journalists have the general responsibilities of telling the truth and minimizing harm. However, these responsibilities take on a specific meaning in journalism. …

These principles are in constant tension" (2010, p. 3). A study of Australian journalists, after a wave of avian influenza cases in 2005, showed that one of the most important roles as perceived by them was to "question and critique" the people and institutions they were covering (Leask, Hooker and King, 2010). This approach also prevented journalists from being seen as supporting a particular agenda.

> The media is not the public relations wing of the health department. We are not there simply to report what they want to tell the public—though we will usually do that also. But our role is to ask challenging, independent questions. (Newspaper medical reporter)
> Leask, Hooker and King, 2010, p. 5

Therefore, even if health officials act in the public interest to control a pandemic, many journalists still see it as their professional duty to question and challenge health policies and decisions, and voice the criticism of third parties. This approach relates to the watchdog or adversary function of journalists, which the SPJ includes in its Code of Ethics. Journalists should: "Recognize a special obligation to serve as watchdogs over public affairs and government. Seek to ensure that the public's interest is conducted in the open, and that public records are open to all" (SPJ, 2014). As the early days of the pandemic have shown, scientists can also have blind spots in their thinking, and thus health journalists could pay attention to the following advice: "When consuming expertise it helps to be able to distinguish between what what [sic] the experts know with confidence and what is speculation, and to explore the implications of different assumptions" (Freedman, 2020).

Criticism towards public health policies during the pandemic was common in the British media, ranging from business owners bemoaning the closing of their premises due to lockdowns (BBC News, 2021; Partington, 2021) to public concerns about specific social distancing rules and how they were applied in practice (BBC News, 2020a; Barmer and Cawley, 2021), to vaccine hesitancy among ethnic groups (Parveen and Barr, 2021; Siddique and Mohdin, 2021) and resistance towards proposed compulsory vaccinations of NHS workers (Luton Today, 2021; Saunders, 2021).

But while scrutiny of public health research and policy may signify the robust functioning of journalism, it may misrepresent the scientific consensus on a topic. Such has been the case with the historical coverage of climate change, where in their pursuit of journalistic balance and the ideal of presenting both sides of the story, journalists have indeed misrepresented the predominant scientific consensus around the anthropogenic contributions to climate change (Boykoff and Boykoff, 2004). "Balanced reporting is actually problematic in practice when discussing the human contribution to global warming and resulting calls for action to combat it", the authors concluded (p. 134).

The balance between journalistic scrutiny and potential for misrepresentation and harm is a difficult one, especially when scientific understanding of a topic is still evolving, as that may result in conflicting findings or conflicting advice to the public. The debate about face masks is a good example of that. In the first months of the pandemic, scientists could not agree on the necessity of using face coverings. Some, including those working with the government, pointed to the lack of evidence and therefore they did not recommend use of face masks for the general public (Bloom and Shadwell, 2020), while others supported the idea that face masks had only small effects on virus spread (Pitas, Sandle and James, 2020). On the other hand, there were stories about why face masks should be worn (BBC News, 2020b). It is important to mention that both narratives referred to "science" and "scientists" to justify the story.

What are some of the main ethical challenges that UK health journalists faced during the COVID-19 pandemic?

Dealing with an infodemic

The COVID-19 situation is unique in many ways compared to previous pandemics. One key difference is that it also triggered an infodemic, which the WHO (2020b) defined as "an overabundance of information—some accurate and some not—occurring during an epidemic" and importantly one that "cannot be eliminated, but it can be managed" (2020b). They pointed out:

> The Coronavirus disease (COVID-19) is the first pandemic in history in which technology and social media are being used on a massive scale to keep people safe, informed, productive and connected. At the same time, the technology we rely on to keep connected and informed is enabling and amplifying an infodemic that continues to undermine the global response and jeopardizes measures to control the pandemic.
>
> *2020a*

These unique circumstances put journalists in the UK and around the world in a very difficult situation due to the volume and diversity of information they had to handle.

The challenges facing health journalists during the pandemic included difficulties with fact-checking information and assuring its veracity, continuous conflict between the pressure of immediacy and the importance of accuracy in reporting, and problems in understanding statistics and interpreting them for lay audiences (Nguyen et al., 2021). All these challenges have ethical implications. They can impact journalists' ability to produce accurate information or correct harmful inaccuracies, and can affect accountability and transparency if journalists struggle to determine how to present uncertain or ambiguous data, while still informing their audiences. These challenges result mostly from internal newsroom pressures and developments in the media industry, which has experienced the reduction of specialist staff positions across newsrooms for years.

Other potential challenges are connected to factors external to newsrooms. They include: fast-changing information and scientific knowledge, which is developing in real time and which has led to uncertainty and conflicting information (see the issue of wearing masks in public discussed earlier); a limited pool of expert sources due to the high complexity of the topic; a wide pool of other sources, who may have competing political agendas and thus may be tempted to tweak the truth (Posetti, Bell and Brown, 2020); risk of information overload for the public, especially related to negative news, which may result in a backlash against the mainstream media; and the ocean of misinformation and disinformation swirling around journalists and audiences, which we discuss later in this chapter. The ethical implications of these challenges are related to the same professional principles of truth seeking, transparency, accountability, aiming to minimize harm and separating fact from opinion. In the case of the latter principle, it may be difficult to achieve if journalists are unclear on how much of sources' statements are based on fact and how much are speculation or opinion.

Competing narratives

The issue of interpreting science is not even about science anymore. Instead, health journalists have been placed at the forefront of competing narratives and influences, which they have had to navigate and negotiate for themselves and their audiences. As a report on the first year of the pandemic stated, "COVID-19 data have been subject to a rather fierce battle between different frames and narratives, in which science had to compete—not always successfully—with religion, culture and, most importantly, politics" (Nguyen et al., 2021, p. 1). These competing influences present an ethical challenge to journalists in terms of which narratives should be emphasised and which should be minimized. Further, the "external" challenge of dealing with sources and including them in the narrative complicates matters even more, as those sources come with their own agendas and misinterpretation. Nguyen et al. (2021, p. 2) presented the situation faced by the British media: "In the midst of confusion, anxieties and fears, the public found mis/disinformation not only on social media but also, and rather deplorably, in press briefings and interviews by ministers and MPs." A similar trend appeared worldwide too, as international journalists identified "politicians, elected officials, government representatives and State-orchestrated networks as top sources of COVID-19 disinformation" (Posetti, Bell and Brown, 2020, p. 3).

Thus, journalists had to take difficult decisions about science and statistics, fact-checking, trust (or mistrust) of sources all within a matter of hours or sometimes even minutes. An excerpt from Nguyen et al. (2021, p. 4) is very revealing of the added pressure of tight deadlines:

> The heightened importance of data-based stories makes matters worse by imposing substantial pressure on journalists to deal with data and their sources as quickly as possible. For afternoon newspapers like the *Evening Standard*, the pressure to "get the morning news on the street quickly" was permanent, sometimes with only "minutes to work out what the data means", said Ross Lydall, its health editor, who cited its copy deadline is 10 am. "How do you make the right call when you don't have much time?" is the constant question that his team would contemplate, especially when there was such uncertainty in the data.

How significant was the use of information disorder during the COVID-19 pandemic?

Obtaining the right information is important in global health crises such as COVID-19 to keep everyone safe and healthy as much as possible, and for fair and efficient distribution of limited resources such as medicines, vaccines and medicinal devices. The dissemination of incorrect information may cause unwanted consequences like unnecessary widespread panic (Heiat et al., 2021), changed shopping behaviours such as stockpiling (Lehberger, Kleih and Sparke, 2021) and decreased psychological wellbeing (Kurcer, Erdogan and Kardes, 2021; Samal, 2021).

False information can spread as fast as the virus, especially on social media, and when it is about COVID-19 it can take the form of conspiracies about its origins, misinformation about the spread, false information about symptoms and treatment, and rumours about the response by authorities and people (Wardle, Garcia and Doyle, 2020; also, see Chapter 3, Sections on *How do you responsibly cover online/social media conspiracy theories* and *Should the ethically-minded journalist attempt to debunk misinformation and disinformation online, or ignore it?*). This information disorder comprises three distinct forms of content that involve varying degrees of harm and falseness, according to Wardle and Derakhshan (2017), all of which were apparent during the pandemic. As discussed in Chapter 1, these are:

- Misinformation: when false information is shared, but no harm is meant
- Disinformation: when false information is knowingly shared to cause harm, and
- Malinformation: when genuine information is shared to cause harm, often by moving information designed to stay private into the public sphere

Wardle and Derakhshan, 2017, p. 5

The growing trend of information disorder during the pandemic has made journalists' jobs even more difficult and has presented them with new questions to consider. For example, should they cover a new development or press briefing which presents misinformation, disinformation or malinformation, and thus risk giving it more credibility and a wider audience, or should they ignore it for these very reasons? The question becomes increasingly difficult when the person spreading the damaging information is a prominent public figure or government official, such as former US President Donald Trump (Spring, 2020) or British ministers and MPs (Nguyen et al., 2021). The news values, which guide journalistic decision making, would advise in favour of coverage due to the newsworthiness of these public figures. But is there another reasoning to consider? Indeed, correcting harmful inaccuracies is one of the principles of UK codes of conduct, which means that journalists are ethically bound to cover such stories and expose the harmful content contained in them. Walter and Tukachinsky provide another reason why this should happen: such corrections have the potential to revert people's attitudes and beliefs to their baseline pre-misinformation levels, even if not entirely (2020).

Such corrective action has the potential to help manage the flood of information disorder that has characterised the COVID-19 pandemic. It may also improve public trust in the media. The global trust survey, *Edelman Trust Barometer 2021*, which covers a significant period of the pandemic, shows very low levels of trust in the journalism profession and the traditional media. For example, in the UK, only 37% of respondents trusted the media, similar to the level in France, but much lower than the global average of 51% (Edelman, 2021).

Despite the reported low levels of trust in mainstream media, the public's appetite for news stayed strong, according to the Ofcom 2021 report. Interestingly the report found that 37% of online adults used Facebook to access news content during the Spring 2020 lockdown, which makes Facebook the most popular intermediary service for news consumption (Ofcom, 2021). This practice comes with its own problems given Facebook's troubled history of spreading misinformation and allegedly prioritising polarising content (Waterson and Milmo, 2021). The Ofcom report also stated that "the prevalence of misinformation claims is highest on Facebook" (p. 167), which again points towards the distribution of misinformation as a major challenge for the future. On a more positive note, participants reported a gradual decrease in exposure to information they considered false or misleading: from 46% in March 2020 (during the first UK lockdown) to 30% a year later (Ofcom, 2021).

Scaremongering

Scaremongering, "the spreading of alarming reports" (Oxford English Dictionary, 2021), is highly related to disinformation and malinformation, as the main motive behind the action is deliberate and calculated. These messages may include anything to generate fear, such as misuse of data and exaggerated cases.

An article on the BBC's website on 21 September 2020 reported a statement by Sir Patrick Vallance, the UK government's chief scientific adviser, that "at the moment we think the epidemic is doubling roughly every seven days" (BBC News, 2020c). He added that if numbers continue to double each week, the UK could see 50,000 new cases per day and more than 200 deaths per day in mid-October. Stressing that this scenario was not a prediction but an illustration of how quickly the virus could develop, he emphasised the need for swift action.

However, when the Coronavirus (COVID-19) in the UK dashboard reported the number of COVID-19 cases three weeks before the story in question, there were 2,948 new cases on 7 September and 3,330 new cases on 13 September (Gov.uk, n.d.), which is an increase of 13% over a six-day period. Further, there were 2,621 new cases on 14 September and 3,899 new cases on 20 September (Gov.uk, n.d.), indicating an increase of 49%, which is again far from doubling, as the government advisers had claimed. The only week when numbers had more than doubled was between 1 and 6 September: 1,295 new cases on September 1 and 2,988 new cases on September 6 (Gov.uk, n.d.). Until that first week in September, the increase in the total number of reported cases was not only far from doubling but also there were decreases too. Additionally, in Vallance's statement there was no mention of the number of tests performed or the rate of tests versus positive outcomes, as it might change the number of people who tested positive (i.e. more tests means a higher chance of more positive cases).

Vallance's comments were later criticised by the *Financial Times* and *The Telegraph*, amongst others. Journalist Camilla Cavendish noted in the *Financial Times* that although Vallance had to admit that the numbers were not actually a prediction, there was an underlying message. She said: "The point was to try and scare people into changing behaviour: stop households mixing and large groups socialising indoors, the two most potent sources of virus spread." She added: "Fear is a natural response to a pandemic. But if messaging makes people increasingly phobic, the impact on their mental health will be appalling, and their anxiety will ricochet through the economy" (Cavendish, 2020). Science editor of *The Telegraph*, Sarah Knapton, followed up with a news story, in which scientists and economists labelled this presentation of data by the government as "implausible" and "irresponsible". They pointed out that data showed the cases were not doubling every seven days as the growth rate of new infections at the time was between 2% and 7% each day. Knapton quoted a tweet from Professor David Paton, a specialist in industrial economics at the University of Nottingham, to Sir Patrick Vallance and the government's chief medical officer, Prof Chris Whitty. It said:

> If you want to compare with France and Spain, why wouldn't you use their doubling time which is every three weeks, not every week?" Paton added: "Do @CMO_England and @uksciencechief really think it is acceptable to present data in this way?
>
> Knapton, 2020

This example by the government's advisers shows how disinformation and malinformation can also come from public officials and scientists and therefore, those sources, and the information they offer, should be scrutinised as much as all others.

What advice can newcomers in health journalism follow when they report on health or science issues related to COVID-19 and beyond?

Health journalism is an exciting field, where lots of new and impactful developments on COVID-19 and beyond happen regularly. Below is some advices for starting out there.

1. Do not be afraid of science and data. But also, do not take it at face value and instead interrogate its origin, any discrepancies and questions that come up.
2. Develop professional relationships with experts for example scientists and do not hesitate to ask them for clarifications and explanations. Look for experts in your local university. They may be more likely to respond due to working or living in the same community.
3. Tell your audience when we do not know something due to lack of data. Do not oversell the data.

4. Do not sensationalise the situation, as that hurts your credibility and the story itself.
5. Follow the guidelines for responsible reporting of various issues. One such set of guidelines is the Suicide Reporting Toolkit, which also covers major trauma.
6. Tap into resources that are there to help you, such as fact-checking websites, explanatory videos, educational webinars, intermediaries such as the Science Media Centre, and others.
7. Do not do this alone (Nguyen et al., 2021). See Nguyen and colleagues for more advanced advice on how to work with health data.

Ethics in action: Helen McArdle, health correspondent at *The Herald*: "Look into the small print of the figures, always do it yourself."

Helen McArdle has been a journalist for 12 years. She started as a trainee reporter on the Scottish newspaper, the *Sunday Herald* before moving to its sister paper, *The Herald*. She worked for three years as transport correspondent, before taking on the role of health correspondent in November 2016, covering health news and health-related science. She won the British Journalism Awards category for Health and Science Journalism in 2018, and in 2019 she won News Story of the Year at the UK-wide Medical Journalists' Association Awards for *The Herald's* coverage of NHS Tayside's use of charity funds to augment their weakening finances. She has also been shortlisted for awards at the Scottish Press Awards and UK Regional Press Awards.

How do you decide which topics to focus on when covering COVID-19?

It is a case of what is happening on a particular day more than anything. You are led by maybe certain statistics or problem, so that would dictate what you concentrate on for that day. Or people getting in touch with you about a particular aspect. Sometimes it's just chance and circumstance. And then sometimes if I am reading stuff that is going on elsewhere, I will wonder if there is a Scottish angle to that. I also have to do a weekly column for *The Herald*, which is a chance to provide an analysis of some aspect of COVID. So that gives me an opportunity to discuss what is the most topical aspect of COVID for that week or something that has been overlooked or to bring a Scottish perspective and angle.

When writing stories about COVID-19, how do you make sure that the information you offer is factually correct and how do you avoid false information?

I am always a little bit more wary of things that are put out by different political parties, for example in a press release. These figures are always spun in such a way as it is designed to be an attack on the SNP government (Scottish National Party, the party of government in Scotland). Equally the Scottish government will put out its own figures and try to promote what it thinks is a good angle.

An example where I felt statistics had been spun a bit and I avoided it was the Tories had put out a release where they were trying to argue that acute hospital beds had reduced by about 2,000 in the course of five years. And when I saw that statistic, I thought "that doesn't seem right to me" because I had been looking at statistics on that myself for a different story. And then I realised that they had taken two different sources of the figures and kind of sewn them together. But the way that the numbers had been counted had changed over the five years. So I think you always have to look into the small print of the figures, always do it yourself. We are lucky in Scotland, we have tons and tons of data through Public Health Scotland, through official data published in national records, even the data published by the Scottish government, you can always go back to the data versus what they put out in the press release. Equally, the Office for National Statistics and Public Health England, has tons of data there. So I always think that's the number one thing: go and look at the raw data for yourself.

Social media can obviously be a source of misinformation, but during the pandemic Twitter has also been a source of really good scientific analysis. Over time you gauge the scientists that you can trust because they are the ones who progressively have said something or predicted something that turned out to be true. So you start to discriminate between the scientists who are logical and predict things accurately and those who don't. It's good to start following those scientists on Twitter because they offer explainers or take things that have been misconstrued by politicians and explain them in much more straightforward ways, and that's a good way to cut through the misinformation.

Who do you think should be responsible for addressing the wave of misinformation about COVID-19 which has hit the public sphere?

I think, unfortunately there's probably very little you can do to get rid of it, especially with stuff like social media. All you can do is to present more reliable stuff that's based on actual data and on speaking to people who are better informed in terms of scientists. It's difficult to counter when you as the mainstream media are seen as spreading misinformation.

There are efforts to try and shut down that kind of misinformation on sites like Facebook and Twitter. When you think about it, broadcast media are subject to Ofcom. We in the print media are not as toughly regulated as Ofcom, but we're still regulated [self-regulation via IPSO and IMPRESS, see Chapter 3 for further details]. You can have some sort of regulator, someone you can complain to if people are spreading misinformation. I think that would be the only way.

If you see a story, which science and common sense tell you that is most likely false and may cause harm to audiences but is put forward by prominent people, do you ignore the story altogether because you know that the content is dubious or do you still cover it because it is a newsworthy story?

I think you can still report things like that while giving all the caveats why this isn't a good idea. You cannot not report this stuff, but you can give all the caveats of why it is not right because of a lack of clinical trials or very little evidence it works or things are anecdotal. I do not think you can avoid these kinds of stories, you just have to provide enough of the context. If you do not report it, then it becomes more of a thing of the mainstream media refusing to report on an issue. I think it's better to report them from a trusted source like the mainstream media.

Do you see any difference in how health journalism was practised before the pandemic and how it was practised during the pandemic? Do you think the practice of health journalism has changed?

I am not sure the practice of health journalism has changed, but it has gotten more prominent. In the early days of the pandemic when we had the daily press conferences by Downing Street [the UK government], what used to frustrate me was that they were almost entirely dominated by political journalists. To some extent you also saw it in Scottish briefings. I think that was not always helpful, as sometimes the problems we had in reporting some of the stuff going on was that we had political reporters covering it. When political reporters are asking questions at the briefings, they obviously have their own agenda, they will be looking for a political angle. The science and health journalists would have asked different questions from the political journalists and sometimes that would have helped in understanding the situation better.

What has been your most challenging story during the pandemic so far in terms of ethics? How did you navigate the challenges?

Invariably the toughest story has to deal with patients or with grieving relatives where something bad has happened. That is the toughest thing as a health journalist because you want to do a good job of it. One example would be of a man who died after waiting 40 hours for an ambulance. It was not a difficult story in terms of the actual reporting, but it is always difficult to interview people. There has obviously been a lot more of that over the course of the pandemic. The care homes as well, lots of tragic stories of old people dying in care homes.

Those are situations where you have to be sensitive and you always worry afterwards whether you have reported everything. You are trying to balance what the family wants as well as your duty to the reader to report things. There might be certain things that you think would help explain the story but the family is a bit reluctant maybe for a particular detail to be disclosed because it is quite personal to their relatives.

For all the negatives that the pandemic has caused, do you find any positives to have come out of it for the journalism industry?

This is the first time in years and years when we have received pay rises. I think media organisations have saved so much money by closing offices and switching to smaller offices or having lots of people working from home. They do not have the huge overhead now. They have been saving huge amounts of money and not all of them but some of them have passed this on to staff in the form of pay rises.

In terms of health journalism, it has been nice that health correspondents have been more prominent. Over the years in our company and lots of others, specialists have been cut, and cut, and cut. It has shown the value of having specialists in journalism and having someone who is devoted to the subject and has the contacts and knowledge to be able to explain some of the nuances of things. As I say, there are lots of complexities. For example, people not understanding why are flu vaccinations done in a certain way and what does it have to do with COVID? You can explain that it has to do with the way the GP contracts were drawn a few years ago in Scotland.

Has the pandemic solidified the media's positions and reminded people that they are trusted sources of information?

Yes, I think so. For all that you hear about people complaining about mainstream media and fake news, and other issues, the actual evidence on the ground shows a different story. On our *Herald Scotland* website, traffic is up and digital subscriptions are up. In other newspapers as well, subscriptions have been going up. You have seen that across print as well as television. Who do people turn to when they want information? BBC or Channel 4. When big crises do happen, people do turn back to the mainstream media to get their information. And people have this massive desire for information. I think it has shown the value of that and people's appreciation of that. I have seen it in my own stories. When I do big explanatory pieces on COVID, there are huge readership numbers, huge engagement, even behind paywalls.

The reasons why people are suspicious of the mainstream media often comes from their own biases. If they are very pro-Union (in favour of supporting the constitutional union between Scotland and the rest of the UK), they tend to see everything in the mainstream media as very pro-SNP or vice versa.

What advice would you give to novice health journalists about how to succeed in this field?

Always look out for things that maybe have been underreported or for things that you find interesting or you find a new angle too. Be prepared that you will always feel guilty about the fact that you can never report all the stories that people come to you with. That is an issue with journalism in general, but I think it is particularly problematic in health because sometimes people are coming to you with heart-wrenching stories. But choose your battles and the stories that you cover because your time is precious and you must pursue the stories that you can complete.

Ethical workout

- How would you address the dilemma between the immediacy of the news and the need for accuracy in health reporting?
- Health journalism relies regularly on science and complicated data and it is up to the reporter to translate that complex content for their audiences. What steps can a journalist take to ensure that their story remains true to the science but also tells a good story that captures their audience?
- Is fact-checking the best way to combat misinformation, disinformation and malinformation, or can you think of other ways to address these issues?
- Can you think of additional ways in which health journalism is unique in terms of ethics?

Five takeaways from this chapter

- Health journalism does not only cover health, but also politics, societal movements, social norms and prejudices, as seen throughout the COVID-19 pandemic. Health journalists should be aware that policies are created, decisions are made, and measures are taken by officials not only with public health and epidemiology in mind, but also with regards to socio-economic, political and cultural dynamics.
- Health journalism holds significant potential for causing harm, and therefore information should be scrutinised very carefully and thoroughly.
- As scientific understanding develops swiftly during crisis times, conflicting information can come from sources who are otherwise considered reliable

and trustworthy. This is part of the process, and health journalists should explain that to audiences.
- Health journalists often face the conflict between immediacy and accuracy of the story, and have difficulties interpreting the statistics due to continuous, huge amounts of data flow in a situation like a pandemic. Do not report on the news without confirming the information/data first to be sure of its accuracy, and do not give up on the ethical principles of health reporting in favour of immediacy.
- Misinformation, disinformation and malinformation are growing obstacles for journalists, which they can help to manage via covering those stories and engaging in quick corrections of the inaccurate information. This approach has a chance of repairing some of the damage from misinformation, disinformation and malinformation in the audiences' minds.

Ethics toolbox

- Science Media Centre (UK)—intermediary organisation between scientists and journalists. See www.sciencemediacentre.org/
- Association of British Science Writers. See www.absw.org.uk/
- Guild of Health Writers (UK). See https://healthwriters.com/
- Association of Health Care Journalists (USA). See https://healthjournalism.org/
- International Center for Journalists—provides resources and research on global topics related to COVID-19 and beyond. Further details at www.icfj.org/
- International Journalists' Network—sister organisation of ICJ, provides global opportunities, professional tips, toolkits, and so on. Topics include health and others. Further details at https://ijnet.org/en
- Office for National Statistics—UK's recognised national statistical institute, containing publicly available data on health and other topics on national, regional and local levels. Available at: www.ons.gov.uk/
- Office for Health Improvement and Disparities—part of the Department of Health and Social Care (see www.gov.uk/government/organisations/department-of-health-and-social-care). It focuses on information about health improvement and eliminating health disparities. Available at: www.gov.uk/government/organisations/office-for-health-improvement-and-disparities
- Public Health Scotland—national public health body for Scotland. See https://publichealthscotland.scot/
- UK Coronavirus Dashboard (n.d.). See https://coronavirus.data.gov.uk/
- WHO Coronavirus Dashboard. Available at: https://covid19.who.int/

References

Barmer, I. and Cawley, L. (2021). 'Covid: What the "ping" rule changes mean for small businesses'. *BBC News*. 16 August. Available at: www.bbc.co.uk/news/uk-england-suffolk-58231657 (Accessed: 25 October 2021).

BBC News (2020a). 'Coronavirus: Calls for better workplace social distancing guidance'. *BBC News*. 28 March. Available at: www.bbc.co.uk/news/uk-52076504 (Accessed: 25 October 2021).

BBC News (2020b). 'Coronavirus: Wear masks in crowded public spaces, says science body'. *BBC News*. 7 July. Available at: www.bbc.co.uk/news/uk-53316491 (Accessed: 26 October 2021).

BBC News (2020c). 'Covid-19: UK could face 50,000 cases a day by October without action – Vallance'. *BBC News*. Available at: www.bbc.co.uk/news/uk-54234084 (Accessed: 26 October 2021).

BBC News (2021). 'Small businesses urgently call for more covid support'. *BBC News*. 28 June. Available at: www.bbc.co.uk/news/business-57630349 (Accessed: 25 October 2021).

Bell, M. (2020). 'ITV News Anglia's first interview with Captain Tom Moore'. *ITV News*. Available at: www.itv.com/news/anglia/2020-04-30/one-little-soul-like-me-won-t-make-much-difference-captain-tom-moore-s-first-interview-with-itv-news-anglia (Accessed: 26 October 2021).

Bloom, D. and Shadwell, T. (2020). 'Government says "No Evidence" wearing face masks affects coronavirus spread'. *Mirror*. Available at: www.mirror.co.uk/news/politics/government-says-no-evidence-wearing-21810110 (Accessed: 25 October 2021).

Boeyink, D.E. and Borden, S.L. (2010). *Making hard choices in journalism ethics: Cases and practice*. New York: Routledge.

Boykoff, M. T. and Boykoff, J. M. (2004). 'Balance as bias: Global warming and the US prestige press'. *Global Environmental Change*, 14, pp. 123–136.

Cavendish, C. (2020). 'Scaremongering will damage the UK's fragile economy'. *Financial Times*. 26 September. Available at: www.ft.com/content/044d7d82-c762-4d41-ab0f-9b1e9e49cc6f (Accessed: 26 October 2021).

Cecco, L. (2020). 'Canada's Chinese Community faces racist abuse in wake of coronavirus'. *The Guardian*. 28 January. Available at: www.theguardian.com/world/2020/jan/28/canada-chinese-community-battles-racist-backlash-amid-coronavirus-outbreak (Accessed: 25 October 2021).

Cummins, E. (2020). 'The new coronavirus is not an excuse to be racist'. *The Verge*. 4 February. Available at: www.theverge.com/2020/2/4/21121358/coronavirus-racism-social-media-east-asian-chinese-xenophobia (Accessed: 25 October 2021).

Edelman (2021). 'Edelman trust barometer 2021'. *Edelman*. Available at: www.edelman.com/sites/g/files/aatuss191/files/2021-03/2021%20Edelman%20Trust%20Barometer.pdf (Accessed: 27 October 2021).

Ethical Journalism Network (EJN) (2021). 'Our five core principles of ethical journalism'. Available at: https://ethicaljournalismnetwork.org/who-we-are. (Accessed: 29 December 2021).

Freedman, L. (2020). Scientific advice at a time of emergency. SAGE and Covid-19. *The Political Quarterly*, 91(3), pp. 514–522. https://doi.org/10.1111/1467-923X.12885

Giuffrida, A. and Willsher, K. (2020). 'Outbreaks of xenophobia in west as coronavirus spreads'. *The Guardian*. 31 January. Available at: www.theguardian.com/world/2020/jan/31/spate-of-anti-chinese-incidents-in-italy-amid-coronavirus-panic (Accessed: 25 October 2021).

Gov.uk Coronavirus (Covid-19) in the UK (n.d.). 'Cases in the UK'. Available at: https://coronavirus.data.gov.uk/details/cases#card-cases_by_date_reported (Accessed: 10 January 2022).

Harcup, T. (2015). *Journalism: Principles and practice*. 3rd edn. London: Sage Publications.

Health and Social Care Committee and Science and Technology Committee (2021). 'Coronavirus: Lessons learned to date'. *UK Parliament House of Commons*. Available at: https://committees.parliament.uk/publications/7496/documents/78687/default/ (Accessed: 25 October 2021).

Heiat, M., Heiat, F., Halaji, M., Ranjbar, R., Marvasti, Z.T., Yaali-Jahromi, E., Azizi, M.M., Hosseini, S.M. and Badri, T. (2021). Phobia and fear of COVID-19: Origins, complications and management, a narrative review. *Annali di Igiene: Medicina Preventiva e di Comunita*, 33(4), pp. 360–370. doi: 10.7416/ai.2021.2446

Hswen, Y., Xu, X., Hing, A., Hawkins, J.B., Brownstein, J.S. and Gee, G.C. (2021). Association of "#covid19" versus "#chinesevirus" with anti-Asian sentiments on Twitter: March 9–23, 2020. *American Journal of Public Health*, 111(5), pp. 956–964. https://doi.org/10.2105/AJPH.2021.306154

Human Rights Watch (2020). 'Covid-19 fueling anti-Asian Racism and xenophobia worldwide'. *Human Rights Watch*. Available at: www.hrw.org/news/2020/05/12/covid-19-fueling-anti-asian-racism-and-xenophobia-worldwide (Accessed: 25 October 2021).

Knapton, S. (2020). '"Implausible": Scientists hit out at warning of 50,000 covid cases a day'. *The Telegraph*. Available at: www.telegraph.co.uk/news/2020/09/21/implausible-scientists-hit-warning-50000-covid-cases-day/ (Accessed: 25 October 2021)

Kurcer, M., Erdoğan, Z. and Kardeş, V.Ç. (2021). The effect of the COVID-19 pandemic on health anxiety and cyberchondria levels of university students. *Perspectives in Psychiatric Care*, pp. 1–9. doi: 10.1111/ppc.12850

Leask, J., Hooker, C. & King, C. (2010). Media coverage of health issues and how to work more effectively with journalists: A qualitative study. *BMC Public Health*, 10, 535. https://doi.org/10.1186/1471-2458-10-535

Lehberger, M., Kleih, A-K. and Sparke, K. (2021). Panic buying in times of coronavirus (COVID-19): Extending the theory of planned behavior to understand the stockpiling of nonperishable food in Germany. *Appetite*, 161(105118). doi: 10.1016/j.appet.2021.105118

Luton Today (2021). 'Almost 1,000 Bedfordshire hospitals trust staff unvaccinated'. *Luton Today*. Available at: www.lutontoday.co.uk/health/coronavirus/almost-1000-bedfordshire-hospitals-trust-staff-unvaccinated-3432178 (Accessed: 25 October 2021).

Mercer, D. (2020). 'Coronavirus: Hate crimes against Chinese people soar in UK during COVID-19 crisis'. *Sky News*. Available at: https://news.sky.com/story/coronavirus-hate-crimes-against-chinese-people-soar-in-uk-during-covid-19-crisis-11979388 (Accessed: 25 October 2021).

Milman, O. (2020). 'Trump touts hydroxychloroquine as a cure for Covid-19. Don't believe the hype'. *The Guardian*. 6 April. Available at: www.theguardian.com/science/2020/apr/06/coronavirus-cure-fact-check-hydroxychloroquine-trump (Accessed: 10 January 2022).

MSN (2021). 'The Captain Tom story and how it all started on the Bedford Times & Citizen'. *MSN News*. Available at: www.msn.com/en-gb/cars/news/the-captain-tom-story-and-how-it-all-started-on-the-bedford-times-and-citizen/vi-BB1dIWHk (Accessed: 27 October 2021).

Nguyen, A., Zhao, X., Lawson, B. and Jackson, D. (2021). 'Reporting from a statistical chaos: Journalistic lessons from the first year of Covid-19 data and science in the news'. *Bournemouth University*. Available at: www.bournemouth.ac.uk/news/2021-01-27/reporting-lessons-journalists-first-year-covid-19-data-science-news (Accessed: 26 October 2021).

Ofcom (2021). 'Online Nation 2021 report'. *Ofcom*. Available at: www.ofcom.org.uk/__data/assets/pdf_file/0013/220414/online-nation-2021-report.pdf (Accessed: 26 October 2021).

Oxford English Dictionary (2021). 'Scaremongering, n.'. Available at: www.oed.com/view/Entry/172031?rskey=H4FUc7&result=1#eid24151029 (Accessed: 30 December 2021).

Partington, R. (2021). '"We need more help": Three firms on surviving the UK's Covid-19 economy'. *The Guardian*. Available at: www.theguardian.com/business/2021/feb/12/we-need-more-help-three-firms-on-surviving-the-uks-covid-19-economy (Accessed: 25 October 2021).

Parveen, N. and Barr, C. (2021). 'Black over-80s in England half as likely as white people to have had covid jab'. *The Guardian*. 4 February. Available at:

www.theguardian.com/world/2021/feb/04/black-over-80s-in-england-half-as-lik ely-to-have-had-covid-vaccine (Accessed: 25 October 2021).

Pidd, H. (2020). '"He's just a wonderful man": How Captain Tom became a superstar fundraiser'. *The Guardian*. Available at: www.theguardian.com/world/2020/ may/01/hes-just-a-wonderful-man-how-captain-tom-became-a-superstar-fundrai ser (Accessed: 27 October 2021).

Pitas, C., Sandle, P. and James, W. (2020). 'UK Scientists say face masks have only small effect on coronavirus spread'. *Reuters*. 28 April. Available at: www.reuters.com/ article/us-health-coronavirus-britain-masks-idUSKCN22A2UT (Accessed: 25 October 2021).

Posetti, J., Bell, E. and Brown, P. (2020). 'Journalism and the pandemic: A global snapshot of impacts'. *International Center for Journalists (ICFJ), Tow Center for Digital Journalism*. Available at: www.icfj.org/sites/default/files/2020-10/Journalism%20 and%20the%20Pandemic%20Project%20Report%201%202020_FINAL.pdf (Accessed: 26 October 2021).

Rich, M. (2020). 'As coronavirus spreads, so does anti-Chinese sentiment'. *The New York Times*. 30 January. Available at: www.nytimes.com/2020/01/30/world/ asia/coronavirus-chinese-racism.html (Accessed: 25 October 2021).

Samal, J. (2021). Impact of COVID-19 infodemic on psychological wellbeing and vaccine hesitancy. *The Egyptian Journal of Bronchology*, 15(14). https://doi.org/ 10.1186/s43168-021-00061-2

Saunders, T. (2021). '111,000 NHS workers are still unvaccinated against Covid and yet to receive a single dose'. *i News*. 5 October. Available at: https://inews.co.uk/ news/health/covid-vaccine-nhs-workers-havent-had-jab-uk-mandatory-vaccinat ion-1233173 (Accessed: 25 October 2021).

Shearing, H. (2021). 'Capt Tom donations: What was the £33m spent on?' *BBC News*. 3 February. Available at: www.bbc.co.uk/news/uk-52758683 (Accessed: 27 October 2021).

Siddique, H. and Mohdin, A. (2021). 'Study reveals low covid jab take-up among black people in England'. *The Guardian*. 29 March. Available at: www.theguard ian.com/world/2021/mar/29/study-low-covid-jab-take-up-black-people-england (Accessed: 25 October 2021).

Society of Professional Journalists (2014). 'SPJ code of ethics'. *Society of Professional Journalists*. Available at: www.spj.org/ethicscode.asp (Accessed: 22 October 2021).

Spring, M. (2020). 'Coronavirus: The human cost of virus misinformation'. *BBC News*. 27 May. Available at: www.bbc.co.uk/news/stories-52731624 (Accessed: 27 October 2021).

The Captain Tom Foundation (n.d.). 'Story'. *The Captain Tom Foundation*. Available at: https://captaintom.org/story-1 (Accessed: 27 October 2021).

Turner, C. (2020). 'Bedford man to walk 100 lengths of his garden for NHS before his 100th birthday'. *Bedford Today*. 7 April. Available at: www.bedfordtoday.co.uk/health/bedford-man-walk-100-lengths-his-garden-nhs-his-100th-birthday-2532073 (Accessed: 27 October 2021).

UK Coronavirus Dashboard (n.d.). 'Coronavirus (COVID-19) in the UK'. Available at: https://coronavirus.data.gov.uk/ (Accessed: 30 September 2021).

Walter, N. and Tukachinsky, R. (2020). A meta-analytic examination of the continued influence of misinformation in the face of correction: How powerful is it, why does it happen, and how to stop it? *Communication Research*, 47(2), pp. 155–177. https://doi.org/10.1177/0093650219854600

Wardle, C. and Derakhshan, H. (2017). 'Information disorder: Toward an interdisciplinary framework for research and policy making'. *Council of Europe*. Available at: https://rm.coe.int/information-disorder-toward-an-interdisciplinary-framework-for-researc/168076277c (Accessed: 27 October 2021).

Wardle, C., Garcia, L. and Doyle, P. (2020). 'Covering coronavirus: An online course for journalists'. *First Draft*. Available at: https://firstdraftnews.org/long-form-article/covering-coronavirus-english/ (Accessed: 27 October 2021).

Waterson, J. and Milmo, D. (2021). 'Facebook whistleblower Frances Haugen calls for urgent external regulation'. *The Guardian*. 25 October. Available at: www.theguardian.com/technology/2021/oct/25/facebook-whistleblower-frances-haugen-calls-for-urgent-external-regulation (Accessed: 27 October 2021).

Wilkins, L. (2005). Plagues, pestilence and pathogens: The ethical implications of news reporting of a world health crisis. *Asian Journal of Communication*, 15, 247–254. https://doi.org/10.1080/01292980500260698

Williams, T.-A. (2020). 'Trump-touted hydroxychloroquine does NOT prevent Covid – Major study halted'. *The Sun*. Available at: www.thesun.co.uk/news/11794207/trump-hydroxychloroquine-does-not-prevent-covid/ (Accessed: 10 January 2022)

Woolley, S. (2020). 'Melbourne students assaulted in "disgusting" racist attack'. *7NEWS*. 17 April. Available at: https://7news.com.au/lifestyle/health-wellbeing/coronavirus-university-of-melbourne-international-students-assaulted-in-unprovoked-racist-attack-c-983675 (Accessed: 25 October 2021).

World Health Organization (1946). 'Constitution of the World Health Organization'. *World Health Organization*. Available at: https://apps.who.int/gb/bd/PDF/bd47/EN/constitution-en.pdf?ua=1 (Accessed: 25 October 2021).

World Health Organization (2015). 'WHO issues best practices for naming new human infectious diseases'. *World Health Organization*. Available at: www.who.int/news/item/08-05-2015-who-issues-best-practices-for-naming-new-human-infectious-diseases (Accessed: 25 October 2021).

World Health Organization (2020a). 'Infodemic'. *World Health Organization*. Available at: www.who.int/health-topics/infodemic (Accessed: 25 October 2021).

World Health Organization (2020b). 'Managing the COVID-19 infodemic: Promoting healthy behaviours and mitigating the harm from misinformation and disinformation'. *World Health Organization.* Available at: www.who.int/news/item/23-09-2020-managing-the-covid-19-infodemic-promoting-healthy-behaviours-and-mitigating-the-harm-from-misinformation-and-disinformation (Accessed: 25 October 2021).

Yanovitzky, I. and Bennett, C. (1999). Media attention, institutional response, and health behavior change: The case of drunk driving, 1978–1996. *Communication Research*, 26, pp. 429–453. https://doi.org/10.1177/009365099026004004

10
Battling for news
Reporting war and conflict

Richard Lance Keeble

This chapter explores some of the many ethical issues involved in the reporting of conflict. It focuses on the corporate media and the emergence of the professional war correspondent. Along with a critique of professionalism, it takes in the alternative media and considers the opportunities for progressive journalism within the mainstream. The crucial ethical responsibilities of journalists in both the corporate and alternative sectors in bringing to light the warfare activities of the secret state are also highlighted. In the *Ethics in Action* section, former BBC World Service correspondent, Lara Pawson, reflects on the ethical choices she made while reporting from Africa.

How can we understand, critically, the emergence of the professional war reporter?

The Irishman William Howard Russell (1820–1907) is often described as Britain's first professional war correspondent. Reporting the Crimean War (1854–1856) for *The Times*, he was able to exploit the newly invented telegraph to send vivid battle reports based on first-hand interviews—living and marching with the troops. As Jon E. Lewis writes:

> With combat reportage plus instant communication, the era of the war correspondent had arrived. ... Sales of *The Times* shot up and soon every major newspaper in the Western world had a combat correspondent aboard to satisfy the readers' seemingly insatiable appetite for news of war. After all, war is the ultimate press story—human interest plus the destiny of nations. Nothing compares to it.
>
> 2001, p. xv

Russell, who described himself as "the miserable parent of a luckless tribe", went on to report on the Indian 'mutiny' in 1857, the American Civil War in 1861 and the Franco–Prussian War of 1870, with his despatches from the Zulu War of 1879 for the *Daily Telegraph* being his last. His Crimea reporting came at a critical moment in the history of the British press (Knightley, 2000, p. 2). In 1855, the stamp duties on newspapers—which had effectively limited their readership to a wealthy elite—were finally abolished. This allowed for the emergence of a mass-selling newspaper industry based largely on advertising. In the process, the unstamped (and hence illegal) trade union-based, republican, revolutionary and highly partisan press—which had previously been far more popular than the elite press—was marginalised. The market effectively censored the radical, activist media (Curran and Seaton, 1994, pp. 32–48).

The latter half of the nineteenth century saw the emergence of professionalism – with apolitical corporate journalism (along with other professions such as medicine, teaching and law) and its associated ideologies of objectivity and press freedom being closely integrated into the operations of the bourgeois state. The notion of social closure, first theorised by Max Weber (1978 [1922]) and later developed by Frank Parkin (1979) and Richard Collins (1990), highlights the way in which occupations seek to regulate market conditions in their favour restricting access to a limited group of eligible, mainly middle class, white professionals. The notion can help to explain how the ideologies of professionalism serve to exclude alternative, activist, partisan media even from the definition of 'journalism'. The ideology is so pervasive still that it provides the frame around which much of the debate over media ethics in times of conflict operates today (see Royle, 1987; Owen and Purdey, 2009; Moorcraft, 2016).

How important is the war correspondent's role as eye-witness?

Many journalists who cover conflicts stress their role as eye-witnesses. They do not strike political poses; using their professional skills and ethical awareness, they try to record accurately and honestly what they see. This approach ties in with notions about objectivity, media freedom, the public interest—and the fourth estate which highlights the watchdog role of the professional media keeping a check on abuses of power by both government and other professions. Geoff McLaughlin (2016) rightly stresses the dangers frontline reporters can face. Not surprisingly then, celebrations of journalists as intrepid battlers for the truth appear after they are killed, injured or taken hostage. Following the death of *The Sunday Times*'s intrepid reporter Marie Colvin—famous for wearing an eye patch after being hit during the Sri Lankan civil war in 2001—while covering the Syrian war in 2012, Roy Greenslade praised her in his *Guardian* tribute as "a fearless but never foolhardy war correspondent who believed passionately in the need to report on conflicts from the frontline" (Greenslade, 2012).

And after *The Times* correspondent Anthony Loyd and photographer Jack Hill were attacked while reporting the Syrian civil war in May 2014, the newspaper captured many elements of the dominant ideology when it editorialised:

> War reporters are not omniscient. Their information is inevitably partial. Yet they are honour bound to describe the world as they see it and not according to a set of ideological presuppositions. … *The Times* is not neutral in its editorial views. Informed by the testimony of our reporters, we have no doubt that [President] Assad bears prime responsibility for Syria's torment. Our reporting takes no side, however, but accuracy. … The ability to distinguish fact from propaganda is what our readers expect. It is through the bravery and professionalism of Loyd, Hill and others that we seek to fulfil that obligation.
>
> The Times, 2014

Is it right for the media to back 'our boys' always during wars?

Journalists in the corporate sector tend to be more courageous in criticising the government when British forces are not engaged; when 'our boys' (and a few of 'our girls') are in action, most of the media tend to back it. But is this right? William Howard Russell's famous despatches for *The Times* from the Crimean War chronicled the failings of the army and supposedly led to the resignation of the prime minister at the time, Lord Aberdeen's cabinet. But was he justified in sending his reports? Many commentators who stress the inevitable adversarial relationship between the media and the military focus on Russell's reporting (see Snoddy, 1993; de Burgh, 2000, pp. 33–34). Yet how much is this myth? Phillip Knightley (2000, p. 16) in his seminal history of war reporting, *The First Casualty*, says that while Russell exposed military failures he failed to understand their causes. And while he criticised the lot of the ordinary soldier, he never attacked the officers "to whose class he belonged himself". "Above all, Russell made the mistake, common to many a war correspondent, of considering himself part of the military establishment." Moreover, *The Times* played only a small role in the fall of the government. An important section of the elite was determined on Aberdeen's fall, irrespective of any views expressed in the press.

Were American journalists too outspoken in their coverage of US actions in Vietnam? For the US elite the defeat in Vietnam against a far less technologically sophisticated enemy—accompanied by assassinations, race riots and student upheavals at home—was a trauma of unprecedented proportions. Many blamed the media. Long after the end of the conflict, television images still dominate perceptions of it: a US Marine Zippo lighting a Vietnamese village, the execution of a Vietcong suspect in a Saigon street, a Vietnamese girl running naked and terrified down a road after a napalm attack. Images such as these, along with press criticism of the conduct of the war, are said to have eroded public support.

Yet how much of this is also myth? Surveys showed that media consumption, in fact, promoted support for the war (Williams, 1993, pp. 305–328). And virtually every Vietnam reporter backed the war effort. A Gannett Foundation report commented (1991, p. 15): "Throughout the war, in fact, journalists who criticised the military's performance did so out of a sense of frustration that military strategy and tactics were failing to accomplish the goal of decisively defeating the North Vietnamese forces." Most commentators have seen a shift to more advocacy reporting following the Vietcong Tet offensive of 1968. But such a shift occurred among the American elite with significant sections beginning to question the costs, effectiveness and overall moral/political justification for the war. The media followed the shift in the elite consensus rather than created it (Hallin, 1986, p. 21; Williams, 1987, pp. 250–254; Cummings, 1992, p. 84; Cohen, 2001). Susan Carruthers comments (2000, p. 148): "As elite dissatisfaction with US involvement deepened, journalists (both print and television) began reporting as 'atrocities' American actions which had previously received minimal, or no, attention." Also, after 1968, many in the US military were concerned to show the difficulties and daily frustrations of the war to the American public and welcomed the press as potential allies in conveying this message. Philip Taylor (2003, p. 73) also suggests the power of the media in promoting opposition to the Vietnam War has been widely exaggerated:

> It is too easily forgotten that American troops were not withdrawn from Vietnam until 1973. This was five years after Tet, a period just as long and as significant as US involvement in Vietnam before it—and a period longer than American involvement in the Second World War!

The patriotic imperative lies at the heart of British journalists' culture (Norton-Taylor, 1991). Not surprisingly this patriotic loyalty appears strongest during times of war. Both the BBC and ITN have identified themselves as guardians of national morale and national interest during wars. Significantly ITN's submission to a Commons select committee inquiry into handling of information during the Falklands War of 1982, opposed battlefield restrictions on journalists on these grounds: "Great opportunities were missed for the positive projection of the single-minded energy and determination of the British people in their support of the task force." Max Hastings, former editor of the London *Evening Standard* but most famous for being the first journalist to march into Port Stanley at the end of the Falklands War, commented:

> I felt my function was simply to identify totally with the interests and feelings of that force [the task force] ... when one was writing one's copy

one thought: beyond telling everybody what the men around me were doing, what can one say that is likely to be most helpful in winning the war?
Williams, 1992, pp. 156–157

Other journalists argue that they have a permanent responsibility for bringing the authorities to account and that their dissident role is all the more important when lives are at stake. Censorship, they claim, is too often used to hide military incompetence and inefficiency resulting in the loss of service people's lives.

During the Gulf War of 1991, all Fleet Street significantly backed the 'allied' attacks on Iraq, though *The Guardian* maintained a certain scepticism throughout. In 1999, the Fleet Street consensus again backed the US/UK attacks—this time on Yugoslavia (with *The Guardian* proving to be one of the most jingoistic) and called for a ground assault. Only the *Independent on Sunday* opposed the war, and its editor (Kim Fletcher) was sacked just days after the bombings ended. Some journalists, however, argue that while an editorial line may back a war, balance can be achieved in the coverage by presenting both sides. For instance, while *The Guardian* backed the Kosovo attacks, some of its prominent columnists opposed them and a large proportion of the letters took a similar balancing line. Similarly, while the *Mail* backed the bombings, some of its most prominent columnists were given considerable space to express opposition.

In 2003, with significant opposition to the rush to war being expressed by politicians, lawyers, intelligence officials, celebrities, religious leaders, charities and human rights campaigners—together with massive street protests—both nationally and internationally, the breakdown in Fleet Street's consensus was inevitable. Significantly, an International Gallup poll in December 2002, barely noted in the United States, found virtually no support for Washington's announced plans for war in Iraq carried out 'unilaterally by America and its allies' (see Ismael and Ismael, 2004). And on 15 February 2003, just days before the launch of the US/UK attacks on Iraq, an estimated two million people protested in London in the largest demonstration ever seen in Britain. Here was clearly a market that Fleet Street could not ignore. Yet still for the invasion of Iraq, the vast bulk of Fleet Street backed the action (though columnists and letter writers were divided).

The pro-intervention consensus on Fleet Street remained largely consistent during the Western attacks on Libya which led to the toppling and brutal butchering of President Gaddafi in 2011. And amidst the complex and devastating Syrian civil war which has drawn in multiple foreign powers, both overtly and covertly since it began in 2011, the newspapers have been resolute in their opposition to President Bashar al-Assad and his Russian ally, Vladimir Putin.

In many countries since 9/11, reporters covering conflicts have been intimidated, shot at and killed. What are the reasons and how should journalists respond?

Amazingly during the Second World War, few journalists were killed. For instance, of the 84 BBC radio journalists reporting the conflict, only two—Kent Stevenson and Guy Byam—perished. An estimated 71 reporters died during the Vietnam War (1965–1975), including those lost in Cambodia, Laos and Vietnam (Pyle, 2006), and none were killed in the Falklands conflict of 1982.

But the killings of journalists by US forces in Iraq continued relentlessly, even after the official ending of hostilities by President Bush on 1 May 2003. Unprecedented access to the front lines was the carrot offered the Western media during the invasion, but the stick was always on hand. Fifteen non-Iraqi journalists were killed, two went missing and many unilateral non-embeds were intimidated by the military. Had there been the same death rate for journalists during the Vietnam War, there would have been 3,000 killed. As John Donvan (2003) argues, "coalition forces saw unilaterals as having no business on their battlefield". Unilateral Terry Lloyd, of ITN, was killed by marines who fired at his car; Reuters camera operator Tara Protsyuk and Jose Couso, a cameraman for the Spanish TV channel Telecino, died after an American tank fired at the 15th floor of the Palestine Hotel in Baghdad, while Tayek Ayyoub, a cameraman for Al-Jazeera, died after a US jet bombed the channel's Baghdad office. In all, seven journalists were killed in US attacks. A major report by the Committee to Protect Journalists, *Permission to Fire*, blamed the US army for a breakdown in communication with the media and claimed the attack on the Palestine Hotel could have been avoided. Yet an investigation by the US military, released in November 2004, failed to explain why troops were not made aware the hotel was widely used by journalists (Tomlin, 2008). How many Iraqi journalists perished in the slaughters we will never know. For the most of the Western mainstream media they are non-people.

Of the 127 journalists and media workers killed in Iraq between 20 March 2003 and up until April 2008, at least 16 journalists and six media-support staffers were killed by US forces (Tomlin, 2008; Paterson, 2014). Some 14 reporters died during the Libyan invasion of 2011—including the legendary photojournalist, Tim Hetherington. In 2012, the celebrated *Sunday Times* frontline reporter, Marie Colvin, was killed covering the conflict in Syria—leading many organisations to pull back on their newsgathering activities in dangerous war zones. Colvin was one of 136 journalists who died covering the Syrian conflict between 2001 and 2020, according to the Committee for the Protection of Journalists.

In January 2015, armed men invaded the offices of the satirical, weekly cartoon magazine, *Charlie Hebdo*, in Paris, killing 12 people and injuring 11. More recently, on 16 October 2017, a car bomb killed a prominent anti-corruption blogger, Daphne Caruana Galizia, in Malta. Less than six months later, in Slovakia, Ján Kuciak, who had been reporting on the Italian mafia and alleged embezzlement of EU funds, was murdered. Then, in 2018, the murder and dismemberment of exiled Saudi journalist Jamal Khashoggi in the Saudi Arabian consulate in Istanbul, Turkey, made headlines around the world.

Moreover, the growth of organised crime linked to the operations of drug cartels in Asia, South and Central America, and the Caucasus is putting local journalists in extra dangers. Mexico is now one of the most dangerous countries for journalists as the drug cartels move north from Colombia to the US border (Cottle, Sambrook and Mosdell, 2016, p. 4). According to Donald Matheson and Stuart Allan, at the heart of the problem lies the decline of the notion of the journalist as a neutral observer:

> The extraordinarily high casualty rate among journalists in Iraq during the peak years of the US invasion and occupation is attributable partly to the new freedom with portable communications equipment gave them to enter dangerous areas, but it is also related to the collapse of the notion of the journalist as neutral observer. ... The distinction between combatant and reporter increasingly makes little sense to those fighting modern war
> *Matheson and Allan, 2009, p. 17*

Some commentators even suggest the position of the professional war reporter is now seriously under threat. In their survey of journalists' attitudes to the current dangers, Simon Cottle, Richard Sambrook and Nick Mosdell report (2016, p. 166):

> ... the capacity for belligerents as well as activists to bypass mainstream news media channels and send their own messages direct to their preferred audiences on their own terms and with their preferred images. This, according to many of our respondents, has increasingly undermined the earlier dependence of conflicting parties on news journalists and has thereby positioned journalists, in their eyes at least, as relatively redundant and, therefore, possibly without value.

Conflict zones in Syria, Yemen and Afghanistan are now considered too dangerous to cover by leading Western news organisations. In response, many news organisations have placed an extra reliance on freelances, human rights campaigners, citizen journalists and locally hired fixers (see Murrell, 2013). Yet all this raises a range of tricky ethical/political questions. Sometimes, news organisations are tempted to employ local stringers—most likely lacking proper personal insurance and risk assessment training—who are prepared to go into places considered far too dangerous by Western journalists. Significantly, all the 48 journalists and media workers who were killed in 2019—the lowest figure in 16 years—were locals (International News Safety Institute, 2020).

How ethical is this exploitation of local knowledge and daring? Locals also may prove partisan and highly selective in their sourcing. The death of 18-year-old Reuters photographer Molhem Barakat, in Aleppo, in December 2013, highlighted the difficulties facing news agencies relying on local hires to gather news. BBC news producer Stuart Hughes commented:

> We're entering uncharted territory in terms of the "reportability" of Syria and I fear this is the inevitable result. There's no way Reuters would have put a staffer into Aleppo—but they're prepared to give a teenager camera kit and send him on his way
>
> Pendry, 2020

Moreover, like many other locals working for international news organisations in Syria, Barakat was deeply involved in the conflict, killed alongside his brother Mustafa who was a rebel fighter for the Tawhid militia.

On a broader, international level, journalists have a responsibility to support and publicise organisations highlighting the dangers correspondents face simply in doing their job. These include the Committee to Protect Journalists and the International News Safety Institute. The Dart Center for Journalism and Trauma, a project of the Columbia Journalism School, promotes safety training, the ethical reporting of trauma and a greater awareness among media organisations of the impact of trauma coverage on both news professionals and news consumers. Journalists are also more likely to handle dangerous situations if they work collaboratively. Such ventures include the International Consortium of Investigative Journalists which has investigated private military cartels, Iraq and Afghanistan war contracts and, most famously in 2016, published the *Panama Papers*, a collaboration of more than 100 media partners, exposing the corrupt offshore banking operations of noted personalities and heads of state in over 40 countries. In addition, the Global Investigative Journalism Network brings together around 180 associations from 76 countries.

But surely there is a space for critical, progressive reporting on conflict in the mainstream?

Research confirms that the mainstream, professionalised media, given its close economic ties to the military/industrial/political/entertainment complex, tends to support warfare and downplays opportunities for the peaceful resolution of conflict. Controversies appear but they generally reflect elite disagreements (Herman and Chomsky, 1994 [1988]; Der Derian, 2001; Edwards and Cromwell, 2018). Edward Herman and Noam Chomsky (1994 [1988], p. 2) propose a propaganda system in which "money and power are able to filter out the news fit to print, marginalise dissent and allow the government and dominant interests to get their message across to the public". As Florian Zollmann says in his summary of the propaganda model, heavy market and ownership concentration encourages the recycling of information at the expense of original inquiries while links to external organisations such as banks and other shareholders further increase the dependence on outside actors (Zollmann, 2017, p. 40).

Yet within advanced capitalist economies there are, indeed, spaces for progressive journalism; the system is not monolithic. Indeed, Chris Atton (2004, p. 10) warns against presenting an oversimplified view of separate mainstream and alternative spheres, calling for a "hegemonic approach" involving a "complexity of relationships between radical and mainstream that previous binary models have been unable to identify". Robert Hackett argues from a radical, alternative perspective, that the Herman and Chomsky model is too deterministic and that change is possible from within the mainstream. The model "fails to identify the scope and conditions under which news workers could exercise the kind of choice called for" in a progressive form of journalism and to acknowledge that individual journalists are "active and creative agents" able to combine an involvement in the corporate media with regular contributions to alternative, partisan, campaigning media (Hackett, 2007, p. 93).

Daniel Hallin, in his study of US media coverage of the Vietnam War, identifies various ideological spheres: in the consensus sphere, dominant attitudes go largely uncontested while the sphere of legitimate controversy establishes the limits of acceptable debate. Finally, the sphere of deviance is occupied by attitudes ignored by the mainstream. In this context, it's useful to see the work of progressive journalists within the mainstream as falling within the sphere of legitimate controversy. One example of such a journalist today would be John Pilger. His work can be seen as an example of media hybridity since ideologically it falls both in the margins of the mainstream and in the alternative sphere. While Pilger's investigative work for mainstream media—both print and broadcast—highlighting the lies and crimes of the imperial powers has won him a series of international awards he has also contributed to a substantial range of alternative media, including the *New Statesman*, *coldtype.net*, *wsws.org*, *Socialist Review*, and *Truthdig*.

How important is peace journalism as a critique of mainstream coverage of conflict?

I have always been committed to peace journalism. In the early 1980s, I launched the group, Journalists Against Nuclear Extermination, to campaign for peace through the National Union of Journalists. And similar preoccupations have been ever-present in my journalism and academic writing and practice since then. My PhD examined the press coverage of the 1991 Gulf conflict. It was published as *Secret State, Silent Press: New Militarism, The Gulf and the Modern Image of Warfare* by John Libbey in 1997 with a second, updated edition published by Abramis in 2017 as *Covering Conflict: The Making and Unmaking of New Militarism*. But the thesis was essentially a protest (in appropriate academic prose) at the unnecessary massacres inflicted on defenceless Iraqis by the US-led coalition—and the way the mainstream media hid the reality of that horror behind the myth of heroic, precise warfare. For me, it has always been clear that some of the most important responsibilities of the journalist are to promote peace, dialogue and understanding; to confront militarism in all its forms—and the stereotypes and lies on which it is based.

One of the most original contributions to the debate over its practical and theoretical aspects appears in *Peace Journalism* by Jake Lynch and Annabel McGoldrick (2005); see also Lynch (2002, 2003). Every journalist should be aware of it; every journalism education programme should include it in their reading lists. Most academic analysis of conflict reporting is quick to condemn. But this text is far more ambitious. It both highlights the media's many failings and also offers convincing alternative strategies. Lynch and McGoldrick, drawing on 30 years' experience reporting for the BBC, ITV, Sky News, the *Independent* and ABC Australia as well as teaching peace journalism at four universities, rightly call for a journalistic revolution. Drawing particularly on the peace research theories of Prof. Johan Galtung (1998), they argue that most conflict coverage, thinking itself neutral and objective, is actually war journalism. It is violence and victory orientated, dehumanising the 'enemy', focusing on 'our' suffering, prioritising official sources and highlighting only the visible effects of violence (those killed and wounded and the material damage).

In contrast, peace journalism is solution-orientated, giving voice to the voiceless, humanising the 'enemy', exposing lies on all sides, highlighting peace initiatives and focusing on the invisible effects of violence (such as psychological trauma). Dotted throughout the text are comments from practising journalists and advice from the authors. For instance, to resist war propaganda they advise journalists:

- to be on the lookout for shifting war aims;
- to avoid repeating claims which have not been independently verified;
- to avoid demonising a person or a group; and
- to remind their audience of when war propaganda turns out to be misleading.

In its handbook on reporting crises, the Institute for War and Peace Reporting (IWRP) (2004, pp. 202–204) stresses six core duties for responsible peace journalism: to understand conflict, to report fairly, to present the human side, to cover the background and the causes of conflict, to report on peace efforts and to recognise the media's influence. Journalists also have a responsibility to know international humanitarian law. As IWRP comment:

> ... seeing an army shell a church or other historic site which is sheltering civilians is bad enough; but understanding that such an attack represents a violation of the Geneva Conventions raises it to another level of importance—elevating what may seem a routine article into a breakthrough report on a major shift in the tactics and implications of the conflict.
>
> *ibid., p. 179*

Lynch and McGoldrick focus in their study almost entirely on the mainstream media and thus fail to acknowledge the crucial contribution of campaigning, alternative media (such as those linked to radical left, feminist, environmental, human rights causes) to the promotion of peace journalism.

For example, since its founding in early 1936, *Peace News* has been a site of citizen journalism for the promotion of peace and social justice. Today, it's produced as a hard copy monthly journal with a regularly updated website (see www.peacenews.info/). As part of a statement of principles, the journal says it campaigns for:

> a nonviolent world where war has been abolished and the roots of war pulled up, including the silent, routine violence of hunger, oppression and ecological devastation. Making such a world will require a nonviolent revolution in every area of society.

Editor Milan Rai comments:

> For *Peace News*, citizen journalism has meant activist journalism, with self-reporting by large numbers of social movement activists through the years. ... Throughout the past thirty years, a staple of *PN* coverage has been the self-documentation by members of various peace camps around Britain, most famously Greenham Common Women's Peace Camp in the 1980s and now including Faslane nuclear submarine base in Scotland and the Atomic Weapons Establishment in Aldermaston, Berkshire. The number of *PN* street sellers may have shrunk over the years, but the number of journalist-activists has increased correspondingly
>
> *Rai, 2010, p. 211*

Another function of media such as *Peace News* is to promote a form of counter journalism. By this, Rai suggests searching the output of the mass media

> with diligence and a sceptical eye, cutting through the mass of misrepresentation and fraud to discover nuggets that can help citizens to better understand—and to more effectively alter—the world in which we are living. Part of the purpose of journals such as *Peace News* is precisely to give

neglected facts the attention and context they deserve with the appropriate placement, tone and frequency of repetition.

ibid, p. 217

Rai provides the example of a 2007 *PN* report on a poll in Iraq which indicated a total of 1,220,580 deaths since 2003, a finding which was almost totally ignored by the mainstream media.

Does peace journalism have a special role in the reporting of the 'war on terror'?

The 'war on terror' launched by President Bush in the wake of the 9/11 atrocities in the United States in 2001 heralded an era of perpetual war. There have been costly conflicts in Afghanistan, Iraq, Libya, Somalia, Syria and Yemen; and terrorist attacks across the globe—in Ankara, Bali, Barcelona, Berlin, Boston, Brussels, London, Manchester, Nice, Paris, Melbourne, Moscow, Madrid, Mumbai, Pittsburgh, Sri Lanka, Toronto and elsewhere. The jihadist group Islamic State, also known as Daesh, burst on to the international scene in 2015 when it seized large swathes of territory in Syria and Iraq. By 2019 it had lost much of this territory—but then began immediately to regroup, establishing overseas provinces in India and Pakistan and conducting thousands of attacks in Iraq and Syria.

But the war on terror is essentially a covert conflict and alternative, progressive peace journalism has played a crucial role in covering both the secret states and the secret wars they wage. In 2019, for instance, members of US Special Operations forces—Navy SEALs, Army Green Berets and Marine Raiders among them—operated in 141 countries (Turse, 2020). In the same year, British special forces were engaged in seven covert conflicts—often involving the secret deployment of drones, largely outside parliamentary or democratic oversight—in Afghanistan, Iraq, Libya, Pakistan, Somalia, Syria and Yemen (Curtis and Kennard, 2019). But these conflicts, largely ignored in the corporate media, are best covered on the alternative sites.

Indeed, given the international reach and consumption of the Internet, it is now possible to talk of an international alternative/counter public sphere in which an extraordinary range of publications operate challenging the silences, myths, lies and war-mongering of the dominant media. Such publications involve not just activist journalists but feminists, human rights campaigners, environmentalists, progressive intellectuals, hactivists, anarchists, WikiLeakers and revolutionaries. These include: *www.bigbrotherwatch.org.uk*, *Chomsky.info*, *www.coldtype.net*, *Consortium News*, *www.counterpunch.org*, *Daily Maverick*, Mark Curtis's *Declassified*, *www.greenleft.org.au*, *intelnews.org*, *middleeasteye. net*, *New Matilda*, *www.newsbud.com*, *nsarchive.wordpress.com*, *offguardian*, *peoplesworld.org*, the Wisconsin-based *Progressive*, spyculture.com, tomdispatch.com, http://whowhatwhy.com and zcomm.org/zmag/.

Whistleblowers—why are they so important?

Many defence correspondents loyally promote the Official Line (as on Weapons of Mass Destruction before the Iraq invasion of 2003); after 30 years have passed, top level, highly classified documents are regularly released (though suitably redacted) from the National Archives. But the Official Line is deliberately broken when whistleblowers speak out. Bradley/Chelsea Manning (see Madar, 2012), Julian Assange (Greenberg, 2012; Fowler, 2018) and Edward Snowden (Greenwald, 2014) are only the latest in a long line of men and women who have risked so much in speaking out against the secret state. Manning, an intelligence analyst with the US Army, was originally jailed in 2010 for 35 years for exposing, via WikiLeaks, American war crimes in Iraq and Afghanistan. After seven years behind bars, she was suddenly released by President Barack Obama in an act of clemency during the final days of his presidency. Then, in 2019, she was again jailed after refusing to testify before a grand jury investigating WikiLeaks.

Assange, founder of the WikiLeaks whistleblowing site in 2006, fearing extradition to the United States (and likely torture and jailing) took refuge in the Ecuadorian Embassy in London in August 2012. He was there for almost seven years until April 2019 when he was seized by police and quickly sentenced to 50 weeks in Belmarsh high-security prison for breaching the Bail Act. In June 2019, Nils Melzer, the UN Special Rapporteur on Torture, demanded an immediate end to the "collective persecution" of Assange, condemning the United States and its allies for inflicting "psychological torture" on him (Grenfell, 2019). In early 2022, he was continuing his challenge in the courts to avoid extradition to the United States. And NSA contractor Edward Snowden took refuge in Russia after revealing the global surveillance activities of the Britain and the United States (Snowden, 2019).

All three whistleblowers have received substantial coverage from corporate media—such as *The Guardian*, the *New York Times*, *Der Spiegel*, *Le Monde* and *El Pais*. But the most consistent and detailed reporting has appeared, it can be argued, in alternative media such as *wsws.org*, *johnpilger.com*, *theintercept.com*, *www.cryptome.org* and *lobster-magazine.co.uk*.

Ethics in action: Lara Pawson: "I'm a big fan of doubt"

Lara Pawson worked for the BBC World Service from 1998 to 2007, reporting from Mali, the Ivory Coast, and São Tomé and Príncipe. From 1998 to 2000, she was the BBC correspondent in Angola, covering the civil war. Her investigation into the little-known events of 27 May 1977, when a small demonstration against the MPLA, the ruling party of Angola, led to violent repression and the massacre of thousands, is covered in *In the Name of the People: Angola's Forgotten Massacre* (2014), which was longlisted for the Orwell Prize 2015. Her commentaries, essays and reviews have been published in many places and she reviews regularly for the *Times Literary Supplement*. Her second book, *This is the Place to Be*, is a fragmentary memoir of her experiences.

You were for a number of years BBC correspondent in Africa. What were the main ethical issues you faced during that time?

In total, I reported from several countries on the African continent for close to five years. That wasn't always for the BBC, but mainly. That I'm now a little over 50 years old means that I've only spent a tenth of my life as a correspondent. I think it's important to state this openly and honestly in part because there's often a tendency to exaggerate the work of correspondents, especially so-called foreign correspondents. I like to try to keep it real, if you know what I mean.

So I guess that's one ethical issue in itself: the drama that surrounds the title foreign correspondent and also war reporter. Indeed, I still feel a need to state how uncomfortable I often felt—and still feel on occasion – when people would sort of "ooh and aah" when they heard you were a (drum roll) BBC correspondent. It carries so much status. And it shouldn't.

Other matters? Well, there's race of course—and culture. I am a white European woman from a privileged middle-class family, who grew up in a stable country during peace time (internally at least). I was reporting on and from African countries, two of which—Angola and Ivory Coast—were caught up in war. I had my own baggage. My own preconceptions. My own anxieties. You can never unburden yourself of this stuff, but you can try to be aware of it and be open and honest about it. Don't pretend it doesn't matter or that it's not there.

When I arrived in Angola, I didn't speak more than a few sentences of Portuguese. So language: that's another big ethical matter. I did speak French, which helped in Ivory Coast, of course. But I didn't speak any indigenous languages—only the language of the coloniser. I think that matters a lot. When we lived in Mali it was a huge disadvantage. I began learning Bambara. But really, to stay and live there as a functioning reporter of any worth, I would have needed to learn at least two indigenous languages. Using a translator/interpreter has its drawbacks, for all concerned. It can take a huge toll on the translator/interpreter in particular. It can cost them their life.

When I started out in Angola, in 1998, I don't think I knew what on earth I was doing. So that's another ethical issue. I learned on the job. Some would say that's fine, that all jobs involve this to some extent. And I did. I learned a lot. But (as I often wondered back then) at whose cost? There was very much this idea among former (white British) BBC journalists I spoke to back then that you cut your teeth in Africa—that you make your mistakes in Africa and learn the trade in Africa because Africa doesn't matter as much as the rest of the world. That certainly wasn't how the BBC's African reporters saw things though—by which I mean the reporters who were from the countries in question, the people you rarely hear about, who work away unnoticed by most listeners/viewers of BBC English language broadcasts. This brings me to another ethical issue: the pay imbalance between (usually white) British BBC reporters and (usually black) African BBC reporters. I could talk about this till the cows come home: it's called inequality and discrimination.

You report in your memoir, This is the Place to Be, *of 2016, witnessing some horrific scenes while on assignments. Do you think some sanitisation of news is inevitable? And how did you manage to cope psychologically?*

Generally, I am very much against sanitising the news—or (the necessities of living with COVID aside) sanitising anything for that matter. I don't know how relevant this is, but I don't appreciate the way some adults sanitise life in front of their or other people's kids. I don't think it helps children. And I don't think it helps the world—in this case, the viewing/listening public—to sanitise what is happening in the world. We need to know, for example, what is really happening with global warming—all the forest fires, the rate of ice melt, the disappearance of certain species—and we need to be kept abreast of this all the time. Without this knowledge, it is harder to act effectively. For me, the same goes with conflict. We must know what's happening to people around the world—in Syria, Afghanistan, the Central African Republic, the United States et cetera.

One of the most important films I've seen in recent years was an entirely uncensored—if you like, unsanitised—piece of work from Syria called *Silvered Waters: Syria Self Portrait*. I wrote about it for Verso. Many people watching it covered their eyes at certain points—the violence is relentless—but my eyes were always open, always fixed on the screen. I believe that it's important that we stare into the abyss of life. We must. I think it's an obligation of all citizens. We mustn't look away. It is who we are. It is what we are. Why sanitise it? What's the point? I simply don't understand that approach to the world in which we live.

How did I cope? I'm not sure I ever thought much about that. Perhaps, looking back, the fact that I felt closer to death encouraged me to live more fully in the moment. I had quite a lot of sex and I smoked quite a lot of cigarettes. I drank whisky and I laughed a lot. There were good people around me. I was incredibly lucky. Especially in Angola. I met wonderful people who taught me how to laugh in the face of adversity. I think this is a quality you often see in countries where there are dictatorships or brutal regimes: people learn to laugh, to see the comic side of life. I remember hearing the Egyptian author, Ahdaf Soueif, make this point during a talk about the so-called Arab Spring. She commented on various jokes that Egyptians used to make about Hosni Mubarak, the president who held power from 1981 to 2011. It reminded me of the jokes people made in Angola about the MPLA ruling party (the Popular Movement for Liberation of Angola) and also about the rebel UNITA movement (the National Union for the Total Independence of Angola).

I think the humility of Angolans taught me how to cope. They were coping! And most of them couldn't leave the country as easily as I could. I was in a very fortunate position. I could leave at any point. That said, I think some of what I witnessed in Angola and Ivory Coast did catch up with me later … it came back to bite me. I think that's why I started writing. Maybe that's how I coped. I started writing. But I'm reluctant to emphasise too much the idea of coping. It's a rather loaded idea. Nothing awful ever happened to me. Not really. I didn't have that much to cope with in the grand scheme of things. I was lucky.

You also record in your memoir how over time you became very critical of the whole notion of journalistic objectivity. Could you explain that process?

There's a quite simple idea in journalism, which I don't necessarily dispute. It's the idea that you get, as they say, both sides of the story. For example, you get the response of the government and you get the response of the opposition party. This seems to be the root idea of objectivity in mainstream journalism. It's obviously a lot better than simply giving the ruling party's version of events, which is what you tend to get in dictatorships and one-party systems.

The problem with this approach is that very often there are more than two sides to any story. The nature of political life is more complex than simply what side A and side B have to say. Arguably, in a situation of conflict, it's much more complicated than this. But I think practically everything is more complicated than this!

Truth tends to be more subtle, more fuzzy, more nuanced. I think I began to realise this while living and working in Angola, perhaps because I went to the country with very fixed ideas about its history since the early 1960s. I had very fixed ideas about which side was good, and which one was bad. I'm ashamed to admit this, but I want to be honest! Living in Luanda, I began to realise that the history of the country was much, much more complicated than I had ever imagined. It was much more complicated than had been reported in the books I had read about Angola before I went to live there. Living among Angolans, listening to their views, histories and memories, I began to realise that I had got things very wrong. It was a steep but rapid learning curve. These days, I have little time for people who spout opinions on countries they've not lived and worked in. They rarely know what they are talking about. I strongly believe that you have to live and work somewhere to get beneath its skin.

When I began writing my first book—about the 27 May 1977 uprising in Angola that was followed by an appalling massacre—I dug even deeper into my doubts around objectivity, honesty, truth and the personal. Once I had started on that journey, I couldn't look back. I couldn't go back to the sort of news reporting I had done previously. It wasn't for me. I realised that I was someone—I am someone—who likes to look very thoroughly at everything, to examine it from all sides, from inside and outside, and that often I am reluctant to come to firm conclusions. I'm a big fan of doubt. I'm a big fan of thinking with questions as opposed to coming up with answers. A Zimbabwean friend of mine taught me the importance of good questions. He taught me that questions matter more than answers because they help us to think more deeply. This is what matters.

What role has emotion in the reporting of conflict?

I think emotion can be useful. I'm a big fan of anger! Anger is my engine. It drives me on. And I think nurturing one's emotions matters. Indeed, one of the reasons I began to question my work as a news reporter was that I felt I was becoming too cold in the face of suffering. I didn't think this was a good thing. I wanted to carry on feeling shocked and saddened by the suffering I saw. Of course, on the other hand, too much emotion can get in the way of one's life, of one's work, of one's relationships with other people. I think this is a very individual thing. I wouldn't want to prescribe emotional responses for others. I can only think about it for myself.

Which journalists reporting conflict today do you admire—and why?

Several people stay in my mind. One is the Ivorian photojournalist, Thierry Gouegnon. I was amazed by the work he did when I was living in Abidjan. He was incredibly brave and took brilliant photographs. He showed no fear. I found him very inspiring.

Another journalist I admired hugely when I was living in Angola, was Herculano Coroado, a print and broadcast reporter. We travelled together across the country. He taught me a lot about Angola, and about courage. He took many risks, which inspired me.

Omar Mohammed, who created the blog Mosul Eye, probably wouldn't call himself a journalist. He's a historian and what you might call a citizen journalist. I have so much respect for what he did. What courage! I can't begin to imagine how he did what he did. Absolute and total respect!

Anthony Loyd, the war correspondent for *The Times*, is brilliant. He's outrageously brave and writes phenomenal, often beautiful copy. His book, *My War Gone By, I Miss It So* is a classic. Everyone should read it.

I also hugely admire Lindsey Hilsum, Channel 4 News' international editor. I trust her absolutely. She's as balanced as is humanly possible, she cares deeply, she's very experienced, and she's incredibly clear. I don't know how she does it.

I feel the same about the BBC's chief international correspondent, Lyse Doucet—and I love the way she always prioritises the experiences of the ordinary people on the ground. You sense, in her reports, that she is always mindful of how everyday men and women are experiencing conflict.

Ethical workout

- Do media reports over-sanitise the horrors of warfare?
- Does media coverage of wars alert public opinion and politicians to human rights abuses and help stop them?
- How useful is peace journalism as a critique of mainstream coverage of wars?
- With so many wars today fought in secret—with the deployment of special forces, drones, covert arms sales etc.—how can the media possibly report on them?
- Which war correspondents do you admire today—and why?
- Do you consider whistleblowers such as Julian Assange, Chelsea Manning and Edward Snowden heroes or traitors?

Five takeaways from this chapter

- Professional war correspondents stress their crucial role in reporting accurately and honestly what they hear and see. They are 'eye-witnesses' to history.
- Given the closeness of the corporate media to dominant political, military, economic and ideological interests in society, during conflicts they tend to back the government. And yet there are possibilities for progressive, critical journalism within the mainstream.
- Since 9/11 reporting on wars, particularly from the frontlines, has become increasingly dangerous. As a result many news organisations rely on locals, freelances and citizen journalists. But all this throws up many new ethical dilemmas.

- There are many examples of peace journalism, particularly in alternative media, that offer useful models of the progressive, ethical, accurate and inspirational reporting on issues of war and conflict resolution.
- Whistleblowers such as Julian Assange, Chelsea Manning and Edward Snowden bravely throw light on the operations of the secret state—so critical now since so much of the 'war on terror' is fought covertly.

Ethics toolbox

- Evelyn Waugh's *Scoop*, of 1938, though a hilarious, satirical novel, confronts the reality of the follies of war and the men who report on it in a sharp and memorable way.
- Marie Colvin's collected war journalism—to be considered, as with all texts, critically—is published as *On the Front Line*, London: Harper Press, 2012. Her biography, *In Extremis*, by her friend and colleague, Lindsey Hilsum, London: Chatto & Windus, 2018, is also fascinating.
- Robert Fisk, of the *Independent*, is an outstanding war correspondent. His selected writings appear as *The Age of the Warrior*, London: Harper Perennial, 2009.
- A vital overview of the field is *The Routledge Handbook of Media, Conflict and Security*, edited by Piers Robinson, Philip Seib and Romy Fröhlich, London: Routledge, 2017.
- The War and Media Network (www.warandmedia.org/) brings together academics, professionals and researchers, organises conferences and carries a wealth of useful information on its website.
- All of John Pilger's television documentaries and a large selection of his writings appear at *johnpilger.com*. His full archive is held at the British Library, *bl.uk*.
- Important sites for academic discussions on peace journalism globally include: www.cco.regener-online.de/, http://globalmedia.emu.edu.tr/, *Peace Review* at www.tandfonline.com/loi/cper20, the *Journal of Peace Research* at https://journals.sagepub.com/home/jpr, the *Peace Journalist* at https://issuu.com/peacejournalism and Johan Galtung's www.transcend.org/.
- The Dart Center for Journalism and Trauma (https://dartcenter.org/), a project of the Columbia Journalism School, produces a lot of materials which reporters of peace and conflict issues find invaluable.

References

Atton, C. (2004) *An alternative internet: Radical media, politics and creativity*, Edinburgh: Edinburgh University Press.

Carruthers, S. (2000) *The media at war*, London: Macmillan.

Cohen, J. (2001) 'The myth of the media's role in Vietnam'. Available at: www.fair.org/index.php?page=2526 (Accessed: 13 December 2006).

Collins, R. (1990) 'Market closure and the conflict theory of professions', in Burrage, M. and Torstendahl, R. (eds.) *Professions in theory and history: Rethinking the study of professions*, London, Newbury Park and New Delhi: Sage, pp. 24–42.

Cottle, S., Sambrook, R. and Mosdell, N. (2016) *Reporting dangerously: Journalists' killings, intimidation and security*, London: Palgrave Macmillan.

Cummings, B. (1992) *War and television*, London: Verso.

Curran, J. and Seaton, J. (1991) *Power without responsibility: The press and broadcasting in Britain*, 4th edn. London: Routledge.

Curtis, M. and Kennard, M. (2019) 'Britain's seven covert wars', *Daily Maverick*, 17 September. Available at: www.dailymaverick.co.za/article/2019-09-17-britains-seven-covert-wars-an-explainer/

De Burgh, H. (ed.) (2000) *Investigative journalism: Context and practice*, London: Routledge.

Der Derian, J. (2001) *Virtuous war: Mapping the military-industrial-media-entertainment network*, New York: Basic Books.

Donvan, J. (2003) 'For the unilaterals, no neutral ground', *Columbia Journalism Review*, May/June. Available at: www.cjr.org/year/03/3/donvan.asp (Accessed: 12 July 2003).

Edwards, D. and Cromwell, D. (2018) *Propaganda blitz: How the corporate media distort reality*, London: Pluto Press.

Fowler, A. (2018) *Shooting the messenger: Criminalising journalism*, London: Routledge.

Galtung, J. (1998) 'High road, low road: Charting the course for peace journalism', *Track Two*, 7(4). Available at: https://journals.co.za/doi/abs/10.10520/ejc111753 (Accessed: 4 September 2019).

Gannett Foundation (1991) *The media at war: The press and the Persian Gulf conflict*, Columbia University, New York City: The Freedom Forum.

Greenberg, A. (2012) *The machine kills secrets: How WikiLeakers, hactivists and cyberpunks aim to free the world's information*, London: Virgin Books.

Greenslade, R. (2012) 'Marie Colvin obituary', *The Guardian*, 22 February. Available at: www.theguardian.com/media/2012/feb/22/marie-colvin (Accessed: 4 September 2019).

Greenwald, G. (2014) *No place to hide: Edward Snowden, the NSA and the surveillance state*, London: Hamish Hamilton.

Grenfell, O. (2019) 'United Nations Special Rapporteur: Julian Assange is being tortured', *wsws.org*, 1 June. Available at: www.wsws.org/en/articles/2019/06/01/pers-j01.html (Accessed: 11 June 2019).

Hackett, R.A. (2007) 'Is peace journalism possible?' in Shinar, D. and Kempf, W. (eds.) *Peace journalism: The state of the art*, Berlin: Regener, pp. 75–94.

Hallin, D. (1986) *The 'uncensored' war*, Oxford: Oxford University Press.

Herman, E.S. and Chomsky, N. (1994 [1988]) *Manufacturing consent: The political economy of the mass media*, London: Vintage.

International News Safety Institute (2020) 'Killing the messenger', *with Cardiff School of Journalism*. Available at: https://newssafety.org/fileadmin/Killing_the_Messenger_2019FINALFINAL.pdf

Institute for War and Peace Reporting (2004) *Reporting for Change: A Handbook for Local Journalists in Crisis Areas*, London/Washington, Johannesburg: IWPR.

Ismael, T.Y. and Ismael, J.S. (2004) *The Iraqi predicament: People in the quagmire of power and politics*, London: Pluto Press.

Knightley, P. (2000) *The first casualty: The war correspondent as hero and myth-maker from the Crimea to Kosovo*, 2nd edn. London: Prion.

Lewis, J.E. (ed.) (2001) *The mammoth book of war correspondents*, New York: Carroll and Graf Publishers.

Lynch, J. (2002) *Reporting the world*, Taplow: Conflict and Peace Forums.

Lynch, J. (2003) 'Reporting the world and peace journalism', *Peace News*, December–February 2004, p. 27.

Lynch, J. and McGoldrick, A. (2005) *Peace journalism*, Stroud: Hawthorn Press.

Madar, C. (2012) *The passion of Bradley Manning*, New York: Or Books.

Matheson, D. and Allan, S. (2009) *Digital war reporting*, Cambridge: Polity.

McLaughlin, G. (2016) *The war correspondent*, 2nd edn. London: Pluto Press.

Moorcraft, P. (2016) *Dying for the truth: The concise history of frontline war reporting*, Barnsley: Pen and Sword Books.

Murrell, C. (2013) 'International fixers: Cultural interpreters or "People Like Us"?', *Ethical Space*, 10(2 and 3), pp. 72–79.

Norton-Taylor, R. (1991) 'Pressure behind the scenes', *Index on Censorship*, London, 4/5, p. 14.

Owen, J. and Purdey, H. (2009) *International news reporting: Frontlines and deadlines*, Chichester: Wiley and Sons.

Parkin, F. (1979) *Marxism and class theory: A bourgeois critique*, London: Tavistock Publications.

Paterson, C. (2014) *War reporters under threat: The United States and media freedom*, London: Pluto Press.

Pendry, R. (2020) *Journalists' sources as news producers, 1854–2015*. Unpublished PhD, University of Kent.

Pyle, R. (2006) 'Iraq journalist deaths match number killed during Vietnam War', AP, 31 May. Available at: https://cpj.org/in-the-news/2006/05/iraq-journalist-deaths-match-number-killed-during.php

Rai, M. (2010) 'Peace journalism in practice – *Peace News*: For non-violent revolution', in Keeble, R. L., Tulloch, J. and Zollmann, F. (eds.) *Peace journalism, war and conflict resolution*, New York: Peter Lang, pp. 208–221.

Royle, T. (1987) *War report: The war correspondent's view of battle from the Crimea to the Falklands*, London: Mainstream.

Snoddy, R. (1993) *The good, the bad and the unacceptable*, 2nd edn. London: Faber and Faber.

Snowden, E. (2019) *Permanent record*, London: Macmillan.

Taylor, P. (2003) 'Journalism under fire', in Cottle, S. (ed.), *News and public relations and power*, London: Sage, pp. 63–79.

Times (2014) Editorial: 'The first casualty', 16 May, p. 20.

Tomlin, J. (2008) 'US short on answers', *Press Gazette*, 18 April.

Turse, N. (2020) 'America's commandos deployed to 141 countries', *tomdispatch.com*, 19 March. Available at: www.tomdispatch.com/post/176677/tomgram%3A_nick_turse%2C_america%27s_commandos%3A_what_did_they_do_and_where_did_they_do_it/

Weber, M. (1978 [1922]) *Economy and society: An outline of interpretive sociology*, Roth, G. and Wittich, C. (eds.). Berkeley: University of California Press.

Williams, K. (1987) 'Vietnam: The first living room war' in Mercer, D. (ed.), *The fog of war*, London: Heinemann, pp. 213–260.

Williams, K. (1992) 'Something more important than truth: Ethical issues in war reporting', in Belsey, A. and Chadwick, R. (eds.), *Ethical issues in journalism and the media*, London: Routledge, pp. 154–170.

Williams, K. (1993) 'The light at the end of the tunnel: The mass media, public opinion and the Vietnam War', in Eldridge, J. (ed.) *Getting the message: News, truth and power*, London: Routledge, pp. 305–328.

Zollmann, F. (2017) *Media, propaganda and the politics of intervention*, New York: Peter Lang.

Index

ABC News 185, 231
abduction 140–1
Aberdeen, Lord 224
abuse: extreme pornography and 141; harassment and 110; of power 24; of press freedom 23; sexual 72, 109, 144, 146; trauma and 135, 146; of young women 72
accidents 108, 121–2, 139; road 147
accountability 2, 12, 25, 37, 39–41, 45, 48, 53–4, 60, 102, 114, 139, 154, 200, 205; principle of 6–7
accuracy 2, 15, 36, 40–4, 48, 50, 53, 61, 63, 84, 86, 93, 103, 139–40, 174, 176, 183–4, 186, 200, 204, 214–15, 224: truth and 3
Adams, S., 92
adolescents 157
advertising 1, 24, 59–60, 73–5, 119, 223
advisory groups 10
advisory notices 32, 34, 137
advocacy reporting 225
Afghanistan 24, 228–9, 233–4, 236
African Americans 175
African countries, reporting from 10, 179, 222, 235–6
agenda-setting 13–14
Ahmed, S. 181–2
Ahmed, T. 186
Akunjee, T. 61–2
Al Qasimi, Sheikh Khalid bin Sultan 130
al-Assad, B. 69, 224, 226
Albania 49
alcohol 169; *see also* drunken behaviour
Alexander Mosely Charitable Trust 33
algorithms 177
Al-Jazeera 227

Allan, G. 9, 151, 154, 164
Allan, S. 228
American Association of Suicidology (AAS) 158, 170
Amnesty International (AI) 24–5
anarchism 233
Anderson, A. G. 87
Andersson, J. 187
Angola 234–8; MPLA 235, 237
anniversaries 145, 148, 156
anonymity 4, 123
apologies 34–5, 37, 108, 129
apps 38
Arab Spring 237
Arab world 52
arbitration schemes 32–4
arbitrators 32, 34
Army Green Berets 233
arrests: unlawful 25; warrants 25, 89
artificial intelligence (AI) 5, 20, 177
Ashley, S. 7
Asia: anti-Asian rhetoric 201–2; businesses 187; communities 189, 194; drug cartels 228; faith 189; media 187, 191
Assange, J. 24, 234, 239–40
assassinations 224
assault 109, 139–40, 180–1, 226; allegations 109; stories 180–1
Association of British Science Writers 215
Association of Health Care Journalists 215
Association of LGBTQ Journalists 186
asylum seekers 182
Atkins, Ros 181
Atomic Weapons Establishment 232
atrocities 225, 233

Index

Atton, C. 230
audio clips 105
auditing, ethical 49; self-auditing 48
Auman, A. 58
Ausaf TV 36
Ausaf UK Limited 36
Australia 94, 158, 201, 231; media 163, 169, 185, 203
authentication 62
authenticity 16, 19, 62, 105, 118, 188–9, 191
authoritativeness 84
avian influenza 203
Avicii 160, 168
Ayyoub, Tayek 227

Backholm, K. 138
bail 25, 234
Bailey, I. 177–8
Balkans 52
banking 95, 229–30
Banks, David 110
Barakat, Molhem 229
Barlett and Steele Awards 94
Barmer, I. 203
Barnett, Steven 32, 114–15
Barney, R. 152
Barr, C. 203
Barrett-Maitland, N. 102
Bartlett, R. 70
Bashir, Saad 185
BBC (British Broadcasting Corporation) 30, 35; 50:50 project 85, 97, 181; African reporters 236; China 181; codes of conduct 53, 104, 107; complaints process 36–7; correspondents 234–5, 239; COVID-19 coverage 202–3, 213; death and trauma, coverage of 129, 140, 142; diversity 181–2; editorial guidelines 36, 48, 72, 104; equal pay 182; Executive Complaints Unit (ECU) 37; freedom of expression 109, 119; journalists 31, 70–1, 187, 231; Local Democracy 59; news 31, 60, 203–4, 208, 229; *Newsnight* 63; One 37; positive health reporting 202; radio journalists 227; scaremongering 208; social media 70–72, 77, 78; war coverage 225, 227; World Service 10, 222, 234
Beckham, David 105
Beckham, Victoria 105
Bedford Times & Citizen 202

Begum, Shamima 61, 64
Belgium 47
Bell, Emily 62, 205–6
Bell, M. 202
Bennett, C. 201
Bennett, Thomas 109
Benz, K. 177
bereavement 134, 153, 166
bias: unconscious/implicit 177–9, 193
bigbrotherwatch.org.uk 233
bigotry 175–6
Birmingham Evening Mail 45
Birney, Trevor 89
Bjorkqvist, K. 138
Black Lives Matter (BLM) 69, 175, 190
Blewett, S. 61
blogging 39, 45, 54, 59–60, 62–63, 79, 228
Blood, R. W. 158
Bloom, D. 204
body image 10
Boeyink, D. E. 202
bombings 121–2, 133, 226–8
Bordeaux Declaration 44
Borden, S. L. 202
Bossio, D. 71
bourgeois state 233
Bourne, J. 179
Bowcott, O. 107
Boykoff, J. M. 203
Boykoff, M. T. 203
Bradshaw, P. 79
Brandeis, L. D. 102
brands 14–16, 50, 60, 70–71, 94
Brandwood, J. 106
Breen, Suzanne 89
Brewer, D. 103
Brexit 15, 187
bribery, press 43, 46
Broadcasting Standards Commission 35
broadsheets 84, 199
brutality 4, 141
Buckingham Palace 112; *see also* royal family
Bulgaria 49
bullying 93, 110, 113, 162, 187; cyber- 201
Burgess, Judge 89
Burke, Tarara 180
Bush, George W. 227, 233
Buzzfeed 60, 74
Byam, Guy 227

bylines 72, 118, 180
Byrne, L. 90
Byrnes, S. 180–1

cable services 35
Cairncross Review 59
Cairns, Andy 90
Callamard, Agnès 25
Calver, B. 185
Cambodia 227
cameramen 227
Campbell, Naomi 106
Canada 112, 201
capitalism 230
Captain Tom Foundation 202
captions 18–19
Carey, J. W. 14
Carruthers, S. 225
cartels 228–9
cartoon magazines 228
Cavendish, Camilla 208–9
Cawley, L. 203
CBC Radio 25
Cecco, L. 201
censorship 41, 45, 226
census data 86
Cerel, J. 152
Chakalain, A. 160
Channel 4 30–1, 36, 43, 70, 78, 213, 239
Channel 5 31
Charlie Hebdo 228
Chartered Institute of Journalists (CIoJ) 43–44, 53
Chermak, S. M. 139
children: autonomy of 117; digital content 51, 65, 118; privacy/private life, right to 8, 101–2, 107–8, 117–18, 123; rape of 132; welfare of 117
Childers, N. A. 85
China 17, 49, 52, 181, 201; COVID-19 pandemic 177, 201–2
Chomsky, Noam 229–30, 233
Choudhury, Barnie 9, 174, 184, 187–8, 192
citizen journalists 58, 60, 69–70, 78, 228, 239; *see also* social media
City AM 74
civil war 69, 222–4, 226, 234
Clayton, J. 51
Clegg, Nick 118

Clerwall, C. 14
clickbait 2, 17–18, 66, 112
Cobain, Kurt 168
Cohen, J. 225
coldtype.net 230, 233
Coleman, R. 37, 41
Colombia 228
columnists 90, 189, 226
Colvin, Marie 223, 227, 240
complaints 30–8, 44, 46–7, 53, 113, 120, 137, 182–3
Conde Nast Publications Limited 32
condolence messages 136
confidentiality 41, 88–89, 92, 95, 102
Consortium News 233
conspiracy 18, 24, 52, 64–6, 76, 78, 206; communities 64; theories 18, 52, 64–6, 76, 78, 206; *see also* social media
Cook, J. 14
Cooper, G. 124
copyright 22, 66–7, 75, 110, 112–13
Cornell University's Alliance for Science 17
Coroado, Herculano 238
coronavirus *see* COVID-19 pandemic
coroners 159, 165
corruption 23, 25, 45, 68, 83, 102, 115
Cottle, S. 228
Couso, Jose 227
COVID-19 pandemic 3, 8–9, 14–15, 17, 23–4, 30, 49, 52, 60, 64–65, 128, 136, 187, 199–215, 236; China 177, 201–2; competing narratives 205–6; dashboard 208, 215; face masks 204–5; infodemic 52, 204–5; information disorder 17–18, 206–8; lockdowns 73, 200, 202–3, 207–8; scaremongering 208–9; sources of information 148, 210–14; trust in journalism 14–15; *see also* health journalism
Craft, S. 7
Crerar, Pippa 73
Crew, J. 93
Crimean War (1854–1856) 222, 224
criminality 160, 178
Cromwell, D. 229
cross-checking 84, 95; *see also* fact-checking
crowdfunding 66
crowdsourcing 40, 62, 66
Crowley, John 148

Crown Prosecution Service (CPS) 91
culture: of fear 188; of intrusion 120; of plausible deniability 20; of secrecy 24; of tolerance 141
Cummings, B. 225
Cummings, Dominic 73
Cummins, E. 201
Curran, J. 223
current affairs 31, 35, 70, 85, 181
Curtis, Mark 233
Cyprus 49

Daesh 233; *see also* ISIS (Islamic State of Iraq and Syria)
Daily Mail 17, 90, 107, 112
Daily Maverick 233
Daily Telegraph 222
Dart Center for Journalism and Trauma 148, 170, 229, 240
Davidson, L. 158
Davidson, Ruth 118
Davie, Tim 71
Davis, S. 106
DCMS 8
De Burgh, H. 224
deadnaming 187
deafness 185
death, coverage of 128–48; ethical issues 128–31; *see also* bereavement; funerals; grief; road crashes; shock; suicide; violent crime
Debatin, B. 102
deepfake videos 20
Deeptrace 20
defamation 7, 22, 32, 34, 66, 109
democracy 21, 23–4, 45, 53, 59, 96
depression 163–4, 167
Der Derian, J. 229
Der Spiegel 234
Derakhshan, H. 206–7
derogatory language 66, 163
Di Stefano, M. 68
Diana, Princess of Wales 112
Díaz-Campo, J. 45, 70
dictatorships 237
digital journalism: codes of conduct 44–5
dignity 12, 41, 102, 114, 123, 130, 153, 174, 176
disabilities 9, 174, 184–5, 193; non-disabled persons 185

Disaster Action 133
disasters 103, 116, 123, 128, 136, 138, 148
disclaimers 72
disclosure 34, 88, 90, 103, 115, 156
discretion 122, 129, 182
discrimination 5–6, 9, 41–2, 49, 102, 174–7, 179, 182–5, 201, 236
disease 14, 17, 122, 160, 200–1, 204; *see also* COVID-19 pandemic
dishonesty 50, 115
disinformation 3, 12, 15–16, 50, 52, 64, 76, 205–9, 214–15
displacement camps 61
diversity 35, 85, 174–94; *see also* bias; disability; discrimination; ethnic minorities; LGBT+ community; women
Dix, Pam 133–4
Dixon, Avril 135
Dixon, Rose 135
documentaries 112, 240
documentary evidence 62
domestic violence 128, 144
donations 33, 59, 202
Donvan, J. 227
Dorking Advertiser 120
Doucet, Lyse 239
Dowler, Milly 118, 122
Downing Street 91, 191, 212
Doyle, P. 206
drones 112, 233, 239; footage 2, 5
drowning 159
drugs 25, 106, 130, 141, 159, 169, 201, 228; abuse 141; addicts 106; administration 201; anti-drug campaigns 25; cartels 228; dealers 25; overdose 130, 159; poisoning 201
drunken behaviour 19, 71; *see also* alcohol
due diligence 16
Duggan, Mark 190
Duncan, Sallyanne 1, 8, 12, 30, 92, 101, 128, 132–3, 147, 151, 154–5, 159–60, 162–4, 174
Dunn Johnson, Taya 136
Duterte, Rodrigo 25
Duwe, G. 140
Duxbury, S. W. 178
dwarfism 185
Dworznik, G. 138

Eastern Eye 187
eating disorders 10

Index

eavesdropping 67–8
Ecker, U. K. 14, 65
Eckler, Petya 9, 199
economics 63, 200, 209
Edelman Trust Barometer 207
Edinburgh Evening News 118
Edwards, C. 114
Edwards, D. 229
Egypt 49, 237
elections, political 35, 37, 51
Elvestad, E. 59
email 90, 92
embedded journalists 86–7; *see also* sources
embezzlement 228
emergency powers 23
emergency services 84, 86
Emmy Awards 94
emotion 88, 93, 128, 143, 238
empathy 134, 153, 179
employment 43, 71, 85–6, 181
encryption 95, 97
Engineer 88
Englehardt, E. 152
environmental issues 232–3
epidemics 160, 204, 208
epidemiology 200, 214
epilepsy 118
equality 53, 97, 176, 180–2, 185, 194
Erdogan, Z. 206
ethical journalism: core principles of 1–10; influences on 12–25
Ethical Journalism Network (EJN) 2–3, 4–5, 6, 8, 30, 39, 45–54, 98, 201
'ethical vacuum' 58, 60
ethnic groups 182, 203
ethnic minorities 9, 15, 174, 182–4
ethnicity 157, 176, 178, 181, 188
European Court of Human Rights (ECHR) 88, 91
Everard, Sarah 140–1, 187
Evon, D. 20
execution 224
expression, freedom of *see* freedom of expression
extradition 24, 234
extrajudicial killings 25
extramarital sexual behaviour 106
eye-witnesses 59, 223, 239

face veils (*niqab*) 182
Facebook 17, 20, 25, 50–2, 59, 66–8, 71, 75–7, 88, 121, 135, 142, 168, 207, 211
fact-checking 3, 15–19, 61–3, 204, 206, 210, 214
fair representation *see* diversity
fairness 2, 12, 35–6, 41, 45, 53, 83, 85, 103, 174; fundamental principle of 4–5
faith-based attacks 183
fake news 14, 16, 20, 25, 50, 64, 90, 213
Falklands War (1982) 225, 227
false information 3, 16–17, 163, 206–7, 210; types of 18–20
falsehoods 20, 32, 34, 50, 64–5, 75–6
far-right activism 68, 71, 178, 183
Farrow v Lancashire Evening Post 135
Faslane nuclear submarine base 232
Fawcett Society 181, 194
Federal Drug Administration (FDA) 201
Fekete, S. 157
feminism 232–3
Fengler, S. 39
Fenton, Amy 72
Ferret Fact Service 3, 34
Fieschi, C. 114
filmmakers 75
films 89, 236
financial journalists 41; investigations 95, 202
financial model 14, 96
financial penalties 36, 119
Financial Times 31, 37–8, 45, 47, 53, 68, 208
Fincham, K. 71–2
fines 32, 34–5
Finland 15
Firmstone, J. 187
Fisk, Robert 240
Flack, Caroline 106, 160, 168
Fleet Street 115, 226
Fletcher, Kim 226
Fletcher, R. 13–14
Floyd, George 69, 85, 190
footballers 51, 185, 189
Fowler, A. 234
Fox News 59
framing 18, 140, 154, 163
France 111, 201, 207, 209
Francis, Pope 19
Franco–Prussian War (1870) 222
fraud 25, 232

freebies 74
Freedman, L. 203
freedom of expression 4, 7, 12, 20–5, 41–3, 45, 54, 89, 91, 101, 107–9, 114–15, 118, 123, 183; crisis, during 23–4; free media and 24–5; importance of 20–5; journalism's responsibilities 21–2; limits to 22–3
freedom of information 23–4, 87
freedom of speech 113
freelancers 1, 8, 31, 34, 73, 79, 118, 228, 239
Fröhlich, Romy 240
Frost, C. 20–4, 39–41, 44, 54, 60, 66, 68, 70, 109, 116, 124
function-based rights 41–2
funding 31, 33, 199
fundraising 121–2
funerals 9, 128, 136–8, 143

Gaddafi, Muammar 226
Galizia, Daphne Caruana 228
galleries 157
Galloni, Alessandra 15
Gallup polls 226
Galtung, Johann 84, 231, 240
Gannett Foundation 225
Gans, H. 84
Garcia, L. 206
gardens 104
Gardiner, B. 72
Garvey, A. 138
gas explosions 104
gatekeeper media 58, 61
Gates Foundation 179
gender 41, 49, 53, 85, 157, 174, 176, 178–82, 188, 193–4; angle 179, 193; balance 181; discrimination 182; equality 53, 180–1, 194; identity 176, 180; imbalance 181; parity 179; representation 85; rights 49; *see also* girls; LGBTQ+ community; sexual orientation; transgender community; women
German journalism 95, 112
Gibson, M. 136
Gibson, O. 106
gifts 4
girls: images of 185, 224; violence towards 141
Giuffrida, A. 201
GLAAD Media Reference Guide 186, 194

Global Charter of Ethics for Journalists 3–4, 44
global warming 203–4, 236
glossaries 49
Goethe, Johann Wolfgang von 157
Goldsmith, N. 177–9
good faith 38, 66
Good Morning Britain 112–3
Goodwin, Bill 88
Google 77
Gopsill, Tim 44
gossip 77
Gouegnon, Thierry 238
Gould, M. 158
Gracie, Carrie 181–2
Grant, Hugh 39
Grant, Katie 63
Green, D. 186–7
Greenberg, A. 234
Greenham Common Women's Peace Camp 232
Greenslade, R. 109, 223
Greensmith, G. 142
Greenwald, G. 234
Grenfell, O. 234
grief 131–4; grieving families 66, 121–2, 128, 131–3, 134, 138–9, 155; grieving relatives 132–6, 147, 169, 212; social media content 134–6
gross intrusion 23
groundwork 85, 133, 147
Grundlingh, L. 140
Guardian 8, 31, 37–8, 45, 47–8, 51, 53, 58–9, 62, 72–5, 79, 181, 223, 226, 234
Gulf War (1991) 226, 231

Hacked Off 39, 108, 183
Hackett, R. 230
hacking 39, 46, 74, 111, 118–19, 122; phone-hacking 13, 39, 46, 11, 118–19, 122
Hafez, K. 40–1
Hagan, S. 86
Hall, S. 84
Hallin, D. 225, 230
Hammarberg, T. 102
hanging, death by 159
Hanif, F. 178, 182
Hanitzsch, T. 13

harassment 22, 32, 34, 73, 110, 122, 130, 180–1; anti-harassment advice 32
Harcup, T. 1, 59, 84, 199
Harris, N. 43
Hart, Luke 141–2
Hart, Ryan 141–2
hashtags 180, 202; see also #MeToo movement
Hastings, Max 225
hate 5, 48–9, 51, 53, 182–3; crimes 218; speech 5, 48–9, 51, 53, 182
Haugen, Frances 51, 88
Hawton, K. 158
headlines 1, 18, 50, 61, 65–6, 74, 76, 78, 141, 145, 155, 160, 184, 228
Healey, Jo 9, 128, 133–5, 142, 147
health journalism 9, 199–215; advice for newcomers 209–10; COVID-19 pandemic 204–14; ethical challenges 204–6; ethical issues 200–4; expansive nature of 200; harm and 201–4; importance of 199–200; positive health reporting 202; uniqueness of 200–4; see also COVID-19 pandemic
hearings, court 110, 112, 187
Heawood, J. 109–10
Heiat, M. 206
Heitzig, N. A. 178
helplines 9, 151, 153, 156, 163–4, 169–70
Henshall, P. 106
Herald 10, 210, 213
Herman, Edward S. 229–30
heroin overdose 130; see also drugs
Hetherington, Tim 227
Hewett, J. 72
Hicks, W. 92
hidden cameras/recordings 5, 96
Hill, Jack 224
Hilsum, Lindsey 239–40
Himelboim, I. 40
Hinduism 189
hockey 62–3
Hollywood 180
Holmes, Eamonn 64
Holt, E. 23
homelessness 144, 186
homicide 148
Hong, S. C. 105
Hooker, C. 203
Hopkins, Katie 183

horoscopes 21
hospitals 35, 84, 104, 199, 200, 211
hostage-taking 223
Howell v Metro.co.uk 116
Hoy, Sir Chris 137
Hswen, Y. 202
Huffington Post 31, 38, 53
Huffpost 38, 60
Hughes, Stuart 229
human interest 153, 174, 191, 222
human rights 20, 22, 25, 44–5, 52, 88–9, 91, 101–2, 109, 120, 182, 184, 201, 226, 228, 232–3, 239
Human Rights Act (1998) 20–1, 101, 109, 120
Human Rights Watch 52, 201
human services 158
human trafficking 25
humanity 2, 12, 21, 40–1, 45, 48, 53, 153; principle of 5–6
humility 188, 237
humour 138
Humphreys, Emma 144
Hungary 49
hunger 232
Hunt/Black plan 31
hydroxychloroquine 201
hyperlinks 19
hyperlocal sites 30–1
hypocrisy 40, 102, 114, 120

Iceland 95–6
ideology 223–4
iMediaEthics 39
impartiality 2, 4–5, 12, 18, 36, 38, 40–1, 45, 48, 52–3, 71, 140, 157, 160, 188; principle of 4–5
IMPRESS (Independent Monitor for the Press) 30, 33–4, 37, 40, 42–4, 47–8, 53, 103–4, 107, 110, 117, 129, 199, 212
imprisonment 88; see also jail sentences; prison
impunity 60, 119, 190
inclusivity see diversity
independence 2, 12, 31–2, 41, 45, 48–9, 53, 139, 200; principle of 3–4
Independent Monitor for the Press see IMPRESS
Independent Press Regulation Trust (IPRT) 33

Index

Independent Press Standards Organisation (IPSO) 30–4, 37, 40–4, 47–8, 53, 67–8, 70, 79, 88, 103–5, 107, 116, 119–20, 122, 129–30, 135, 137, 176, 183, 186, 212
Independent 8, 33, 38, 47, 68, 93, 231, 240
Independent on Sunday 226
Independent Television Commission (ITC) 35
India 96, 179, 222, 233
indigenous languages 235
influencers 17, 65
infodemic 52, 204; COVID-19 pandemic 204–5
infographics 49, 169
information disorder 12–25: COVID-19 pandemic and 17–18, 206–9; definition 16; trust and 16
information overload 19, 205
iniquity 96
injustice 120, 140–1, 144
inquests 33, 145, 155, 159, 162, 165, 170
inquiries 145, 155, 230
Instagram 51, 75, 77, 135
Institute for War and Peace Reporting (IWRP) 232
intelnews.org 233
Intergovernmental Panel on Climate Change (IPCC) 87
International Center for Journalists (ICJ) 148, 215
International Consortium of Investigative Journalists (ICIJ) 94–7, 229
International Federation of Journalists (IFJ) 3–4, 6–7, 44–5, 53–4, 182
International Freedom of Expression Exchange (IFEX) 45
Investigatory Powers Act 2016 (IPA) 91
IRA (Irish Republican Army) 89
Iraq 24, 226–9, 231, 233–4; Iraqi journalists 227
Ireland 94
ISIS (Islamic State of Iraq and Syria) 61, 233; *see also* Daesh
Islam 178, 182–3; Islamic law 160; Islamophobia 183; *see also* Muslim community; Sharia law
Ismael, J. S. 226
Ismael, T. Y. 226
Italy 201, 228

ITN News 31, 176, 225, 227
ITV News 31, 112–13, 202, 231
Ivory Coast 234–5, 237

Jack, I. 93
jail sentences 23, 46, 89, 144–5, 160, 234
James, W. 204
Japan 201
jets: bombings 227; private 111
Jews 182
jihadist groups 233
JML Direct 36
JML Media Limited 36
Joannides, L. 181
johnpilger.com 234, 240
Johnson, Boris 90, 182
Jones, J. M. 13
Joseph, S. 84
Journalists Against Nuclear Extermination 230
Joy, I. 68
juries 91, 190, 234
justice 24–5, 34, 43, 109, 122, 232
Justice for Women 144

Kansara, R. 69
Kapur, N. 69
Kardes, V. C. 206
Karlsson, M. 14
Kassova, L. 179–80
Keeble, Richard L. 2, 10, 40–1, 59, 84, 140, 151, 174–5, 185, 188, 222
Keng, Wilfredo 25
Kennard, M. 233
Kenya 179
Khashoggi, Jamal 228
kidnappings 141
King, C. 203
King, Joshua 8, 101, 118
'kiss-and-tell' stories 107
Kleih, A.-K. 206
Knapton, S. 209
Knight, A. 59
Knightley, P. 223–4
Knowlton, S. 61
Koch, T. 87
Kosovo 226
Kozinski, K. 69
Kuciak, J. 228

Kurcer, M. 206
Kwateng-Clark, D. 181
Kyd, Sally 139

Laitila, T. 41
Laker, L. 139
Lamb, J. 186
Lambley, E. 180
Lammy, David 183
Lancet 23
Laos 227
Lashmar, Paul 91
Latino men 178
Lawrence, Stephen 190
lawsuits 109
Le Monde 234
Lehberger, M. 206
Leveson Inquiry 22, 30–3, 37, 39, 46–8, 54, 60, 118–19, 129
Lewandowsky, S. 14
Lewis, J. E. 222
Lewis, Paul 62
Lewis, S. C. 13–14
LGBTQ+ community 9, 174, 185–7, 194
Libbey, J. 231
libel 25, 129; cyber- 25
Liberty (campaign group) 91
Libya 226–7, 233
licensing, broadcast 20, 35–6
lifestyle magazines 8
Limor, Y. 40
literacy, media 7–8, 37, 45, 53, 92
literary journalism 10
live streaming 104
Liverpool 8, 10
Liverpool Daily Post and Echo 8
Liverpool Echo 61
Llewellyn, Sue 72
Lloyd, Terry 227
lobbying 71
Locke, John 20
Lockerbie flight disaster (1988) 133
logos 19
loutishness 71
Lowe, Kristine 59
Loyd, Anthony 224, 239
Lydall, Ross 206
Lynch, J. 102, 231–2

Machlin, A. 163
Macnamara, J. 87
Macsai, E. 157
Madar, C. 234
mafia 228
magazines 8, 18, 30–2, 88, 111–13, 175, 228
Mail on Sunday 108, 110–13
Mail Online 17, 110–11, 130, 226
Majid, A. 17–18, 175–6
Maksl, A. 7
malaria 201
Malcolm, J. 93
Mali 234–5
malicious falsehood 32, 34, 50
malinformation 3, 12, 15–16, 207–9, 214–15
Malta 228
Mance, Lord 106
Manchester Arena bombing 122, 233
Mangrove Nine 190
Mann, Justice 109
Manning, Chelsea 234, 239–40
Mantar, Ozan B. 9–10, 199
marines 224, 227, 233
Markle, Meghan 110, 115, 175; see also Meghan, Duchess of Sussex
Markle, Thomas 111–12
Marshall, A. 106
mass audiences 58
mass communication 59
mass media 232
mass shootings 9, 62, 142, 148, 178
mass surveillance 90; see also surveillance
Matheson, D. 228
Matthews, J. 86
Mayes, Ian 38
Mayhew, F. 175
McArdle, Helen 10, 210
McCaffrey, Barry 89
McCann, J. 141
McCann, Madeleine 129–30
McDonald, H. 89
McGoldrick, A. 231–2
McKee, Lyra 24
McKinley, J. C. 61
McLaughlin, G. 223
McStay, A. 124
Meghan, Duchess of Sussex 8, 101, 108, 110–14, 119; see also Markle, Meghan
Melzer, Nils 234

Index

memoir 235–7
memorials 122, 156; pages 136; services 168; sites 161
Mencher, M. 140
mental health 51, 106, 113, 119, 148, 160, 162–5, 168, 170, 174, 178, 209
mental illness 162–3, 165, 167, 170, 176, 178
Mercer, D. 201
Messenger Davies, M. 108, 118
#MeToo movement 180–1
Mexico 228
micro-publishers 31
migration 13, 45, 49, 53, 182–3
Milano, Alyssa 180
militarism 231
military databases 24
Mill, John Stuart 21
Milman, O. 201
Milmo, D. 207
Milton, John 20
Mishara, B. L. 160
misinformation 3, 12, 15–17, 49, 64–5, 76, 205–8, 211–12, 214–15
misrepresentation 18, 43, 68, 204, 232
missing persons 152–3, 165–6
Mitchell, Andrew 91
mobile technology 59, 90
Mohammed, Omar 238
Mohdin, A. 203
Momo hoax 65
monarchy 113; *see also* royal family
Montenegro 49
Moorcraft, P. 223
Moore, Captain Sir Tom 202
Moosavian, R. 108
morality 162
Morgan, Piers 74, 112–13
Morris, B. 108, 118
Morris, N. 179
Morton, B. 24
Mosdell, N. 228
Mosely, Max 33
Moses, Alan 183
Mossack Fonseca 95
Mosul Eye 238
MPs (Members of Parliament) 84, 183, 191, 206–7
Mrs Hazel Cattermole v Bristol Evening Post 137

MSN News 202
Mubarak, Hosni 237
multimedia 30, 164
Muratov, Dmitry 24–5
murder 9, 25, 108, 128, 135–6, 138–42, 144, 147, 187, 189–90, 228; murder-suicide 9, 141, 170
Murdoch, Rupert 119
Murray, Ian 175–6
Murrell, C. 228
musicians 107, 121
Muslim community 178, 182–4, 189, 194; anti-Muslim attacks 182; *see also* Islam

Narcotics Anonymous 106
National Health Service (NHS) 199, 202–3, 210
National Records of Scotland (NRS) 151, 169
National Union of Journalists (NUJ) 43, 53, 67, 71, 74, 89, 91, 158, 162–3, 170, 183–4, 231; code 43–4, 48, 88, 103, 199
Navy SEALs 233
NCTJ Student Council 118
Neil, Andrew 37
Nessa, Sabina 187
Netherlands 47
neutral coverage 224, 228, 231; neutral language 139, 160
New Matilda 233
New Zealand 62, 108; Christchurch shooting 62; Media Council 131
Newman, N. 14–15, 60
Newmark, Brooks 68
Newquest 72
News of the World 46, 111, 118–19, 129
newsgathering 4, 8, 43, 58, 66, 227
Newsnight 63
Newsome, Melba 85
newspaper industry 47, 223; skills 10
newsworthiness 9, 68–9, 75, 116, 128, 135, 143, 151, 207, 212
Newton, Jackie 8, 83, 92–3, 132–3, 147, 160
Nguyen, A. 204–7, 210
niche-oriented groups 13
Nicolaou, E. 113
Nieman Lab 97
Nigeria 179
NLGJA (Association of LGBTQ Journalists) 186

Nobel Peace Prize 24–5
non-governmental organisations (NGOs) 25, 33
non-profit journalism 54
norovirus 183
North East and North Cumbria Suicide Prevention Network 164
Northern Ireland 24, 89; Statistics and Research Agency (NISRA) 151, 169; Troubles-era murders 89
Norway 24, 47
Norwegian Nobel Committee 24
Nottingham 209
Novaya Gazeta 25
novice journalists 85, 92–3, 214
nuclear weapons 230, 232

O'Carroll, L. 107
O'Connor, C. 86–7
O'Neill, D. 84, 86–7
O'Neill, Prof Onora 21
Obama, Barack 20, 234
Oborne, Peter 90
Ofcom (Office of Communications) 8, 16, 31, 34–7, 43–4, 47, 53, 103, 105, 107, 113, 129, 176, 192, 199, 207–8, 211
Oftel (Office of Telecommunications) 35
Olson, R. 162–3
Olsson, J. 109
ombudsmen 37–8, 48, 89
Onion 18
online groups *see* social media
openDemocracy 24
Orwell, George 10, 235
Oswald, M. 118
'othering' 178
Overseas Press Club of America 94
Owen, J. 223

Pakistan 95, 233
Palestine 49, 227
Palmer, Ruth 67, 93–4, 116
Panama Papers 8, 83, 94–6, 229
Pandora Papers 8, 83, 94, 96
paparazzi 111–2
Papyrus 157
Paradise Papers 8, 83, 94
paramilitary activities 24
parental consent 107, 117

Parkin, Frank 223
parody 18
Partington, R. 203
Parveen, N. 203
Paterson, C. 227
Paton, D. 209
patriarchal norms 180
patriotism 225
Pawson, Lara 10, 222, 234
paywalls 59, 213
PBS 13
peace journalism 10, 230–4, 239–40; importance of 230–3; war on terror 233–4, 240; *see also* war correspondents
Pearson, Matthew 138
Peele, Jordan 20
Pelosi, Nancy 19
penalties 36, 51, 119, 189
Pendry, R. 229
pensions 184
Philippines 24–5
Phillips, A. 59
Phillips, D. P. 158
phone hacking *see* hacking
photographers 32, 75, 137, 224, 229
photojournalists 227, 238
photoshopping 19
Pickstock, H. 66
Pidd, H. 202
Pilger, John 230, 240
Pink News 186
Pirkis, J. 158, 163
Pitas, C. 204
PJS v News Group Newspapers Ltd 106–7
plagiarism 7
Plaquenil 201
Plebgate incident (2012) 91
podcasts 38
Poland 49
police 59, 69, 73, 84, 116, 119, 130, 159, 190; Metropolitan 91, 140–1; Northumbria 166, 168; PSNI 89; South Yorkshire 109
political correctness (PC) 175
Politkovskaya, Anna 25
Ponsford, Dominic 68, 91, 108, 115
populism 52
pornography 141
Portugal 129
Posetti, J. 91, 205–6

postal industry 31, 34
'post-truth' era 45, 50
poverty 49, 186
Poynter Institute 39, 54
prejudice 6, 176, 183–4, 200, 214
Press Association 32
Press Complaints Commission (PCC) 31–2, 46, 120, 137
Press Recognition Panel (PRP) 33
Prince Harry, Duke of Sussex 110–15, 175
prison 24–5, 89, 104, 144, 234; Belmarsh 234; high-security 24, 234
Pritchard, D. 191
privacy: basic right to 110–16; celebrities' private lives 105–8; children 117–18; extent of media intrusion 107–8; 'Harry and Meghan' case 110–16; ordinary people 116–17; regulatory bodies 103–5; rights, respect for 101–3; Sir Cliff Richard case 109–10; social media and 118–23
professionalisation of communication 40, 87, 92
professionalism 6, 10, 78, 175, 222–4
propaganda 4, 24, 224, 230–1
protests 69, 175, 226
Protsyuk, Tara 227
psychology: effects 138; scars 162; torture 234; trauma 231; wellbeing 206
public interest 5–6, 8, 22–3, 30, 33, 42–3, 67–8, 88–92, 94–7, 101–110, 115, 117, 119–21, 123, 130–1, 136, 140, 152, 159, 203, 223; *see also* sources
Pulitzer Prize 94
Purdey, H. 223
Putin, Vladimir 226
Pyle, R. 227

quality journalism 14, 60, 83
Quinn, F. 104
quotes: use of 1, 18, 59, 67, 76, 93, 163

racism 49, 51, 113, 175, 183, 187–90
Radio Authority 35
Radio Ikhlas 36
Radiocommunications Agency 35
Rai, M. 232
Randall, David 93
rape 132, 139, 140–1, 144
Rappler 25

Ratcliffe, R. 24
Raven, D. 61
redundancies 86
referenda 15, 35–6
Regulation of Investigatory Powers Act 2000 (RIPA) 91
regulatory bodies: advantages of 40; codes of conduct 39–45; disadvantages of 40–1; other forms of regulation 37–9; privacy rights and 103–5; UK 30–9; values 41–2
Regulatory Funding Company (RFC) 31–2
Reich, Z. V. I. 84
religion 35, 41, 176, 188–9, 205
Reporters without Borders (RSF) 23–4
Responsible Suicide Reporting (RSR) 9, 151, 154–6, 169; *see also* suicide
Ressa, Maria 24–5
Reuters 15, 72, 227, 229
Reuters Institute 14–5, 60, 72
Reynolds Journalism Institute 39, 85
Ribbans, Elizabeth 38
Richard, Sir Cliff 109–10, 119
Richards, Julian 24
Riesmeyer, C. 87
rights-based clauses 41
right-wing views 182
riots 24, 51, 190, 224
road crashes 116, 128, 138–9
Roberts, C. 41
Roberts, J. 59
Robinson, J. 13, 129
Robinson, P. 240
Robinson, S. 13–4
Roma community 182
Royal Charter 30, 36, 47
royal family 110, 112–14, 118; weddings 110–11
Royle, T. 223
Ruge, Mari 84
rumours 18, 61, 63–6, 78, 123, 129, 159, 206; social media 61–4
Rusbridger, Alan 38
Russell, William Howard 222, 224
Russia 24–5, 226, 234; Chechnya, war in 25; Crimea, war in 222, 224
Rwanda 49
Ryle, Gerard 8, 83, 94

Sacco, V. 71
salaries 182

Salmond, Alex 37, 118
Samal, J. 206
Samaritans 153, 157–8, 160–1, 170
Sambrook, R. 228
Sample, I. 20
Sanchez, J. 185
sanctions 34–6
sanitisation of news 236
Santos, Reynaldo Jr. 25
Sao Tomé and Principe 234
satellite services 35
satire 18, 228, 240
Saudi Arabia 228
Saunders, T. 203
scammers 66
scandals 13, 39, 46–7, 68, 77, 119
scaremongering 208–9
scepticism 41, 84, 226
Schudson, M. 14
scientific consensus 203
Scotland, Baroness Patricia 187
Scotland on Sunday 118
Scotsman 8, 101, 118
Scottish National Party (SNP) 37, 211, 214
Scottish Sun 130, 137
Seib, P. 240
self-care 153, 164, 170
self-regulation 30, 39, 45–9, 53, 60, 212
sensationalism 130–1, 140–2, 147, 156–8, 160–1, 163
Serbia 49
serial killers 140
sex 109, 130, 144, 176, 236
sexism 175, 187–8
sexting 68
sexual abuse 72, 109, 146
sexual assault 109, 146, 148, 180; *see also* rape
sexual behaviour 106, 141
sexual conduct 107
sexual diversity 185
sexual harassment 180–1
sexual offences 33, 131
sexual orientation 41, 174, 176, 188; *see also* gender
sexual violence 148, 181
Shadwell, T. 204
shaming, public 6
Sharia law 160
Shearing, H. 202

shock 67, 131–7, 159
showbiz personalities 84
Siddique, H. 24, 203
Sir Lenny Henry Centre for Media Diversity 194
Sky News 30–1, 90, 231
Slovakia 49, 228
Smith, N. 177
smuggling 25
Snoddy, R. 224
Snoopers' Charter 91
Snopes 19
Snowden, Edward 234, 239–40
social media 50–2, 58–79; citizen journalists 69–70; closed groups and journalists' identity 68–9; comments, engaging with 72–4; conspiracy theories 64–6; content, use of 66–8; death and grief, coverage of 134–6; fake 68; industry reform 74–7; online content 58–61; online groups 66–8; online rumours 61–4; personal accounts of journalists 70–2; privacy rights and 118–23; 'RIP' posts 135–6; suicide and 161; witness contributors 69–70
socialism 14
Socialist Review 230
Society of Editors 175–6
Society of Professional Journalists (SPJ) 3–4, 6–7, 106, 129, 199, 201, 203
Somalia 233
Soueif, Ahdaf 237
sources 83–98; anonymous 88–90; choice of 83–6; embedded journalists 86–7; interviewees 92–4; news management 86–7; public disclosure 90–2; public interest 94–7; *see also* transparency
South Africa 179
South Korea 201
Spain 209, 227
Speed, Gary 168
sport 86, 90, 121; personalities 108, 137
Sri Lanka 233; civil war (2001) 223
Sridhar, Prof Devi 17
stabbings 144
stalkers 105
Starbucks 86
Steel, J. 102
Steindl, N. 13

stereotypes 46, 155–6, 162, 178–9, 184, 189, 193, 231
Stevenson, K. 227
stigmatisation 160, 162, 164, 184
stillbirth 128
Stokes, Ben 108
Stonbely, S. 191
Stonewall 186, 194
Storm, Hannah 148
storytelling 79, 140, 153–5
subjectivity 140
subscriptions 59–60, 213
subterfuge 68, 92
Süddeutsche Zeitung 95
suicide 5, 9, 33, 44, 49, 65, 106, 128, 142, 144, 151–70, 210; bereavement 153–4; copycat 9, 151, 157–60, 169; explicit details, avoidance of 158–9; glamorising 160–1; harm, minimisation of 156–8; harmful content, avoidance of 162–3; helplines, links to 163–4; language and tone 160–1; missing persons 152–3; responsible coverage 151–5; social media, responsible use of 161; stereotypes, avoidance of 162–3; stigmatising stories, avoidance of 162–3; Suicide Reporting Toolkit 164; working under pressure 154–5; *see also* Responsible Suicide Reporting (RSR)
Sun 91, 108, 111–12, 175–6, 183; *Scottish Sun* 130, 137
Sunday Herald 210
Sunday Mirror 68
Sunday Politics 37
Sunday Times 223, 227
Supreme Court (UK) 106
surveillance 90–2, 234; electronic 91
surveys 13, 16, 70, 175–6, 193, 207, 225, 228
Swire, B. 65
Syria 49, 61, 69–70, 223–4, 226–9, 233, 236

tabloids 13, 60, 75, 84, 106, 110–13, 129–30, 140, 175, 199
Tanzi, A. 86
Tawhid militia 229
Taylor, P. 225
teachers 68
teenagers 51, 137, 157, 229
Telecino 227

telecommunications 31, 34–5, 91
telegraph 222
Telegraph 17, 90, 182, 208–9, 222
telephone 92, 104
teletext 35
television 20, 35–6, 84, 94, 182, 213, 224–5, 240; clips 182; commission 35; documentaries 240; images 224; licensing 36; news 20; programming 94; soaps 84
Tell MAMA 182
tennis 177–8
terrestrial services 35
terrorism 62, 90, 178; anti-terrorism 22; terrorist attacks 62, 116, 123, 128, 136, 138, 233; war on terror 233–4; *see also* peace journalism; war correspondents
testimony 51, 83, 146, 224
Thurman, N. 62–3
Tik Tok 121
Times Literary Supplement 235
TMZ website 111
Tobitt, C. 15–6, 64, 71, 73, 139, 183, 186
Toews, R. 20
Tomlin, J. 227
Tomlinson, Ian 59
torture 234
trade unions 43
trafficking *see* human trafficking
tragedy 8, 111, 136, 141, 145, 148, 170
transgender community 33, 186; *see also* gender
transparency 4, 37, 44, 48, 51, 53, 63, 71, 83, 92, 97, 104, 199, 205
trauma, coverage of 128–48; ethical issues 128–31; Trauma Reporting training 142; *see also* death, coverage of
trolls 69, 73
Trump, Donald 14, 19–20, 177, 201–2, 207
trust: importance of 12–15; COVID-19 pandemic and 14–15; distrust 13–14; false realities 13–14; information disorder and 16; recovery of 14–15; zero-trust society 20
trustworthiness 13, 73, 84, 188, 215
truth: principle of 3; truth-seeking 15, 21; truth-telling 41, 45, 53, 163, 174, 176
Tukachinsky, R. 207
Tuneva, M. 184
Turkey 45, 49, 52, 228
Turse, N. 233

Turvill, W. 15, 137
Twitter 19, 25, 50, 61, 63, 67, 70, 72, 74–5, 77, 135, 168, 202, 211; tweets 2, 19, 61, 63, 67, 72–3, 75, 77, 113, 121, 168, 177–8, 180, 202, 209
typecasting 84

undercover investigations 5, 68
undergarment policy 178
under-representation 9, 12, 174, 176, 179, 193
unethical behaviour 34, 43; journalism 42, 44; news 42
unilaterals 227
United Arab Emirates (UAE) 130
United Nations (UN): Educational, Scientific and Cultural Organization (UNESCO) 91; Special Rapporteur on Torture 234
unlawful arrest 25
untrustworthy sources 12–3, 15
US Marines 224, 233
Usher, N. 13–4

vaccination 10, 203, 213; anti-vax movement 65, 71
Vallance, Sir Patrick 208–9
Van Dalen, A. 13
veiling practices 182
Velting, D. M. 158
Verdecchia, L. 117
verification 3, 16, 62–3, 67, 84–6, 87, 118
Verso 236
victims: blaming 141; experience of 131; of press abuse 32–3; road crashes 139; 'slippery stories' 50; survivors and 142; of terrorist attacks 136; of tragedy, witnesses 148; victimization 140; of violent crime 147; vulnerable 139
Vietcong 224–5
Vietnam War 201, 224–5, 227, 230
Vincent, Rebecca 23
Vine, Jeremy 182
violence: nonviolence, campaigns for 232; assaults 140; attacks 148; crime 9, 139–42, 147; repression 235; threats 178
viral 63, 75, 77, 116, 157, 180, 202; communications 50; viral storm 6
virtual reality (VR) 5
voicemail 74, 118

volunteers 116
vox pops 66, 185
vulnerability 106, 108, 162; groups 48; interviewees 6, 142; people 9–10, 41–2, 44, 151, 153, 157–8, 160–1, 169, 176; victims 139

Wall Street Journal 88, 177
Walter, N. 207
war correspondents 222–40; eye-witnesses, role as 223–4; frontline reporting 223, 227, 239; intimidation and violence, responses to 227–9; mainstream media 229–30; patriotism and 224–6; professional 222–3; *see also* peace journalism
war on terror: 9/11 attacks, US (2001) 233
war zones 227–8
Warby, Justice 112–3
Ward, S. J. 58, 60, 62–3
Wardle, Claire 16, 18–20, 64–6, 206–7
warfare 10, 222, 229, 231, 239; *see also* civil war; war correspondents
Warren, S. D. 102
wars 24, 224–5, 233, 239
Warsi, Baroness 183
Washington Post 14, 38
Wasserman, I. M. 158
watchdogs 4, 14, 35, 87–8, 203, 223
Waterson, Jim 8, 58, 63, 65, 74, 108, 182, 207
Waugh, Evelyn 240
Weapons of Mass Destruction (WMDs) 234
weather 128
web analytics 155
Weber, Max 223
webinars 210
Weinstein, Harvey 180
Weisstub, D. N. 160
welfare 107, 117
well-being 102, 107, 117, 148, 200, 206
Weller, Paul 107–8
Werther effect 157
Westminster politics 8, 90
WhatsApp 65, 68
wheelchair users 185
Whelan, P. 177–8
whips, government 91
whistleblowers 33–4, 49, 51, 88, 90–1, 96, 234, 239–40; importance of 234
White, Aidan 2–8, 12, 30, 45, 83

White, Charlene 176
white criminality 178
white journalists 85, 175, 189–90
white supremacism 178
whitewashing 182
Whitty, Prof Chris 209
widows 66, 145
WikiLeaks 24, 95, 233–4
Wilkins, L. 37, 41, 201
William, Prince of Wales 112
Williams, K. 225–6
Williams, Robin 159–60, 168
Williams, T. A. 201
Williams, Venus 178
Willsher, K. 201
Wimbledon tennis championship 177–8
Windsor Castle, UK 111
Winfrey, Oprah 113
wireless technology, 5G 64
witness contributors 69–70; *see also* citizen journalists *and* social media
Wolfe, L. 180–1
women: bylines 180; fears 141; health 199; representation of 179–82; rights 194; *see also* gender
Women in Journalism (WIJ) 179
Women's Aid 141
Women's Media Center 180

Women's Peace Camp 232
Wong, J. S. 140, 147
Woolley, S. 201
Woolworths 63–4
Works, W. 140, 147
World Health Organisation (WHO) 52, 138, 152, 158, 161, 169–70, 184, 200–1, 204, 215
World Press Freedom Index (2021) 23–4
World War II 225, 227
wrongdoing 34, 42, 46, 68, 75, 83, 92–3
WTOE 5 News 19

xenophobia 201

Yahoo 31
Yanovitzky, I. 201
Yemen 228, 233
Yeoman, Frances 7–8, 58
YouGov 13
Young, Stella 185
YouTube 17
Yugoslavia 226

Zollmann, F. 230
Zoom calls 68, 134
Zuckerberg, Mark 20, 51

Taylor & Francis eBooks

www.taylorfrancis.com

A single destination for eBooks from Taylor & Francis with increased functionality and an improved user experience to meet the needs of our customers.

90,000+ eBooks of award-winning academic content in Humanities, Social Science, Science, Technology, Engineering, and Medical written by a global network of editors and authors.

TAYLOR & FRANCIS EBOOKS OFFERS:

- A streamlined experience for our library customers
- A single point of discovery for all of our eBook content
- Improved search and discovery of content at both book and chapter level

REQUEST A FREE TRIAL
support@taylorfrancis.com

Routledge
Taylor & Francis Group

CRC Press
Taylor & Francis Group

Printed in Great Britain
by Amazon